Curating Italian Fashion

Curating Italian Fashion

Heritage, Industry, Institutions

Matteo Augello

BLOOMSBURY VISUAL ARTS
LONDON · NEW YORK · OXFORD · NEW DELHI · SYDNEY

BLOOMSBURY VISUAL ARTS
Bloomsbury Publishing Plc
50 Bedford Square, London, WC1B 3DP, UK
1385 Broadway, New York, NY 10018, USA
29 Earlsfort Terrace, Dublin 2, Ireland

BLOOMSBURY, BLOOMSBURY VISUAL ARTS and the Diana logo
are trademarks of Bloomsbury Publishing Plc

First published in Great Britain 2022
This edition published 2024

Copyright © Matteo Augello, 2024

Matteo Augello has asserted his right under the Copyright,
Designs and Patents Act, 1988, to be identified as Author of this work.

For legal purposes the Acknowledgements on p. x constitute
an extension of this copyright page.

Cover design by Adriana Brioso
Cover image: A fashionable Moroni portrait, photograph by Daniele Fummo, 2021

All rights reserved. No part of this publication may be reproduced or
transmitted in any form or by any means, electronic or mechanical,
including photocopying, recording, or any information storage or retrieval
system, without prior permission in writing from the publishers.

Bloomsbury Publishing Plc does not have any control over, or responsibility for,
any third-party websites referred to or in this book. All internet addresses given
in this book were correct at the time of going to press. The author and publisher
regret any inconvenience caused if addresses have changed or sites have
ceased to exist, but can accept no responsibility for any such changes.

A catalogue record for this book is available from the British Library.

A catalog record for this book is available from the Library of Congress.

ISBN: HB: 978-1-3502-3077-4
PB: 978-1-3502-3081-1
ePDF: 978-1-3502-3078-1
eBook: 978-1-3502-3079-8

Typeset by Newgen KnowledgeWorks Pvt. Ltd., Chennai, India
Printed and bound in Great Britain

To find out more about our authors and books visit
www.bloomsbury.com and sign up for our newsletters.

Contents

List of Illustrations	vi
Preface	viii
Acknowledgements	x
Introduction	1
1 Constructing Italian fashion heritage	11
2 Industry and corporate heritage in Italy	29
3 Corporate heritage and institutions	51
4 A history of fashion curation in Italy	75
5 Industry and curation: A critical commentary	131
6 Concluding remarks	157
Notes	163
References	175
Index	193

Illustrations

4.1	The display of Italian fashions by Rosa Genoni at the International Exhibition of Milan in 1906	78
4.2	The last room of the exhibition *La leggenda del filo d'oro, Le vie della seta* (*The Legend of the Golden Thread, the Silk Routes*)	83
4.3	The Sala Bianca of Palazzo Pitti was set as a procession of bishops, with mannequins wearing liturgical vestments from the eighteenth and nineteenth centuries	93
4.4	A vitrine of the exhibition *I protagonisti della moda. Salvatore Ferragamo (1898–1960)* [*Leaders of Fashion. Salvatore Ferragamo (1898–1960)*]	100
4.5	The exhibition *La Sala Bianca: The Birth of Italian Fashion* was commissioned by Pitti Immagine	105
4.6	The exhibion *Il motore della moda* (*The Style Engine*)	107
4.7	The installation of Gianfranco Ferré for the Biennale della Moda	109
4.8	A view of the exhibition *Uniforme. Ordine e Disordine* (*Uniform. Order and Disorder*)	114
4.9	The exhibition *L'abito per Pensare* (*Dress for Thought*)	118
4.10	A view of the section *Woven pattern*, dedicated to figured textiles in the exhibition *Gianni Versace. La reinvenzione della materia* (*Gianni Versace. The Reinvention of Matter*)	119
4.11	The exhibition *Salvatore Ferragamo. Evolving Legend 1928–2008*	120
4.12	*Italiana. L'Italia vista dalla moda 1971–2001* (*Italiana. Italy Through the Lens of Fashion 1971–2001*) was a retrospective display of the golden age of Italian fashion production	123
4.13	The exhibition *Il Nuovo Vocabolario della Moda Italiana* (*The New Vocabolary of Italian Fashion*)	124
4.14	The exhibition *Antonio Marras: nulla dies sine linea. Vita, diari e appunti di un uomo irrequieto* (*Antonio Marras: Never a Day Without a Line. Life, Diaries and Notes of a Restless Man*)	125
5.1	*Il museo effimero della moda* (*The Ephemeral Museum of Fashion*) was the first exhibition inaugurating the programme of the Galleria del Costume	142

5.2	The exhibition *Emilio Pucci e Como. 1950–1980* (*Emilio Pucci and Como. 1950–1980*)	146
5.3	The display *Vintage. L'irresistibile fascino del vissuto* (*Vintage. The Irresistible Charm of the Past*)	148
5.4	The exhibition *La camicia bianca secondo me. Gianfranco Ferré* (*The White Shirt According to Me. Gianfranco Ferré*)	149
5.5	This room of the exhibition *Un Palazzo e la Città* (*A Palace and the City*) recreated the art gallery of Luigi Bellini	154

Preface

This book is the result of many visits to exhibitions and archives, and even more conversations with colleagues. I am a fashion historian working across Italy and the UK, where I have had the chance to collaborate with institutions of different kinds, both public and corporate, and I was able to observe first-hand similarities and differences, comparing curatorial and cultural approaches. In a country like Italy where there is only a national state fashion museum with relatively limited resources, the archives and collections of companies are fundamental in preserving material evidence, therefore I started analysing corporate archives and museums as institutions, how their policies are developed and what impact these have had on the development of curation. Furthermore, I noticed that English publications examined the Italian fashion industry and its relationship with international markets – for example White (2000), Steele (2003) and Stanfill (2014) – but rarely acknowledged Italian curation.

These reflections triggered the idea of a publication which could be a critical introduction to the history of fashion curation in Italy. I have drawn from existing literature, which I used as primary source and as a record of specific curatorial approaches. Because of the focus on the relationship between industry and curation, I have analysed the type and content of documents made accessible by companies as further evidence of their will to provide services to society and this approach informs the analysis of a particular type of text: forewords and credits in catalogues and books. These are usually written by the representatives of the sponsors and the public institutions supporting the project to which the publication is dedicated. I have witnessed, in my professional life, that these texts are not always written by the declared authors, yet the latter still validate them and the opinions expressed in them can thus be considered as representative of the declared authors' position. Sponsors may give interviews during the promotion of an exhibition or event but the statements are usually too broad or brief to be analysed as evidence, while the texts here analysed – forewords and introductions – are the lasting and most thorough documents articulating the perspective of the sponsors.

This book is therefore written from my position as an informed historian to provide a critical commentary on the processes that I have witnessed and contributed to in my career. It hopes to provide an understanding of the relationship between industry and curation that is as nuanced as the actual practice, as I have experienced it. Most importantly, it is a tribute to the many scholars and curators who have developed this practice in Italy and especially to those who were kind enough to share their expertise and memories with me.

A note on translations: the adoption of English as *lingua franca* means that some published texts are not the exact words of an author but an interpretation of a translator. As a result, their lexical choices may not have been entirely precise and, for this reason, I have paid close attention to translations and have retranslated texts when I deemed the original translations imprecise.

Acknowledgements

This publication is the result of a doctoral degree, so my first thanks are to my supervisors Amy de la Haye, Donatella Barbieri and Jeffrey Horsley – you are the most wonderful and encouraging mentors one could ever hope to find. My colleagues – whom I can luckily call friends – provided invaluable support and advice both during the PhD and the preparation of this book: Enrica Morini, Margherita Rosina, Jenna Rossi-Camus and Lucia Savi. And then, of course, my family and friends who have lovingly ensured that I always kept my feet on solid ground so I could complete the long journey towards my first publication.

I would like to thank professionals I greatly admire, who took the time to chat with me about their work: Rita Airaghi, director of the Fondazione Gianfanco Ferré; Maria Luisa Frisa, curator and director of fashion at IUAV University; Filippo Guarini, director of the Museo del Tessuto in Prato; Giannino Malossi, curator; and Stefania Ricci, director of the Museo Salvatore Ferragamo.

My appreciation also goes to the following institutions for granting the free use of their images in this book: Archivio Genoni Podreider, Camera Nazionale della Moda Italiana, Fondazione Antonio Ratti, Fondazione Gianfranco Ferré, Fondazione Musei Civici Venezia, Gallerie degli Uffizi, Museo Salvatore Ferragamo, Museo del Tessuto Prato, Pitti Immagine and Triennale Milano.

The cover of this book is particularly precious to me as it is a tribute to Renaissance portraiture – in particular the artist Giovanni Battista Moroni – and fashion historian Grazietta Butazzi, whose book *La donna fatale* I hold in my hand. The photograph is the result of an outstanding team of young Italian creatives: Daniele Fummo, photographer; Sofia Lai, stylist; and Chantal Amari, make-up artist. I would like to thank Nicola Neri for his networking abilities and charm; Marco Pavoni for making scenographic suggestions; and Erika Marzano for helping on the day of the shoot. I would also like to thank Ligne Roset Hampsted and Rosie Johnson for kindly lending their beautiful Curule chair; and Istituto Marangoni London and Nicola Favaron for their support and allowing me to use their photo studio.

Last but not least, a most sincere thank you to Bloomsbury and especially to Frances Arnold and Rebecca Hamilton for making this happen.

Introduction

What's Italian about fashion curation?

I dedicated a PhD and a book to this question, trying to figure out if it even makes sense, and in the process of doing so I had to address a broader question that entertained many scholars before me: what is Italian fashion? What emerged was an investigation of this practice in Italy – which has not been well-studied outside of Italy itself – and of how curatorial practices were used to construct and represent an 'Italian style' and the central role played by the textile and fashion industries.

Fashion curation is a critical practice that entails the study and presentation of fashion through artefacts, traditionally in museum environments, as well as their care and preservation (Vänskä and Clark, 2017). With fashion, I employ the interpretation of Valerie Cumming (British dress historian and former president of the UK Costume Society), who includes dress and textiles, when presented as part of a history of fashionable dress, or when presented as part of a system (Cumming, 2004). Fashion has long been a part of textile collections (Cumming, 2004; Fukai, 2010; Taylor, 2002, 2004), and exhibitions of historical fashion have a complex history (Petrov, 2019). However the popularity of fashion displays was significantly enhanced in the 1970s by the work of Cecil Beaton at the Victoria & Albert Museum (V&A) in London (Clark and de la Haye, 2014) and of Diana Vreeland at the Metropolitan Museum of Art (Met) in New York (Clark and Frisa, 2012). Since the 2000s, the number of these exhibitions has exponentially increased, together with the collaborations between brands and institutions, even ones without fashion collections. A turning point was the 2000 retrospective of Giorgio Armani held at the Solomon R. Guggenheim Museum in New York. The display was much criticized (Taylor, 2005) and raised concerns whether the products of operating fashion companies should be displayed in museums. Alexandra Palmer (Senior Curator of Fashion and

Costume, Royal Ontario Museum, Toronto) later recorded how many North American costume and textile collections had been created or supported by the fashion industry and denounced how the agendas of the latter 'may often be the driving force, instead of collections care' (2008: 54). Despite the criticism, the collaborative model of the designer monograph exhibition has become an established practice within fashion curation and brands too have contributed to its development. The interaction between the industry and institutions has since undergone a change towards a more collaborative nature and museums are now part of the fashion system and new types of relations have arisen between industry and institutions (Riegels Melchior and Svensson, 2014).

Commerce and culture are often positioned in a binary system which fails to capture the complex intertwinement with market forces throughout the history of fashion exhibitions, as unfolded by fashion curator Julia Petrov (2019) and demonstrated in this book. Corporate interests were at play at the boom of museums in the late nineteenth century: taking the example of textile study rooms, Sarah Fee (2014) – Senior Curator, Global Fashion and Textiles at the Royal Ontario Museum, Toronto – highlighted how the promotion of national production and consumption was one of the functions of museums, just like the great exhibitions from which many museums originated. The textile and fashion industries have long supported cultural outputs – the textile-related merchants and guilds were among the richest patrons in early modern Europe – through activities such as patronage and sponsorship. Companies have also engaged with their own corporate heritage: they have produced exhibitions themselves and toured them to promote new collections, flagship stores and corporate anniversaries, as well as establishing corporate institutions. To identify these operations, I propose to use the term *corporate cultural policy*, which can be used to describe all the ways in which a company promotes various aspects of culture, related or unrelated to the business of the company. Because the management of corporate heritage has been extensively discussed in business, marketing and organizational studies, there is a focus on the benefits for companies but limited reflections on the value of corporate cultural operations for society. When companies present their work as an aspect of society, they are communicating their importance but also highlighting the importance of the products they produce. Considering the recent academic and museal recognition of fashion's cultural relevance – though it has always been a relevant part of culture – I argue that, at least in Italy, the corporate cultural policies of the industry have played a fundamental role in the development of curatorial approaches.

In order to understand how the fashion industry interacts with cultural heritage and institutions, it is essential to move away from the equations culture-art and museums-art, which can be detected especially outside fashion and cultural studies. The term *museum* has been used in non-museum studies to describe all sorts of display spaces, and even archives with no display spaces, therefore a discussion of this term is warranted, as well as the employment of 'institutions' as a more suitable umbrella term. I will review existing literature on corporate museums and fashion exhibitions, bridging fashion, marketing, organization and museum studies in order to define a theoretical framework that supports this argument. The first part of the book (Chapters 1 to 3) is devised to tidying up existing discourses: Chapter 1 on the construction of Italian fashion identity and the tools employed to do it; Chapter 2 on the preservation of corporate heritage and the different approaches employed over time; and Chapter 3 explores the system of corporate institutions and defines the various uses of corporate heritage. Through Chapter 4 I have attempted to provide a historical overview of fashion curation in Italy, combining secondary sources, exhibition catalogues and key publications, with the aim of weaving the corporate thread throughout this history. Italian readers and fashion scholars may be already familiar with the events and publications referenced, but hopefully they will find the framework refreshing and, most importantly, convincing.

This book is centred on two points. First, the strategic use of the past has been used from the beginning of what we may refer to as 'Italian fashion', that is heritage marketing is intrinsically connected to Italian fashion – and curatorial tools were essential in this process. Second, at least for Italy, the agency of the fashion and textile industries must be examined to understand why fashion curatorial practices have evolved in the way that they have: through indirect and active engagement, these industries supported projects that aligned with their marketing strategies. For this reason, I frame exhibitions and publications as 'narratives with a purpose'. These should not only be understood as disseminators of scholarship, but also as engaging experiences – especially exhibitions – which can make consumers aware of the cultural dimension of fashion. Corporate storytelling may be the main purpose of curatorial projects but, when the purpose of exhibitions and publications is also to contextualize fashion as a social practice and products as cultural artefacts, then these become tools for sense-making provided to consumers. The contribution of this book is developing a discourse on curatorial practices which centres on corporate agency and this is why efforts were made to bridge literatures in different fields and languages, especially as corporate agency is an important driver for fashion curation outside of the English-speaking sphere and the approach of this book will hopefully inspire similar case studies on other countries. The next sections are dedicated to this bridging by defining the key terminology used in this publication and situating Italian fashion curation in academic literature.

0.1 Defining corporate terminology

The term *corporate museums* has been employed as an umbrella term to identify all forms of corporate institutions and facilities, and companies have named these places in a variety of ways, regardless of the specialist meaning of the titles employed (archive, gallery, museum). The term *corporate* is here used in line with existing literature in this field and not in its legal acceptation, that is related to a corporation, when a firm is legally recognized and exists as an entity separate and distinct from its owners (Dahlsrud, 2008). In marketing, organizational and business studies, the adjective corporate is used in relation with a business or commercial activity, for example as in the expression corporate social responsibility (Carroll, 1999; Dahlsrud, 2008). Although the first publication on the institutions established by companies was entitled *Company Museums* (Coleman, 1943), the term mostly employed is corporate. In archival practice, institutions associated with companies and industry associations are referred to as 'business archives'. The International Council on Archives (ICA) has a section dedicated to Business Archives and the UK has Business Archives Councils. I hereafter use the term corporate with the same understanding.

For the definitions of museum and archive, I use as point of reference that of international associations of professionals and scholars working in the respective fields. This choice is particularly apt given the multilingual nature of this research project. The ICA, founded in 1948, defined archives as 'the documentary by-product of human activity retained for their long-term value' (ICA, 2022). The International Council of Museums (ICOM), founded in 1946, states that 'a museum is a non-profit, permanent institution in the service of society and its development, open to the public, which acquires, conserves, researches, communicates and exhibits the tangible and intangible heritage of humanity and its environment for the purposes of education, study and enjoyment' (ICOM, 2007). This definition of museum will be used throughout the book and the institutions that fulfil it are referred to as traditional museums.

Clarifying the use of *corporate* was instrumental to reflect on how it could be used to describe the strategies employed by companies and associations to engage with culture. The expression *cultural policy* is usually applied to the operations of governments and public institutions, but it has also been applied to 'trade unions, colleges, social movements, community groups, foundations, and businesses' (Miller, 2010). In the latter case, the primary purpose is the benefit of a company, even when the only return is image or addressing corporate social responsibility and, for this purpose, I propose the addition of *corporate* to identify this specific case and declare the interests at play when analysing the operations aimed at the 'production, dissemination, marketing, and consumption' (Rentschler, 2002: 17) of 'the arts (including the for-profit cultural industries), the humanities, and the heritage' (Schuster, 2003: 1).

With the addition of *corporate* to *cultural policy*, the *heritage* it engages with is not only that of a community but also that of a brand and of the industry at large. A key definition of *brand heritage* was provided in 2007 by Mats Urde (professor of Brand Management at Lund University), Stephen Greyser (Professor Emeritus of Marketing at Harvard Business School) and John Balmer (professor of Corporate Marketing at Brunel University). They define brand heritage as 'a dimension of a brand's identity found in its track record, longevity, core values, use of symbols and particularly in an organisational belief that its history is important' (Urde, Greyser and Balmer, 2007: 4). They used this definition to articulate the concept of heritage brand, that is a brand 'with a positioning and a value proposition based on its heritage' (Urde, Greyser and Balmer, 2007: 5). This definition has become the main reference, with this article cited more than six hundred times according to Google Scholar.

0.2 Situating Italian fashion curation

Italy is a particularly suited case study because the lack of a central, national museum dedicated to fashion and the limited support provided by the state in the support of industrial heritage contributed to the active role of companies and trade associations. Given the geographical fragmentation of the Italian fashion system, companies worked within the local institutions for the cultural promotion of fashion. Italy has been described as the country with the highest number of corporate institutions, including museums, archives, galleries and visitor centres (Amari, [1997] 2001; Bulegato, 2008). It is also the country where most research on the phenomenon has been undertaken, primarily within marketing and organizational studies. Italy has a long tradition of fine arts museums and funds and efforts are usually invested there, resulting in the neglect of industrial heritage (Bulegato, 2008). In the 1950s and 1960s entrepreneurs engaged in activities of patronage and sponsorship but, over the years, they have taken on a more active role in the preservation and communication of their heritage, effectively substituting the state in this role. This phenomenon has consistently increased in scale since the 1990s: in 2009, Istat (Italy's National Institute for Statistics) published a report on foundations in Italy and recorded that the corporate foundations established between 1996 and 2005 represent 64.1 per cent of all foundations operating in 2005 (Monteverdi, 2009).

There is limited research on the role of companies in the development of corporate heritage studies, especially in specialist publications on fashion and textiles. In the 2010 *Berg Encyclopedia of World Dress and Fashion* there are but a few mentions: corporate museums are listed in the article 'Dress and Fashion Museums' by Akiko Fukai, who described them as 'fashion museums celebrating either the oeuvres or the names of famous designers', and added that 'designers also establish museums for their own work' (Fukai, 2010: 292). Fukai briefly discussed the Musée Christian Dior in Granville, the Balenciaga Museum in Guetaria and the Fondation Pierre Bergé – Yves Saint Laurent in Paris. She mentioned the 'specialized fashion museum' (Fukai, 2010: 288) yet she included the V&A, a decorative arts museum, in the discussion and did not state whether these designer museums can be considered specialized fashion museums.

An evaluation of corporate institutions is critical to develop a more nuanced understanding of fashion curation as a part of the fashion system in which both research and commercial aims can be achieved simultaneously, and Italy is a particularly rich example given the role played by the industry in the evolution of fashion curation. This book proposes a critical history of fashion curation in Italy and positions it within existing international discourses on this practice, which have favoured the UK, the US and French examples. In 2004 British dress historian Lou Taylor published *Establishing Dress History* (Taylor, 2004), a seminal work, particularly from a methodological perspective, in which she analysed the development of fashion history and the role of collections and institutions. As a British scholar, Taylor primarily focused on the UK, as well as New York and Paris, but there is no discussion on Italy. The absence was also present in another pivotal publication on this topic, *Understanding Fashion History* by British dress historian Valerie Cumming (2004). The tenth volume of the *Berg Encyclopedia of World Dress and Fashion* presented two articles dedicated to fashion curation (Druesedow, 2010; Thompson, 2010). The Galleria del Costume of Palazzo Pitti, the only state funded museum dedicated to fashion in Italy, was present in one, 'Dress and Fashion Exhibits' by Jean Druesedow: in a discussion on private collecting, the museum was mentioned for the donation of the collection of the costumier Umberto Tirelli (Druesedow, 2010). The absence of Italy is largely caused by language barriers, since most catalogues of Italian exhibitions were not published with an English translation and were therefore inaccessible to foreign scholars. Yet, an evaluation of fashion curation in Italy would allow to assess the role played by companies in the preservation and dissemination of fashion heritage, as a close relation between industry and scholarship can be detected since the early stages of fashion studies in Italy and I argue that it can be considered its characterizing trait. What emerges is the recurring employment of a strategic use of the past to communicate and enhance the social and cultural value of fashion, which helps frame how the industry has impacted on curatorial approaches.

In order to critically analyse the history of fashion curation in Italy, it was essential to compile a chronological account of this practice upon which to build a commentary. Three British publications informed the compilation of this account: *The study of dress history* (2002) and *Establishing dress history* (2004) by Lou Taylor and *Understanding fashion history* (2004) by Valerie Cumming. They are focused mainly on activity in the UK, but include extensive references to France and the United States. The first issue to address was the definition of the field of enquiry: Taylor used the term *dress* while Cumming preferred *fashion*. In fact, Cumming reflected at length on the terminology and observed how the fragmentation of the subject is linked to the multitude of approaches to the study of clothes, informed by the background of each scholar. She stated that, while preferring *clothes* and *dress*, these terms appear 'to exclude fashion' (Cumming, 2004: 16) and she therefore decided to opt for that word. Both Taylor and Cumming included textiles in their studies and I employ the term fashion with the same inclusive acceptation. Another approach was deployed in relation to the term *curation*. Taylor effectively discussed museum collections, exhibitions and the interpretation of dress choosing the term *history* (Taylor, 2004). Taylor started her account from 1900 in France as she described the first costume exhibition mounted at the Palais du Costume during the International Exhibition in Paris. A similar operation from an equally authoritative source was the article on the history of fashion curation by Akiko Fukai in the *Berg Encyclopedia of World Dress and Fashion*, edited by Joanne B. Eicher in 2010. Fukai's analysis focused on a shorter timeframe, as does the one presented in this book, and also divided the history in three phases, a division which I have borrowed and adapted to interpret the Italian context. Fukai also employs the term *fashion*, which she intended in its broadest acceptation, including discussions on textiles collections as well as developments within fashion theory. The breadth of Fukai's account provides then an authoritative model for the account on Italian fashion curation here presented.

The account does not aim to be exhaustive, but rather focuses on identifying pivotal authors, similarly to Cumming's identification of specific texts, how they inter-related and were influential in the development of the subject (Cumming, 2004). In addition to this, I stress which companies and industry associations supported each project and how their agenda might have influenced them. One fundamental publication was the collection of proceedings (Morini, Rizzini and Rosina, 2016) of the conference dedicated to Grazietta Butazzi (Italian dress historian), held at the Fondazione Antonio Ratti in Como on 20 June 2014. Butazzi was a pivotal figure in the development of fashion theory and curation in Italy and the reconstruction of her biography by Marialuisa Rizzini (Italian lace and dress historian) effectively served as a partial chronology of the field from the 1970s to the 1990s (Rizzini, 2016). Butazzi herself presented an overview of the field entitled 'Studi e Ricerca sul tema Moda e Costume: la situazione in Italia' (Fashion and Costume Research and Study: the situation in Italy) at the first Costume Colloquium in Florence in November 2008 (only the audio recording is available). Another paper from that 2014 conference was 'Oltre trent'anni dopo "Moda. Arte, Storia e Società"' ("Fashion. Art, History and Society": thirty years later) by Maria Giuseppina Muzzarelli (Professor of History and Culture, University of Bologna), who undertook a similar operation to Fukai and identified three eras, each associated with a different fashion scholar. These sources provided the foundation for the historical account which I compiled by integrating them with information from primary sources, mostly exhibition catalogues and conference proceedings, as well as the valuable research by Simona Segre Reinach (2017) and Gabriele Monti (2019). The account provides the evidence to demonstrate the central role played by the industry, as sponsor first and as cultural producer later, that corporate needs can be addressed alongside civic needs and scholarship. Reflecting on the industry can contribute to a more nuanced understanding of the practice and of how it adapts to a changing industry to which it is inextricably linked to.

0.3 Structuring the book

As indicated by the title of this book – *Curating Italian Fashion: Heritage, Industry and Institutions* – fashion curation in Italy is discussed from three perspectives and a chapter is dedicated to each: heritage (Chapter 1), industry (Chapter 2) and institutions (Chapter 3). After these elements are contextualized in the Italian landscape, an informed historical account of fashion curation is provided by Chapter 4, followed by a critical commentary in Chapter 5, which uses the factual evidence and theoretical framework of the previous chapters to unfold the complex relationship between industry and curation.

Chapter 1 examines the construction of Italian fashion heritage and highlights how fashion companies and associations have employed a strategic use of the past, effectively a form of heritage marketing, since the start of the Italian fashion industry. Key events are discussed to investigate why the Renaissance is a recurring historical narrative used to convey Italianness in fashion.

Chapter 2 looks at the preservation of corporate heritage in Italy and outlines the reasons which led the industry to invest in preserving their own heritage. It introduces the expression of corporate cultural policy to identify the operations undertaken by a company to support culture in the broader sense and then lists four different modes of interaction between industry and culture. Lastly, it examines the role of the industry in the development of studies on corporate heritage in Italy.

Chapter 3 delves into corporate institutions to trace the differences between foundations, archives, collections and museums. Collecting policies are analysed to understand how different interpretative approaches to heritage evidence how companies engage with customers as well as the communities they inhabit. This chapter also explores the differences between institutions, exhibition facilities and stores, in order to unfold the complex system of operations connected to corporate heritage.

Chapter 4 proposes a historical account of fashion curation in Italy and its evolution is divided into four stages: 1900s–1940s, 1950s–1970s, 1980s–1990s and 2000s–2010s. The division is discussed and compared with existing histories of fashion curation and models are specifically sought in British publications. The account centres on pivotal events and figures and underlies the role of the industry at each stage.

Chapter 5 provides a critical commentary on the impact of the industry on curatorial practices. It first investigates the role of the industry as sponsors and as cultural producers. It then proposes that corporate cultural policies and the active engagement of the industry specifically contributed to the focus on manufacture and technique because of the dual purpose of promoting the industry while disseminating industrial and artisanal knowledge. Lastly, it reflects on how corporate and civic needs can be equally addressed.

1

Constructing Italian fashion heritage

From the moment of its unification in 1861, various aspects of culture were addressed to establish an Italian national identity. The process of cultural and social unification is arguably still taking place and Italy's fragmented history has often worked against it. Though it is precisely its variety that is now recognized as one of the key features and success factors, Italy is understood as a container of different realities, sometimes at odds, which have shared histories and golden ages (Ortoleva, 1999). There exist many localized golden ages which focus on specific geographical areas: they resulted from the different configurations of the political, social and cultural entities which make up Italy, and at the same time the historicization of these localized golden ages has strengthened the identity fragmentation. Among these, one has been celebrated globally and is often identified as the beginning of modern European history: the Renaissance. I use this term with the same understanding as Carlo Marco Belfanti, professor of economic history at the Università degli Studi di Brescia: 'the term Renaissance is intended in its widest sense and, at least, partially, is deliberately imprecise: the Renaissance is "simply" the period of the primacy of Italian civilisation in Europe' (Belfanti, 2015a: 76). Its centrality in historical narratives is a complex matter and these are currently being challenged in Italian studies, yet this discussion eludes the aims of this publication and I will focus on why the Renaissance was chosen as the beginning of Italian style and how the fashion industry located in this era its originating myth.

Dress was among the tools employed to manifest Italian identity and traditions during Risorgimento, the process of unification of the Italian peninsula which took place in the third quarter of the nineteenth century. Patriots promoted the adoption of an invented traditional costume as a uniform to manifest their ideas, known as *costume all'italiana*: 'a way of dressing that evoked Italy's distant and more recent past, through the display of an attire that included a jacket in velvet and a hat with a feather' (Romani, 2015: 11). The costume was made mainly of black velvet for both men and women and this choice can be framed as political. The colour black 'conveyed an aura of moral sobriety' (Romani, 2015: 16) and stood for 'the national martyrdom suffered during the recent fights for independence' (Romani, 2015: 11). Velvet was equally charged as it represented 'the international prestige Italy enjoyed during the Renaissance' (Romani, 2015: 11). Gabriella Romani, professor of Italian at Seton Hall University, noted that this was part of a nationalist discourse present in the contemporary Risorgimento press and the fashion periodicals, which advocated against the 'tyranny of foreign influences, especially from France, a country that had dominated the Italian fashion market since the eighteenth century' (2015: 12).

The same nationalist message is at the core of the work of Rosa Genoni (1867–1954), an Italian couturière who has recently been the subject of studies which analysed her work as a feminist and the first advocate for an Italian fashion (Morini, 2020; Paulicelli, 2015a; Soldi, 2018). Genoni was a *première* at the Milanese atelier of Maison Haardt et Fils but independently participated in the 1906 International Exhibition in Milan where she presented her own creations, the first attempt to articulate Italianness through contemporary fashion. In the booklet accompanying the display, she wrote:

> So why imitate and slavishly reproduce the hairstyles from beyond the Alps, when Italy can try to do it by itself and much better? ... It is not just a question of patriotism – it could make people smile as we're talking about fashion – but it is a question of history, because nothing is more characteristic than the art of dressing, which, just like language, has always marked the genius of a race, of a people, of a lineage: and no country, like Italy, is called the classical land of art. (Genoni, 1906: 3)[1]

By framing fashion as 'the art of dressing' – which Genoni understood as an expression of a society and its culture – and by reminding viewers that Italy is the classical land of (fine) art, she traced a genealogy which directly linked the Renaissance – chosen as the golden age of Italian art – with contemporary fashion. She made these links visible by exhibiting a collection of twelve models inspired by great Italian masters: the most cited is a dress dedicated to Botticelli's *La Primavera*, with embroidery motifs taken from the painting. Morini (2020) noted that the silhouette could still be linked to Paris and borrowing decoration motifs from art history was a common practice, as evidenced by the work of Charles Frederick Worth (Trubert-Tollu et al., 2017), therefore limiting the claims to Italian authenticity. Nevertheless, the formal reference generated an impact and Genoni was eventually awarded the International Jury Grand Prix for two of her garments, including the *Primavera* one. Eleven of the twelve models were inspired by Renaissance paintings (Genoni, 1908) and the international reputation of Italian painters from this era was likely a reason for the success with foreign visitors.

The prominence of the award and Genoni's attachment to the Italian feminist movement led to her participation at the 1908 National Congress of Italian Women in Rome. She attended as a delegate of the Società Umanitaria di Milano, a philanthropic institution where she taught dress history. During her speech, Genoni discussed the rationale behind her creations at the 1906 exhibition and proposed how traditional costumes from different regions could be used as further inspiration for Italian models. She stated that women had the responsibilty to contribute to this campaign and asked for help 'to fight against foreign production, to refine their concepts, to assert themselves with a genuine and original Italian character, in short, to create a truly national decorative art' (Genoni, 1908: 6).[2]

Though Genoni's work remains an isolated operation and the first systematic construction of an Italian fashion identity by borrowing cultural capital and market value from the Renaissance would take place in the 1950s, she demonstrated that the Renaissance could 'boost the sense of national identity through style' (Caratozzolo, 2014: 48) and that a link with art could 'ennoble the operation from the cultural point of view, endowing it moreover with a label that had certain drawing power at an international level' (Belfanti, 2015a: 78). Caratozzolo (2014) and Belfanti (2015a) agree that Genoni was the first to draw a link between the Renaissance and contemporary fashion to highlight a continuity which they both identify in the craft tradition. This may be true with hindsight, given the contemporary focus on craftsmanship and the reputation of excellency of Italian manufacture (Caratozzolo, 2014), however I would argue that Genoni aimed at an aesthetic continuity which, as mentioned above, did not exist since the models cannot be considered independent from Parisian styles. Genoni's contribution lies instead in the construction of a historical narrative which was expanded and adapted by subsequent marketing operations but has remained, to this day, the main narrative in the marketing of Italian fashion heritage.

1.1 Renaissance as Italianness

Following Genoni, there are other examples of formal references to Renaissance art in fashion design, such as Germana Marucelli in 1949 (Belfanti, 2015b) or Emilio Pucci, who made extensive use of Italy's artistic heritage in his 1950s print designs (Rosina and Chiara, 2014). After designing collections inspired by resort locations (Capri in 1952) and artistic and cultural heritage (Sicily in 1956), Pucci engaged with Tuscan Renaissance for the remainder of the decade, notably with the collections *Palio* (1957) and *Botticelliana* (1959). Pucci implemented what Caratozzolo defines as 'the dissemination of Italian heritage in the form of a fashion commodity' (2014: 57). Literal references have a *souvenir effect* which can 'reawaken in the consumer overseas, provided he or she was informed of the place of origin' (Morelli, 1987: 59). Yet in the 1950s, the construction of a national fashion identity seemed to be more a preoccupation of fashion promoters than of creators. There was a competition between Turin, Rome, Florence and later Milan to become the centre of Italian fashion; these cities competed up until the end of the 1960s to find their own identities within a broader system which did not have a clear identity. While Genoni's attempt at establishing Italian fashion was rooted in nineteenth-century patriotism and nationalism, 1950s operations were directed by different needs: convincing foreign buyers of choosing Italian products over others; for what concerned fashion, the competitor was Paris.

The existence of a clear identity is of utmost importance in fashion which can be defined by its commercial 'consumption of stereotypes' (Ortoleva, 1999: 55), especially when products are intended or at least mainly consumed by foreign markets, as was the case of Italian fashion and American consumers in the post-war era. Apart from a recognition of the skills of Italian craftsmen, Italy 'did not have any form of intangible cultural heritage to balance against that of *Haute Couture*' and 'had to find a source of cultural reputation at the international level' (Belfanti, 2015a: 86–7). There was an existing tradition of 'picturesque views' of Italy, that is, 'idealized and stereotypical representations' (Caratozzolo, 2014: 48) built over time by foreigners and Italians alike. These represented the cultural and artistic heritage against which Italian fashion would be defined: 'not entirely represented by an autonomous, self-referential language, but rather located in an external creative dimension' (Caratozzolo, 2014: 48). Due to the post-war economic conditions in which Italy was verging and the tight exchange with the United States (White, 2000), Italian fashion and its representations were constructed 'for the use and consumption of an international public' (Belfanti, 2015a: 77). As Italian fashion could not compete with Paris on fashionability, it focused its communication on Italianness.

Italianness required an immediate reference with which the audience could engage and the Renaissance eventually became the main historical narrative employed in communication. Its association with Italian fashion 'was the product of a marketing strategy' aimed at placing it 'in the centre of a well-known, appreciated, not to say indisputable, tradition of "good taste"' (Belfanti, 2015a: 74). The expression *Renaissance effect* was in fact coined to describe the link with the Renaissance, despite it being based on vague definitions (Corbellini and Saviolo, 2004). The Renaissance served as 'a kind of *ante litteram* guarantee of provenance – a "country branding" – recognized throughout the world, which, at the same time, evoked the splendour of a period in which Italian taste was a model to follow and imitate' (Belfanti, 2015a: 74). This was the era when fashion was established 'a social institution of modernity [which] exercised power in the creation of taste, desire, consumption choices' (Paulicelli, 2015b: 3), thus Italy could be interpreted as a legitimate voice in the fashion industry, even older than France.

The consistent representation of Italianness as Renaissance was in response to expectations deriving from stereotypical views by foreigners. It was a process directed at conveying authenticity, that is 'a form of impression management that focuses on the development of a unique image of the organisation and its products for external audiences' (Foster et al., 2017: 1186). The effectiveness of representations of Italianness is assessed by how authentic these are perceived to be by the intended audiences. An eminent example is given by the words of the American photographer Karen Radkai who, in 1950, 'acquired for herself only those works from the designers that she found "sufficiently Italian"' (Brin quoted in Caratozzolo, 2014: 51). This was part of the report of Radkai's stay in Italy compiled by the fashion journalist Irene Brin. Italian fashion products were welcomed when they 'matched an image that was indeed established in advance, but at the same time suggested very new possibilities' (Brin quoted in Caratozzolo, 2014: 51).

Italy's artistic heritage was used as a backdrop for the presentation of fashion not only via fashion shows but also with photography. It was the proximity of a new product (Italian fashion) with an existing product (art and architecture) which allowed the value associated with one to be transferred onto the other. 'The image of Italy in fashion photography, therefore, as a prop, a propaganda element' (Bonetti, 2005: 60). This strategy was on the one hand configuring Italian creations within a setting that was expected of by foreign buyers and on the other promoted an idea of Italianness which reinforced existing models, thus presenting a 'picture postcard' version of Italy (Bonetti, 2005: 61). This version, based on 'Art and landscape, the classical and the Mediterranean, folklore and high society' (Bonetti, 2005: 62) was the main narrative in the 1950s and early 1960s and, though new narratives would be introduced with the rise of ready-to-wear and *stilismo* (Stanfill, 2014) in the 1970s, they can still be detected in current designers. For example, after the restructuring in the early 2010s, Dolce & Gabbana rebuilt their whole image on this specific version of Italy, organizing fashion shows and events in locations that served as cultural props for the interpretation of their creations.

In the 1950s, Giovanni Battista Giorgini, an Italian exporter who had worked with American department stores before the Second World War, promoted Italian fashion to the American market and developed a systematic strategy directed at foreign consumers to build authenticity based on existing ideas on Italianness. The strategic use of historical narratives was common practice in collective events and trade shows (Foster et al., 2017). The 1950 exhibition *Italy at work. Her Renaissance in Design Today* (Brooklyn Museum, New York City, then tour) was organized by American institutions and the Italian government and drew a parallel between past and present (Pinchera and Rinallo, 2017). Giorgini framed the Renaissance as an originating myth and articulated it through an interconnected series of operations, which made it ultimately successful. As Italy could not compete with France on fashionability, whose originating myth was rooted in the eighteenth century (Steele, 2017), Giorgini's promoted a parallel genealogy which went back even further than the French counterpart and used the tangible manifestations of 'Florence's historical, artistic and architectural heritage' to provide 'the material and symbolic bases to infuse the collections showcased at the Pitti Palace with resonant cultural meanings' (Pinchera and Rinallo, 2017: 10). The staging of fashion shows in the *sala bianca* of Pitti Palace provided a display of Italian culture and heritage at each show as background for the garments but it was the collateral events which provided a historical experience to the attendees. From the first show in 1951, guests were invited to galas and urged to wear conspicuously Italian garments (Belfanti, 2015b) while balls and parades had historical themes and this performance of history became literal in 1953 with the re-enactment of the 1584 wedding between Eleonora de' Medici and Vincenzo Gonzaga (Pinchera and Rinallo, 2017).

Giorgini's events in Florence were instead focused on the continuity between a vague history with contemporary fashion, without a precise genealogy of style situated only within clothing. A parallel between historical dress and contemporary fashion – as Genoni had attempted – would have highlighted a continuity within the boundaries of costume, while literal connections across different practices conveyed continuity in style. Furthermore, experiences of the past were staged for those who attended the fashion shows and collateral events: participants enjoyed the architectural and artistic heritage when in Florence and attended events which ranged from gala dinners in historic locations to actual historical re-enactments (Belfanti, 2015b). Fashion was presented as the key to the consumption of the past, which Giorgini realized was a commodity of great value in foreign markets.

The successful operation which Giorgini mounted in the 1950s to sell Italian fashion to American buyers was rooted in an effective strategy of nation branding, intended as 'the diffusion of meanings resulting from coding and encoding processes that use selective readings of the past and which other actors often contest and contrast' (Pinchera and Rinallo, 2017: 2). The branding was centred around the Renaissance, which was able to support Italy's claim to fashionability by leveraging on the artistic leadership in the early modern era and by tracing the lineage of high-quality craftsmanship to Renaissance workshops (Belfanti, 2015b; Pinchera and Rinallo, 2017). The latter was particularly instrumental in strengthening country-of-origin effects which would later allow the 1980s Made in Italy campaign to thrive.

The Made in Italy campaign was launched in 1980 but it built on existing country-of-origin effects (Pinchera and Rinallo, 2017) and was equally rooted in a process of nation branding with the US and other foreign markets as interlocutors. In fact, the expression Made in Italy was 'an established term of reference to make sense of the subsequent market offering originating in the Belpaese' (Pinchera and Rinallo, 2017: 21) and its very formulation in English rather than Italian attests the intended foreign audience. From the 1950s to the 1970s, Italy had established itself as a fashion producer and there already existed a country-of-origin effect, which the Made in Italy reinforced by creating content 'based on product imagery built on the country's material and symbolic resources as well as on selective, strategic readings of its history' (Pinchera and Rinallo, 2017: 21).

Centring the narrative on artistic heritage, the Renaissance and a *dolce vita* lifestyle was also effective nation branding as it differentiated Italy in ways that foreign markets would be able to understand and thus value. Nation branding is 'a territorial form of collective branding that is built over time and requires the orchestration of firms and other stakeholders with regard to joint promotional efforts' (Pinchera and Rinallo, 2017: 21). In Italy, territorial clusters connected different entities within a region with the aim to build the local and national branding. This is particularly evident from the 1980s, when Marco Rivetti – president of the Gruppo Finanziario Tessile (GFT) – took the leadership at the association managing the Florentine Trade show and employed a breadth of tools – from publishing to education and to sponsorship – to relaunch Florence as the cultural centre of fashion in Italy, discussed in Section 4.3.5.

Made in Italy is not solely a country-of-origin feature but also 'represents a vehicle for the symbolic value of Italian culture and its artistic heritage' and there exists a close relationship between cultural and creative industries with cultural heritage (Lazzeretti and Oliva, 2020: 3). This campaign communicated 'a group of products with a high degree of cultural content that reflects the values and heritage of a specific territory' and devised strategies to make this cultural content tangible (Lazzaretti and Oliva, 2020: 3). With the outsourcing of production and globalization, came what the curator Sonnet Stanfill calls the 'ambiguity in relation to the perceived authenticity of Italy's premium fashion houses [which] comes from foreign ownership and production outsourcing' (2014: 28). In the 1990s, Italy was already identified as a 'Designed-in Country', rather than a 'Made-in Country: an origin with recognized cultural value which 'may influence consumer evaluation of product attributes' (Malossi, 1999: 28). Nowadays, the expression *made in Italy* stands less for the manufacturing value of products and has strengthened the cultural framing of products as being conceived in Italy rather than produced (Giumelli, 2016).

1.2 The strategic use of the past

Organizations, whether public or private, may build upon existing narratives or develop new ones, in order to stress the connection which the organization has with local or national communities, cultures and events. This is a process of 'history-telling' devised to highlight 'an existing past shared with individuals and groups as well as with broader collective arrangements' (Foster et al., 2017: 1177). In the critical review of Italian fashion history, we find two different pasts: the past of Italianness, to which post-war designers, photographers, events promoters referred to, centred around the Renaissance as a former golden age and interpreted as the key to open the doors to a new golden age; and the past of Italian fashion, 'a "grand history" of the corporation that is framed as a detailed, truthful account of who did what, when, and where in a coherent and integrated set of events' (Foster et al., 2017: 1178).

The use of historical narratives required evidence upon which to build them. It is an established practice to commission archival research to professional historians, so that they can develop realistic historical narratives (Foster et al., 2017). An example is provided by the commission by Italy's then largest clothing manufacturer, GFT, to the Piedmont section of CISST (the national association of textile and costume historians) in the 1980s to organize the corporate archive

(Rizzini, 2016). This commission led to two outcomes. In 1989, two volumes were published to present the findings of the study of the archive (Berta, 1989). The research on corporate history led to further reflection on the history of ready to wear which triggered the organization of a conference in 1990 dedicated to this theme. It was conceived by dress historian Grazietta Butazzi, who had contributed to the study of the GFT archive, and was organized by the Lombardy section of CISST in Milan, with the financial support of the GFT (CISST, 1991b). Interestingly, the volumes on the GFT history were gifted to all conference participants – an effective way of disseminating research findings in a specialist community of scholarship. The strategic use of historical narratives can enhance 'the credibility of managerial claims to uniqueness' (Foster et al., 2017: 1182) and, as Rivetti wrote in the preface to the conference proceedings, it can also 'provide points of reflection on contemporary issues' (1991: xi). Fashion historian Enrica Morini further elaborated that, at the time, the Italian fashion system was experiencing an exponential and fast-paced growth, therefore commissioning historical research was valued as an aid to understand and frame what was happening.[3]

There can be detected two approaches to history: a realistic approach, with 'a narrative that mirrors the past' and a constructivist approach, with 'a narrative that interprets the past from the perspective of the present' (Foster et al., 2017: 1183). Though there is no wish to place these approaches in an evolutionary trajectory, I argue that they can be ascribed to specific aims. The realistic approach can be used to interpret the work of scholars belonging to CISST and the first exhibitions on still-active fashion brands – one for all, the 1985 exhibition on Salvatore Ferragamo at Palazzo Strozzi in Florence – which were preoccupied with the rigour of the methodology and presentation of findings. The preoccupation was rooted in the lack of recognition of fashion's cultural relevance and in the belief that a practice of overt commercial interests had no place in cultural institutions. The professionals working with this approach may be identified as historians and often came with a defined academic or institutional background (e.g. Grazietta Butazzi and Kirsten Aschengreen Piacenti). The second approach emerged in the 1990s and may be linked to the rise of the role of curators, intended as professionals with disciplinary expertise who employed curatorial practices beyond the established field of costume and textile curation (e.g. Giannino Malossi and Maria Luisa Frisa). In this case, narratives are often focused on themes existing both in the past and in the present – rather than histories – highlighting continuity rather than chronology. Heritage marketing employs a constructivist use of history, as will be highlighted in Chapters 4 and 5 by the exhibitions and publications commissioned by Pitti, for example, *La Sala Bianca* in 1992, curated by Giannino Malossi, which celebrated forty years of fashion shows in Florence. This approach was openly declared by Raffaello Napoleone, CEO of Pitti Immagine, in the foreword to the catalogue of the 1999 exhibition *Volare: The Icon of Italy in Global Pop Culture*:

> Cultural research, once again, is in step with – and in a certain sense, leaving aside the issue of the independence of initiative, is an expression of – the work of marketing that we are currently undertaking through our trade fairs and the communications projects that normally accompany those fairs. (Napoleone, 1999: 23)

The constructivist approach is an effective strategy for fashion promotion because the fashion system is rooted in the 'consumption of stereotypes' and can be particularly successful when it can draw from a country like Italy with 'a composite identity, comprising not only various regional identities but also various "golden ages"' (Ortoleva, 1999: 55). In fact, fashion does not only build upon existing stereotypes but it also 'contributes over time to the construction of a durable and flexible repertory' (Ortoleva, 1999: 55). As noted by Simona Segre Reinach, associate professor of fashion studies at Bologna University, Italian fashion is inevitably associated with the country's heritage and Italian brands 'need to promote themselves alongside the national image, which is constructed and reconstructed through an ongoing process' (Segre Reinach, 2010: 205). Within this perspective, curation is a practice which can offer multiple solutions to research, interpret and communicate heritage and it is employed, either directly or by commission, by both trade associations like Camera della Moda Italiana, promotion organizations such as Pitti Immagine and individual brands, especially those identified as *heritage brands*.

Heritage was used strategically for the development of Florence as the cultural centre of Italian fashion, a process to which all actors took part, from trade associations to brands and independent professionals. Strategies in the 1950s – centred around the work of Giorgini – and in the 1990s and 2000s – organized by or in collaboration with Pitti Immagine – were successful because they borrowed the cultural capital associated with the Renaissance first and with contemporary art later. This capital was made conspicuous by the chosen venues and the city of Florence at large, 'expressing an immediately recognizable aesthetic has become an important corollary to communicate political and economic strength' (Segre Reinach, 2011: 270).

The most extensive constructive approach which we can detect in the analysis of the Italian fashion system is the 'Renaissance effect' (Corbellini and Saviolo, 2004), which described the continuity between the craftmanship of early modern workshops and the production of contemporary fashion houses. As Belfanti explains, this continuity 'has been elaborated through "manipulations" of history which are in part simplistic and in part distorted' (Belfanti, 2015b: 54). The Renaissance was and is still used as a guarantee for the good quality of Italian products, and Made in Italy is linked to 'artisan creativity' which is a considerable historical falsehood, since 'made in Italy' was born from abandoning artisan work for industrial fashion (Segre Reinach, 2010: 209). Nevertheless, this constructivist history was essential to successfully locate Italian fashion within the existing panorama and to strengthen an identity which would become identified in the Made in Italy label.

1.3 Fashion, heritage and artification

A discussion on Italy's artistic heritage and its employment by fashion requires to address the strategic engagement of the arts by luxury brands. Sociologist Roberta Shapiro introduced the term *artification* to indicate a phenomenon of social change by which non-art objects are perceived as art by a specific group of people (2006), with a focus placed on the processes required for this to take place (Shapiro and Heinich, 2012). Diane Crane, Professor Emerita of Sociology at the University of Pennsylvania, applied it to fashion to explore its relationship with art and detected a partial artification in the ways fashion is produced and displayed (2012). She stated that 'practitioners of cultural forms that are relatively uninstitutionalized … develop institutions that evaluate and regulate these forms of culture, thereby socially constructing them as art forms' (2012: 99) though she dedicated only a brief paragraph to fashion exhibitions and corporate museums. Similarly, Jean-Noel Kapferer, Emeritus Professor at the École des hautes études commerciales de Paris, addressed this process, discussing 'the growing multiplication of associations of luxury brands with artists, galleries, and museums' (Kapferer, 2014: 371). He described art as an effective tool to provide luxury with 'a much-needed moral and aesthetic endorsement, noncommercial connotations, and a paradoxical legitimization of its high prices' by way of highlighting the artistic and cultural relevance of its products (Kapferer, 2014: 375). The cultural dimension of luxury products is especially important for exports as brands can present themselves as 'active elements of the culture and ambassadors for a country's art' (Kapferer, 2014: 376), leveraging on the international recognition of art's value – a strategy even more effective when a country is considered a leader in artistic heritage and production as is the case of Italy. Because of this focus and the influence of Kapferer's article, most of the attention in subsequent literature was paid to collaborations with artists and art institutions, and art-based strategies by luxury brands have been mainly discussed in relation to the exclusiveness which artification can provide (Masè and Cedrola, 2017). Limited attention was instead paid to heritage marketing and strategic uses of the past, which are equally contributing to building and communicating the cultural dimension of luxury brands. There appears to be an equation beteween heritage management tools, museums and the 'art' world, which is not exact as was eloquently demonstrated by Petrov who explored the roots of fashion curation in trade exhibitions as well as in art curation (Petrov, 2019). It is indeed the intersection between these two fields which has led to the most effective curatorial strategies to create value, as they addressed two of the four major ways of creating value which Kapferer ascribed to artification: celebration of heritage and awareness of cultural agency of brands and industries at large (2014: 376).

The term artification is also used to describe the 'multiplication of legitimizing bodies' (Massi and Turrini, 2020: 4) which can generate art, including corporate institutions and exhibition spaces. The Fondazione Prada is an example of a private contemporary art institution which was originally legitimized by the directorship of an established curator, Germano Celant, and over the course of three decades has become one of the leading institutions in the Italian landscape, a position acquired in part for the recognized quality of its collection, in part for the collaborations between Miuccia Prada and her brands with artists, and also thanks to the extensive resources which the institution has access to. Fondazione Prada does not exhibit the heritage of the brand so it cannot be stated that it contributes to the artification of the fashion products Prada produces, however it continues the Western tradition of corporate patronage (further discussed in Section 2.3.1), and the reputation of collector-brands contributes to the recognition of the cultural significance of corporate institutions and their operations. Existing literature groups together sponsorship, patronage, heritage management and different forms of institutions – collections, archives, museums, foundations – under the *artification* umbrella (Massi and Turrini, 2020) but it is fundamental to highlight the different natures of these in order to understand how their operations may contribute to artification as well as to heritage valorization. Institutions will be discussed in Chapter 3.

The key aspect of artification which extensively contributes to the recognition of fashion heritage as culturally relevant, is displacement: 'to be artified, an object must be taken out of the contexts it belongs to' (Massi and Turrini, 2020: 6). Displacement is an effective process that triggers reflections and shifts value from container to contained. It was used in artistic practices throughout the twentieth century (Duchamp's urinal remains a model of artistic displacement today), and contemporary fashion has a long tradition of being included in museums but the legitimacy of its presence in fine arts institutions has only been recently accepted (Petrov, 2019).

The presentation of garments on models within historical settings was at the core of the imagery that Italian fashion proposed in the 1950s and 1960s, and the photography of garments on sculptures was also allowed, for example the furs by Jole Veneziani photographed by Pasquale de Antonis (Frisa, Bonami and Mattirolo, 2005). The use of spaces of established fine arts institutions was granted to brands for events but when Fendi organized the retrospective exhibition *Un percorso di lavoro. Fendi – Karl Lagerfeld* (A Work Path. Fendi – Karl Lagerfeld), at the Galleria Nazionale d'Arte Moderna in 1985, the criticism against a fashion exhibition was such that a senator asked the prime minister during a senate hearing whether this was to be considered a statement of intent on how national arts institutions would be used (Mannucci, 2015). The Biennale della Moda in Florence in 1996 was a monumental attempt at displacement, or rather at demonstrating that the exhibition of fashion alongside art should not be considered displacement (Celant, Settembrini and Sischy, 1996), yet the thesis underlying the project was not understood univocally and many perceived the event as wanting to demonstrate that fashion is art, a statement that even designers who took part in the event such as Manolo Blahnik rejected (Zambiasi, 1996). The installations of designers across Florentine museums also received mixed reviews, with Valentino's installation of red-clothed mannequins nearby Michelangelo's David usually mentioned as the least successful installation. Conversely, a similar approach was employed by the Palais Galliera in 2011 when they curated an exhibition of Madame Grès, displaying her creations alongside the sculptures of Antoine Bourdelle at the Musée Bourdelle in Paris, which was positively received by the press as well as academics. The 2000 retrospective of Giorgio Armani at the Guggenheim Museum in New York is likely the most discussed displacement of fashion, yet it was also a turning point as the extensive discussion across generalist and specialist channels brought about reflections that likely allowed more welcoming approaches in arts institutions towards fashion. The relationship between luxury brands and established arts institutions is only one manifestation of artification, and not the main one in Italy. What instead was crucial to the institutionalization of Italian fashion heritage was the strategic use of the past made by brands and trade associations, by way of heritage marketing and the establishment of corporate institutions.

1.4 Fashion as Renaissance legacy

Together with setting the beginning of Italian fashion in the Renaissance, heritage marketing and the corporate cultural policies of the industry ensured that Florence would be perceived as the birth of the Italian fashion system.

Prominent scholar Eugenia Paulicelli discussed Italian fashion extensively (2004, 2014, 2015a, 2015b) and has highlighted the connection between Italian style and the early modern era (2014, 2016). She has pointed out that 'the theorization of the dressed body and the recognition of the affective power of objects and clothing come very much to the fore in early modern Renaissance Italy' (Paulicelli, 2014: 159). Whilst this supports the declared genealogy rooted in this era, Paulicelli also noted that Italy is a 'composite and multi-layered nation' and its 'multi-locality, its long history, its plurality of fashion cities and their cultural, sartorial, and textile traditions that debunk a deterministic and monological notion of identity and also, as a consequence, a monolithic and linear history of Italian fashion' (2014: 158).

Despite the historical centrality of the Renaissance is now being challenged by contemporary Italian studies, a multifaceted history of Italian fashion has not emerged due to the importance of this centrality for the Made in Italy brand and the heritage marketing of Italian companies, who have over time strengthened this myth. The corporate cultural policies of Pitti Immagine heavily relied on the Renaissance because it would automatically place Florence at the centre of Italian fashion history and their aim was to establish Florence as the birthplace of Italian fashion and its cultural capital. In fact, the historicization of Giorgini's work and the shows in the Sala Bianca at Palazzo Pitti are the result of an effective campaign of heritage marketing. For example, already back in 1987, historian Arturo Carlo Quintavalle questioned the mythmaking processes employed in fashion history:

> That there exists an 'Italian fashion', for instance, is a matter of opinion; that it exists independently and autonomously, as if conjured up by the magic wand of Giorgini in 1951, is doubtful. Moreover, the very idea of an 'Italian fashion', with

the touch of nationalism that lies behind it, seems to have reached the end of its rope. (Quintavalle, 1987: 50)

In particular, Quintavalle questioned the myth of Italian fashion being born from Florence. Yet, the strategies employed by Marco Rivetti through Pitti for the relaunch of Florence as the cultural centre of Italian fashion strengthened this myth and are proof of the influence of corporate cultural policies on the construction of identities. In 1992, an exhibition was commissioned by Pitti to celebrate forty years since the first show in the Sala Bianca of Palazzo Pitti, a residence of the Medici family, which was already hosting the only state-funded museum dedicated to fashion in Italy, Galleria del Costume. Although the first show organized by Giorgini in 1951 had been held in his residence, the exhibition looked over this event to strategically place the birth of fashion in one of Florence's most celebrated Renaissance buildings. The exhibition was entitled *The Sala Bianca: The birth of Italian fashion*, curated by Giannino Malossi. It was inaugurated during the June edition of the Pitti fair in 1992 and held for three months at Palazzo Strozzi, another outstanding example of Renaissance architecture due to its rusticated façade, which had already hosted the retrospective of Salvatore Ferragamo in 1985. *La Sala Bianca* was a historicizing display which traced the beginning of Italian fashion to a Renaissance architecture.

This exhibition served the purpose of establishing an originating myth – which coincided with the originating myth of Renaissance and the Italian language in Florence – so that Florence could claim the rights to a leadership in fashion. The research underlying the exhibition had been carried out by Galleria del Costume, who had planned to publish the results in a book, until Pitti proposed to stage an exhibition. In the exhibition catalogue, the curator Kirsten Aschengreen Piacenti (director of the Galleria), stated that the key success factor of the 1950s shows were their presentation within an artistic environment, through which Giorgini aimed at presenting fashion as an artistic expression (Aschengreen Piacenti, 1992). The display was designed by the architect Gae Aulenti and the theatre director Luca Ronconi, two leading figures of contemporary Italian culture. Each room had a white set which represented a rocky formation upon which stood sculptures, in line with the themes of the four sections: Europe, the Americas, Africa and the Orient. The mannequins stand in dynamic poses, always suggesting movement towards one end of the display and, at times, in the position of running. As Aulenti pointed out in her foreword, it was the kind of display through which 'the commissioner wanted to promote (maybe to demonstrate once again) the talent, originality and creativity of made in Italy'(Aulenti, 1992: 7).[4] This is further demonstrated by the fact that the exhibition toured in 1993 to the Musée des Arts Dècoratifs in Paris. This example demonstrates the agency of the industry had in how Italian fashion was and continues to be framed both domestically and internationally.

The historicization resulting from heritage marketing is imprecise and there exists ample evidence that Italian fashion was not born in Florence in 1951. Nevertheless, it has been demonstrated that Italian fashion intended as 'specific Italian style' and a 'cultural identity' did not exist prior to this date, which resulted in a lack of an 'international legitimization that would allow the new form to compete with the dominant haute couture of Paris' (Belfanti, 2015b: 53). Renaissance was the strongest historical framework of Italian heritage in modernity with international recognition which could be used to construct and maintain an Italian fashion identity. It was initially employed as a guarantee for artistic content in the 1950s:

> Efforts were being made in those years to give Italian output and style characteristics of their very own, drawn from the historical and artistic heritage of the country. References to the past represent the *leitmotiv* of Italian High Fashion, as well as of some of the earliest examples of ready-to-wear High Fashion. (Butazzi, 1987: 7)

With the development of industrially produced, luxury ready-to-wear and the Made in Italy, the focus later shifted to a culture of excellence in making. As Belfanti points out, 'in the rhetoric of entrepreneurs, managers and marketing experts, the Renaissance has become almost an integral part of the DNA of Italian fashion' (Belfanti, 2015b: 54) and fashion, from a broader national cultural identity, has been marketed as the manifestation of the legacy of the Renaissance artistic tradition.

The idea of continuity was first proposed by Giorgini who had employed it as a holistic cultural framework, 'far more ambitious than that referring to craft know-how or to the artistic tradition' (Belfanti, 2015a: 82). Through his operations, Giorgini proposed 'that Italian fashion descended from a Renaissance culture of fashion that had been dominant and that was the product of artists of the calibre of Leonardo da Vinci and Michelangelo' (Belfanti, 2015a: 82), thus constructing the originating myth of Italian fashion. This statement was vague and only partially true, and this is precisely why the Renaissance effect (Corbellini and Saviolo, 2004) triggered by Giorgini became a long-term marketing strategy. As a result, Italian fashion was built on the 'swinging between the tradition and modernity' (Caratozzolo, 2014: 48). Within the broad pool of Renaissance references, Italian fashion brands and professionals were able to identify the narratives which best suited their own nature: the artist-genius, the arts patron, the ancient crafts. Presenting fashion within a historical frame allowed visitors to detect similarities of style and, because the historical frame included other cultural frameworks and not fashion itself, what emerged was a trans-temporal dialogue between artistic expressions, of which fashion was the contemporary one whilst being anchored to the past.

Renaissance-centred narratives are still at the core of marketing strategies aimed at fostering country-of-origin effects and nation branding. The operations of corporate cultural policies were fundamental in the construction of 'the sense of self, image, and character that have been identified as Italian' (Paulicelli, 2014: 165). The construction of a cultural identity for a fashion system is not unchartered territory and studies have analysed the complex strategies and events which made and maintained Paris the leading fashion city (Rocamora, 2006; Steele, 2017 and 2019; Kurkdjian, 2020). Within these strategies, trade shows have always been key tools for marketing purposes, especially 'universal and international exhibitions' (Kurkdjian, 2020: 384). Italy did not have a single city around which a whole fashion system was built and therefore we find processes of nation branding. This was fundamental for the establishment of the Italian fashion industry in those decades and one of the policies which determined its success was the 'differentiation of the marketing strategy through collateral promotional events for exporting the Italian fashion image abroad' (Lazzeretti and Oliva, 2020: 7). Because there existed no history of Italian fashion and the differentiation factor was rooted in the Italian artistic tradition, a broader history of Italian culture was used to project values onto the contemporary fashion offer. Therefore, a process of heritagization, that is a strategic use of history for the benefit of the present (Ashworth and Larkham, 1994; García, 2018), became intrinsic to the very nature of Italian fashion. From this perspective, the role of curation was fundamental to construct a national identity and an analysis of the history of fashion curation in Italy can show how the identity was differently framed over times to mirror changes in the fashion industry.

For this reason, I argue that the need to construct heritage narratives led to the employment of archival and curatorial tools by individual companies and associations, first by commissioning work to external professionals and later by directly managing their own corporate heritage. More importantly, I argue that the awareness of the strategic importance of the past is the reason why companies have increasingly retained more agency in the development of curatorial approach and, ultimately, of the symbiotic relationship between industry and scholarship in Italian fashion curation. This awareness may also be the reason why the industry has (consciously or unconsciously) never committed to any project for a state museum of Italian fashion. Rather than allowing external institutions to thrive, they have institutionalized their own corporate cultural policies and increased their control over the manager of corporate heritage.

2

Industry and corporate heritage in Italy

Since the economic boom of the 1950s and 1960s, Italian entrepreneurs have supported the preservation of the Italian cultural heritage (Amari, [1997] 2001; Bulegato, 2008; Martino, 2010) and have had to invest their own resources in the preservation of industrial heritage. The Italian state does not consider all industrial products as cultural artefacts and, therefore, has not put in place systematic policies for their preservation and study. In 2004, the government commissioned the compilation of the Codice dei beni culturali e del paesaggio (Code of Cultural Heritage and Landscape), a Consolidated Act aimed to combine existing legislation into a unified text. However, the Italian jurisdiction had favoured fine arts over industrial products since the first legislation on the 'Protezione delle cose di interesse artistico e storico' (Protection of artefacts of artistic and historical interest, law 1089, 1939) and the overlook over industrial heritage continued in the 2004 legislation (Carucci, 2006; Delfiol, 2012; Montemaggi and Severino, 2007), which defined *cultural artefacts* as

> Every artefact that can adequately and meaningfully testify both the spiritual and the material culture of man: photographs, cinematographic works, audiovisual works or sequences of images whose production is older than 25 years are cultural artefacts; transportation means with more than 75 years; the artefacts and tools of technology and science with more than 50 years. (Montemaggi and Severino, 2007: 49)[1]

The law decrees that industrial goods produced after 1972 (fifty years to the publication of this book) cannot be considered 'cultural artefacts'. This reflection is particularly relevant given that the Italian fashion industry boomed in the 1970s with the high-end industrial production of ready-to-wear clothing (Stanfill, 2014): the preservation of the majority of the corporate heritage of the fashion and textile industry in Italy is not contemplated in the Italian jurisdiction. As a result, when companies decided to take an active role in the management of their heritage, which required significant financial investments, they employed the results of the projects on their heritage for marketing purposes to ensure returns on the investment made. This combination of research and marketing – I argue – is at the core of corporate cultural policies, however it is first necessary to contextualize corporate heritage in Italy. While this book explores the heritage of the fashion and textile industries as an example, these are not the only industries that have promoted research on their heritage and this chapter aims to highlight this phenomenon which is particularly evident in Italy. In the next sections, I will discuss the reasons which led Italian companies and trade associations to invest in the preservation of corporate heritage.

2.1 Corporate heritage: An Italian perspective

The study of corporate culture developed in organizational theory (Gorman, 1989), where it was defined as the combination of 'values, norms, feelings, aspirations and hopes that are subtly hidden from view, but distinctly recognisable' of a company (Gorman, 1989: 14). It has also been referred to as 'organisational culture' (Ogbonna and Harris, 1998). In 2010 Confindustria, Italy's national association of industrialists, to celebrate the 100th anniversary of the association, published the *Manifesto della Cultura d'Impresa* (Manifesto of Corporate Culture), which was defined as 'the shared story of the daily practice that characterizes the commitment of a company, its projection towards the whole industry and towards society' (Confindustria, 2010: 1). Confindustria's statement declares the collective interpretation of corporate culture as 'a story that goes beyond the company boundaries and is able to fully and forcefully represent the real value of the company for the economic, social and civil development of the country'[2] (Confindustria, 2010: 1). This definition of corporate culture includes not only the internal structures and characteristics of the company, but also the relations with other companies and with society. The recurring statement in the document is the need to acknowledge and promote the role of companies in society: 'The widespread and precise knowledge of the world of a company, of its stories and its projects is the best tool to create awareness of the value of the company for economic and social progress'[3] (Confindustria, 2010: 10). With this social perspective, Confindustria shifts the focus of corporate culture beyond individual companies, and therefore their past is presented as collective past (Martino, 2010). The elements of corporate culture which were established in the past and have legacy in the present constitute corporate heritage. The tangible evidence of corporate heritage is usually preserved in a corporate archive and corporate heritage institutions manage the relationships between a company and its stakeholders (Balmer, 2013). These institutions are the tools that companies use to actively demonstrate their responsibility towards society and to manage their 'social, environmental and economic impacts' (Dahlsrud, 2008: 6). Corporate heritage institutions can be helpful in all these areas and, according to Maria Cristina Bonti (Professor of Economics and Management, University of Pisa) 'can be considered a way for companies to be socially responsible' (Bonti, 2014: 144).

While companies strive to be socially responsible and present their corporate heritage and culture as evidence of their responsibility, they also achieve an internal aim, which is to build the 'cultural legitimization of the company'[4] (Sapelli, 1998: 48). This process was highlighted as early as 1998, at the first conference on corporate museums organized by Assolombarda, the association of industrialists from the northern Italian region of Lombardy. Giulio Sapelli, former president of the Centro sulla Storia dell'Impresa e dell'Innovazione (Centre for the History of Business and Innovation) in Milan, discussed the role of companies in the preservation of industrial heritage and stated that corporate institutions should 'allow an interactive relationship and at the same time offer to the potential subject of this relationship different analytical perspectives which are in fact those of the companies'[5] (Sapelli, 1998: 48). What emerged from subsequent research is that the different analytical perspectives can be grouped in two aims: companies use corporate heritage to underline their contribution to 'the territory, local communities, public institutions or private associations' while also achieving 'compatible goals related to marketing policies with a commitment to the communities in which the museums (and the companies) are situated' (Bonti, 2014: 144). The combination of socially relevant narratives and marketing-effective actions is at the core of corporate heritage management, as will be evidenced throughout this publication.

2.2 Investing in corporate heritage

The absence of support by the Italian State towards the preservation and dissemination of industrial heritage led companies to actively manage their own heritage and eventually set up corporate institutions (Mazzotta, 2018). Unlike governmental bodies, such as the Ministry of Cultural Heritage and Activities, whose aim is the preservation of the national heritage, the operations of companies are moved by a logic of profit, understood both as monetary income and intangible benefits (Bulegato, 2008; Martino, 2010; Montemaggi and Severino, 2007). Due to the investment required to undertake such action, companies seek to ensure the highest return on their investment: on the one hand, the preservation of corporate heritage holds cultural and social relevance; on the other, the communication of corporate heritage holds marketing value. Starting from the first publication on corporate institutions in Italy, the simultaneous presence of these two needs has been identified as one of the key elements through which to interpret operations on corporate heritage: when 'the problem of protecting the industrial memory arose, the first ones to address this issue were companies'[6] (Amari, 2001: 13). Companies commissioned research on their history and established institutions for a systematic preservation, but also employed the outcomes of these operations in their communication strategy (Amari, 2001).

Companies in Italy have increasingly invested more resources into culture and have sought more control on the outputs they finance, following the logic of investments. In 2000, *Il Sole 24 Ore* – Italy's prime financial newspaper – commissioned a national survey of the attitudes of Italians towards corporate investments in culture. It recorded that 70 per cent of the sample visited museums and exhibitions (Finzi, 2000), and they detected a 'strong personal interest in cultural activities supported by businesses' (Finzi, 2000: 101). In the list of projects supported by companies, corporate museums registered the lowest interest, at 24 per cent (Finzi, 2000). Despite this, corporate institutions still retained national relevance: in 2000, they were visited by 1.2 million people (Amari, 2001).

The law and support by the state is another reason underlying corporate cultural policies. On the one hand, the lack of large, established and internationally recognized institutions where to donate one's heritage for its preservation. Moreover, in 2001, the law 342 granted financial incentivization and companies were allowed 'full deductibility from the corporate income of the donations in favour of both the cultural heritage and activities, in compliance with the requirements of the law'[7] (Martino, 2010: 47). The deductibility is applicable both by sponsors and sponsees: as pointed out by the Research Report compiled by the Bocconi University in 2003, the law structured 'a new system of tax breaks in order to incentivise liberal donations for the realisation of initiatives of cultural interest and promote patronage'[8] (Università Bocconi, 2003: 11).

This legal incentive provided a boost to the phenomenon of corporate institutions, which can be eligible sponsees as long as they comply with all the requirements. There are no restrictions regarding the relationship between a corporate institution and its parent company but the corporate institution must guarantee accessibility, operating at least five days a week with set opening times (Università Bocconi, 2003). The presence of these two clauses implies that any institution, to be eligible for tax deductions, must guarantee accessibility to the public. Nevertheless, the Italian legislation is by no means prescriptive from a practical perspective and in fact, the Code of Cultural Heritage and Landscape – while aiming at unifying existing legislation – did not take into account the various disciplines and how their practices may be affected by the Code (Carucci, 2006). In an effort to bridge the gap between the Code and practice, in 2010 the Ministry of Cultural Heritage and Activities and Tourism nominated a committee to define the 'minimum levels of quality for activities of valorisation' (livelli minimi di qualità delle attività di valorizzazione). The proceedings edited by the Committee (Montella and Dragoni, 2010) are, however, not regulatory but merely serve as guidelines for institutions, with the consequence that most archives and museums continue to adopt the guidelines described by the respective international associations, for example the International Council on Archives (ICA) and the International Council of Museums (ICOM).

The Italian legislation does not identify not-for-profit as a necessary requirement for cultural institutions, unlike the International Council of Museums which includes not-for-profit in the definition of museums (ICOM, 2007). Profit – whether tangible or intangible – moves all corporate operations and cannot be prescinded when discussing corporate institutions: as will be demonstrated throughout this publication, the presence of profit does not hinder the relevance of the cultural outputs of corporate institutions. Given that in Italy the phenomenon is widely disseminated, it could be argued that the legislation implies the possibility of the combination of profit and scholarship. Section 4 demonstrates the fundamental role played by corporate institutions in the establishment of corporate studies in Italy. Furthermore, the discussion on the curation of fashion heritage evidences that it was precisely the combination of profit and scholarship which led to the development of curatorial practices.

2.3 Corporate cultural policies

The concept of cultural policy was developed in the 1960s at UNESCO to describe the laws, actions and resources that governments employ to promote culture and make it accessible (UNESCO, 2021). This concept can also be applied to the financial support that many companies provide to cultural projects. The expression 'corporate cultural policy' can be used to describe all the ways in which a company promotes various aspects of culture, which can be related or unrelated to the business of the company. The principal reason for introducing the expression *corporate cultural policy* is precisely to address the dual aims of operations on corporate culture and heritage. In literature, there is a separation between corporate culture and the marketing operations using corporate culture (Urde, Greyser and Balmer, 2007), while the Confindustria manifesto (2010) implies their intrinsic coexistence. Diego Robotti, a state archivist for the Superintendence of Piedmont and Aosta Valley, stressed the difference between corporate culture and corporate communication (understood as marketing): 'The culture of a company is that combination, stratified over time and peculiar, of knowledge, skills and professionalism that determine the success of a company, communication is the image of itself that the company intends to present'[9] (Robotti, 2012: 68). This distinction is fundamental as it helps highlight that companies engage with culture as a manifestation of society – not only as their corporate culture – because culture is a language 'more universal than any other … capable of building up the corporate "reputation" '[10] (Martino, 2010: 14). *Corporate cultural policies* not only describe operations addressing corporate heritage, but culture in general. In fact, before corporate heritage operations, companies employed culture (unrelated to their production) as a tool for communication and only in recent times they have engaged in the production of cultural events themselves. This book focuses, however, only on corporate heritage and corporate cultural policies will be discussed through this lens.

The interactions between the luxury industry and the arts have been analysed through the framework of artification (Section 1.3). In existing literature there appears to be a focus on arts institutions when discussing how companies engage with culture (Massi and Turrini, 2020). As the literature on these interactions is limited and there is no established terminology to differentiate them, I will draw on the work of Valentina Martino, researcher in Communications at the Sapienza Università in Rome, who has dedicated two publications to corporate culture and heritage (2010, 2013). Martino surveyed the relationship between industry and culture in Italy and identified four models of interaction: patronage, sponsorship, partnership and investment (Martino, 2010). These models could be read as 'mutually exclusive and sequential from a historical perspective, the result of a linear evolution'[11] (Martino, 2010: 41), but they now coexist and companies employ a combination of modes in their corporate cultural policies (Martino, 2010). Nevertheless, there appears to be an evolution since the 1950s, both in Italy in general and specifically in Italian fashion curation, in which companies have taken an increasingly active role in the management of their own heritage. With regards to corporate cultural policy, these modes imply different degrees of control of the company and – when dealing with its own heritage – a company generally exercises a high degree of control.

2.3.1 Patronage

Within the corporate environment, there exist two types of patronage (Martino, 2010): traditional patronage is the support of artists and the acquisition of their works, and in this case the founder or CEO of the company is usually identified as the patron; corporate patronage is the commission of works of art on the company, to be employed in corporate communication. Many companies have commissioned artists to design logos, produce images and entire advertising campaigns, sometimes establishing long-term collaborations such as between Salvatore Ferragamo and the futurist artist Lucio Venna (Fidolini, 1987) or between the Milanese department store La Rinascente and the illustrator Marcello Dudovich (Bandera and Canella, 2017). The artworks produced constitute corporate art, defined as art that is commissioned and used by a company for marketing and communications purposes (pptArt, n.d.). In existing literature, the expression 'corporate art' is indifferently used to indicate company-commissioned art and company-owned art, even when the artworks are not connected to the production of the company (Wu, 2003; Kottasz et al., 2008). Despite the objects inscribed in these expressions having similar forms, they are conceptually opposite: in company-owned art the role of the company is that of the collector, in company-commissioned art the role of the company is that of the commissioner, wherefore companies retain more control.

Commissioning corporate art is a widely endorsed practice as shown by the *Corporate Art Awards*, created by pptArt, an 'Italian-based crowdsourcing platform offering bespoke art-related services to corporations and individuals' (pptArt, n.d.: online). The *Corporate Art Awards* were a short-lived yet meaningful initiative with only three editions – 2016, 2017 and 2018 – which aimed at acknowledging the contribution of the industry to the art world. The awards were sponsored by the Business School at Libera Università Internazionale degli Studi Sociali (LUISS) in Rome, the Italian Ministry of Cultural Heritage and Activities and Tourism, and Museimpresa, the national association of corporate institutions. They had categories such as 'best corporate collection' or 'best art award programme' but the rationale was that a scientific committee would evaluate corporate art operations from the previous year and award the best practices.

Patronage is linked with the ideal of the patron, an individual – usually the entrepreneur, owner or president of the company – who collects art to satisfy an artistic or collecting need. In Italian, patronage is translated by the term 'mecenatismo', derived from Gaius Maecenas (68 BCE–8 BCE), an important advisor to Emperor Augustus, who was a wealthy, generous and enlightened patron of the arts (Martino, 2010). Apart from English, most European languages used this word to identify patronage of the arts. Patronage itself in English, although also used in politics, is usually understood as support to the arts. Sponsorship, on the other hand, has no specification as to the object of the support. In French, where both terms are used, *parrainage* (sponsorship) refers to the support of an event or association, *mécénat* (mecenatismo) is solely related to art and in the French law, *mécénat* has a more privileged role than sponsorship (Morel, 2005).

2.3.2 Sponsorship

Martino explains the core difference between patronage and sponsorship effectively: patronage is used by an entrepreneur 'for whom culture is a vehicle for social promotion and a status symbol'[12] (Martino, 2010: 66) while sponsorship is instead a 'pragmatic and instrumental involvement, which translates into a conscious orientation to communication'[13] (Martino, 2010: 66). Martino suggests that patronage is not creating a connection between industry and culture, while sponsorship is. With the exclusion of corporate art commissions as previously discussed, patronage is a one-way relationship in which the immediate effect is either ownership of the artworks or financial donation. Making corporate art or company-owned collections accessible to the public creates a link between industry and culture but is achieved not through patronage, but through loans to or organization of exhibitions. With sponsorship, companies have expectations on the returns of the financial support. Companies gain more control than with traditional patronage, though still limited, and their influence on the sponsored subject increases with the long-term support of specific institutions or projects in specific fields, through which the company builds a reputation of contribution to the development of a specific institution or field. In this case, the corporate cultural policy becomes manifest and its reiteration leads to widespread diffusion and recognition of the company's contribution. A historical example of prolonged sponsorship is that of the Olivetti company, first under the guide of Adriano Olivetti, son of the founder, who became the emblematic model of the enlightened entrepreneur in the 1940s and 1950s, thanks to his social and cultural initiatives. Later, with the President Carlo De Benedetti, Olivetti was relaunched in the 1970s also thanks to a programme of international exhibitions (London, New York, Paris and Mexico City) which accompanied the start-up operations and new products of the company (Martino, 2010). The corporate cultural policy proved very effective for marketing purposes and built a strong brand equity; moreover, it contributed to the recognition of the cultural value of the company itself and the archive, which had been established in 1985, was among the first to be declared of historical interest by the Italian State in 1998.

In the 1980s, sponsorship started to be perceived as a limited tool for promotion, for it is 'characterised by a low rate of involvement of the company, and therefore, by low margins of management autonomy, including control over the very outcomes of the communication'[14] (Martino, 2010: 42). In 1994, the Associazione per l'Economia della Cultura (Association for the Economy of Culture) compiled an extensive report on the Italian cultural economy between 1980 and 1990 (Bodo, 1994) and noticed that due to 'the intolerance of some of the major companies in putting their brand on events organized by others' triggered 'their tendency to intervene directly in the organization of cultural events, building on their company culture'[15] (Trezzini in Martino, 2010: 43). The report identified the first indication of this change in the opening of Palazzo Grassi in Venice, bought and entirely financed by the FIAT group and launched as an exhibition centre, where high-quality exhibitions would be held. Palazzo Grassi opened in 1998 with an exhibition programme based on three principles as stated by the then director Paolo Viti: the institution should never pay for loans; the quality of the curation should be exceptional; there would be a restoration project of an object in the exhibition (Viti, 1998). Palazzo Grassi was later bought by the French entrepreneur François Pinault in 2006 who used the palace, in addition to a more contemporary art exhibition program, to display his personal art collection, effectively returning the institution to a more traditional form of patronage.

The 1990s witnessed an increasingly more complex relationship between companies, 'characterized by the search for a deeper interaction between private partners and cultural initiatives'[16] (Martino, 2010: 42). Furthermore, the defiscalization for sponsorship became of interest to the government, which worked towards financial benefits both for sponsors and sponsees alike and sought 'to incentivize the liberal donations for the realization of initiatives of cultural interest and to favour sponsorship'[17] (Università Bocconi, 2003: 11). The law states that companies can deduct the entire sum of the sponsorship from their taxable income and that the eligible beneficiaries must be non-profit institutions with declared cultural aims in their statute. As a result of this defiscalization, sponsorship was favoured over patronage (Mazzotta, 2018). In 1999, *Il Sole 24* commissioned a survey of the attitudes of Italians towards corporate sponsorship, to identify the most successful and promising areas for investments (Bondardo Comunicazione, 2000) and in 2003 Assolombarda commissioned a report on corporate sponsorship, which presented a whole section dedicated to the jurisdiction regulating cultural sponsorship, intended as a guideline with suggestions for companies (Università Bocconi, 2003). The financial benefits derived from investing in culture and establishing corporate foundations have been recognized in previous research as one of the triggers of the boom of this phenomenon in the 2000s (Bulegato, 2008; Martino, 2010; Xu, 2017). Furthermore, in a country like Italy, where private financial support has integrated and at times substituted State support, these operations are very beneficial for both the cultural heritage and the company's reputation (Mazzotta, 2018). However, before analysing what can be considered fully fledged investments, the next section discusses partnerships between established institutions and companies, an intermediate step towards the establishment of corporate institutions.

2.3.3 Partnership

Partnership is a broad concept employed in many fields and existing literature does not provide a specific definition for the cultural industry. Partnership is generally intended as the association of two or more parties in which all parties share profits and liabilities. A rare mention of this mode of interaction in this field is by Martino (2010), who used it to differentiate traditional sponsorship from a form of interaction between culture and industry that has long-term aims and in which the needs of both parties are equally addressed. In the late 1990s and early 2000s – as testified by contemporaneous publications (Kaiser, 1998, 1999 and 2000; Bondardo Comunicazione, 2000) – companies were seeking more interactions with cultural institutions. The interaction between private and public was also promoted by the then Minister for Cultural Heritage and Activities Giovanna Melandri, who advocated to 'encourage genuine mixed public-private management of culture' (Melandri, 2000: 118). In her contribution to the above-mentioned publication by *Il Sole 24 Ore*, Melandri acknowledged the beneficial effects of sponsorship but stressed the need 'to rethink in detail the phenomenon of public/private collaborations and in particular the way in which cultural investments can be incentivized and,

I would say, considered to be interventions in the public interest' (Melandri, 2000: 118).

Martino (2010) specifically identified the project *Intrapresae Collezione Guggenheim* as an attempt to build a partnership between industry and culture. It was a plan for long-term collaboration between a museum, the Peggy Guggenheim Collection in Venice, and private companies. The project was conceived by Michela Bondardo, who had created Bondardo Comunicazione in 1987, the first agency dedicated to the cultural communication for businesses in Italy. *Intrapresae Collezione Guggenheim* was launched in 1992 as an annual membership scheme for companies 'to enjoy a series of classic and innovative benefits that respond to the companies' communication needs' (Bondardo Comunicazione, 2000: 86). Initially only ten companies took part but over the years seventy-one companies have joined the association.

For Italy it was a groundbreaking experiment especially as it was conceived by a communication agency. It was therefore crafted with direct experience of the communication needs and processes of commercial businesses, around which services were devised to be provided by the museum in exchange of financial support. The synergy with and understanding of the needs of companies at the Venice Guggenheim was most likely due to the fact that the Guggenheim Foundation championed the idea of an international museum corporation and pioneered the opening of branches around the world. In 1997, museums opened in Bilbao and Berlin, although the latter closed in 2012. The Abu Dhabi branch was first announced in 2006 but it has still not opened. Two short lived experiences in America were located in Las Vegas, Nevada (2001–8) and Guadalajara, Mexico (2007–9). Helsinki, Finland and Vilnius, Latvia were also announced in the late 2000s but both projects were abandoned.

In 1999, Michela Bondardo, president of Bondardo Comunicazione, was asked to contribute to a conference organized by Assolombarda on corporate museums, where she described the shift in corporate communication which was then taking place. It was part of a cycle of three conferences organized between 1998 and 2000 to reflect on these institutions and their potential. In her presentation, Bondardo recorded that communications had been focused on products up until the 1980s, while now the institutional communication was becoming increasingly more important for companies in order to 'establish a more complex and articulated relationship with the external world (and also internal), aware that the value of their identity and their history have a weight equal to that of their products or services'[18] (Bondardo, 1999: 39). Bondardo, analysing sponsorship from the perspective of the industry, criticized the passive role it allowed companies to have and the limited returns it could provide them. She urged companies to undertake 'more strategic investments' and to change their interaction with culture 'from sponsorship to cultural policy'[19] (Bondardo, 1999: 43).

The role of Bondardo Comunicazione in raising awareness of the importance for companies to develop cultural policies was eminent. Bondardo nurtured contacts with cultural institutions and served as a bridge for companies wanting to invest in culture. It also realized the importance of exposure and, in addition to the communication of projects and events, in 1997 conceived the *Premio Guggenheim – Impresa & Cultura* (Guggenheim Award – Industry & Culture) in order to create a platform for the recognition of excellence in corporate cultural policies. The aim of the initiative was to identify the best examples of corporate cultural projects and demonstrate their ability 'to create value both for the company and for the community'[20] (Bondardo, 1999: 45). For the first four editions (1997, 1998, 1999 and 2000), only one award, the Impresa & Cultura Guggenheim Prize, was given and special mentions were always presented. In 1999 the award was given to Museo Salvatore Ferragamo, which had only been operating since 1995 but was recognized for its effort to align to museological standards (Ricci, 2015) as well as for organizing an extensive exhibitions programme. The prize was a sculpture and a one year membership to *Intrapresae Collezione Guggenheim*. In 2001, six categories were introduced in addition to the main award:

- the Peggy Guggenheim Prize for the most innovative project;
- the Monditalia Prize, promoted by the Ministry for Production and ICE for the company that best used culture as an instrument of world communication;
- the Assolombarda Prize for the best corporate museum or archive;
- the De Agostini Rizzoli Art & Culture Prize for the most effectively communicated project;
- the Regione Veneto Prize for the project having the highest social value; and
- the Il Sole 24 Ore Prize for the best debuting company (Impresa Cultura, 2001).

In this edition, the award for best corporate museum was introduced and was awarded to the Museo dello Scarpone e della Calzatura Sportiva (Museum of Boots and Sport Footwear). The museum is located in the town of Montebelluna in Veneto, known for its production of sport boots, and is run by the association of the production district. While not associated with a specific brand, the museum was still considered a corporate museum as it promoted the corporate heritage of the entire production district. The best corporate museum or archive prize was only awarded in 2002, 2003 and 2004. The award was renamed *Premio Impresa e Cultura* (Industry and Culture Award) in 2002. This second phase of the award was characterized by the inconsistent presence of prizes, each year renamed, introduced or discontinued, according to which company was sponsoring each award. The Award ceremony ran until 2007 and was then discontinued but no reasons were officially declared. Like the *Corporate Art Awards* (mentioned in Section 2.3.1), the *Intrapresae Collezione Guggenheim* and the *Premio Guggenheim* were initiatives by a private company that bridged industry and culture and sought support from business partners and, most importantly, from academic and national institutions, in order to provide authority to the award. These awards were also a reaction to the lack of recognition of the work of corporate cultural policies and corporate institutions by the Italian state (Carucci, 2006). There are currently no awards which include a category dedicated to corporate institutions and the only acknowledgements have come from the world of archives, with the ICA forming a group dedicated to business archives in 1990 and the UK Museum Association creating a group discussion for corporate collections in 2017.

The choice of Martino (2010) to define *Intrapresae Collezione Guggenheim* as a partnership was not supported by a theoretical and practical description of what a partnership should be. In fact, the *Intrapresae Collezione Guggenheim* was a form of corporate membership by an institution, a practice already adopted elsewhere, especially in Anglo-Saxon countries, usually chosen by big corporations (Pino, 2017). Nevertheless, it signalled a shift in the awareness of companies in developing their corporate cultural policies in a structured way and the recognition of the need of companies to have a 'cultural representative' (Bondardo Comunicazione, 2000: 86). This expression is echoed by the current descriptions of the Museo del Tessuto in Prato (Museo del Tessuto, 2007) and the Museo Salvatore Ferragamo in Florence (Ricci, 2015), who view corporate museums as cultural interfaces of the company (in the case of Ferragamo) or a production district (in the case of Prato and its wool manufacturing).

2.3.4 Investment

The three previous forms of interaction between industry and culture can all be considered investments on the part of the companies as they can provide returns in terms of positive image and associations with established cultural institutions. However, all three are characterized by the limited control that companies can have in the cultural outputs they support (Bondardo Comunicazione, 2000). From the 1990s, Italian companies started to seek more active control on the cultural production they supported and eventually established their own institutions. This section is a general overview of the phenomenon in Italy to situate the operations by fashion and textile companies.

In 2000, *Il Sole 24 Ore* published a book edited by Bondardo Comunicazione entitled: *Porta lontano investire in cultura. L'opinione degli italiani sul rapporto impresa-cultura* (*Investing in Culture Takes Far. The Opinion of Italians on the Industry–Culture Relationship*). Sponsorship was defined as a two-way relationship and the texts included in the publication covered a broad range of perspectives: institutional, financial and governmental. In his article 'Culture as Business Software', Gioacchino Gabbuti (then director of the Italian Foreign Trade Institute) wrote that investing in culture for the industry is 'a method for ensuring its own diffusion' (Gabbuti, 2000: 126). Gabbuti drew the line between sponsorship and investment in the manifestation of the funder's expectations and identified the characteristic quality of investment in the 'selfishness' of the investor (Gabutti, 2000), which implies a different reason – pre-envisioned benefits for the company – for investment, as opposed to sponsorship, the benefits of which cannot be predicted with precision. The marked presence of expectations is directly manifested in the subsequent commissions of surveys and research by trade associations to assess the potential benefits of investing in culture.

In 2003, Assolombarda commissioned Bocconi, Italy's prime business university, to produce a research report entitled: *Il ruolo delle imprese per sostenere imprenditorialità, qualità e fruizione nella cultura e nello spettacolo a Milano* (The Role of Companies in Order to Sustain Entrepreneurship, Quality and Fruition in Culture and Entertainment in Milan). It aimed at identifying the key areas of 'interventions in favour of culture', 'the possibly detectable results or the observations that can be formulated on these interventions,' and 'the motivations/modalities for a better collaboration between companies and culture'[21] (Università Bocconi, 2003: 3). The increasing interest of investing in culture was also mirroring the growing public interest in culture and entertainment: 'the spending of Italian families for culture and leisure has gone from 48 billion annually in 1998 to 64 billion in 2008, an increase of 34%'[22] (Martino, 2010: 54). This report demonstrated the validity of culture as a medium through which to promote corporate values and products.

Traditional sponsorship can however be limiting. At best, companies can be perceived as generous benefactors but never as cultural producers: in other words, the product is always separate from the support – or rather, in marketing terms, the endorsement – of already existing institutions or artworks. The nature of the latter is not affected by the operations of the companies. What Martino described as 'investment' (2010) is the active contribution of companies to cultural production. Martino discusses a company's 'own artistic-cultural message' (2010: 82) ('il proprio messaggio artistico-culturale') and states that this can be achieved through 'self-produced cultural events' (evento culturale auto-prodotto) in order to 'allow much broader margins of autonomy in economic, management and communication terms'[23] (Martino, 2010: 82). According to her, the 'organization of independent cultural events, conceived and promoted by the company,' was favoured as it allowed the 'rationalization – at once economic and communicative – of the corporate investment'[24] (Martino, 2010: 83). This observation allows us to inscribe corporate cultural policies in a trajectory whereby companies were then seeking control in their cultural production and this is confirmed by the last edition of the Industry & Culture Award (2006/2007), in which four out of five projects submitted were created by companies themselves. The direct control over cultural events allows companies to be perceived not only as funding cultural activities (which is achieved through sponsorship) but also as producers. This is also evidenced by the history of fashion curation presented in Chapter 4, in which the late 1990s and early 2000s emerge as a key phase in the shift of the industry from sponsor to cultural producer.

Italy's prime corporate institutions by fashion brands have employed different museological models based on the aims of their policies. For example, Prada appointed Germano Celant, one of Italy's most influential art curators, as director of the art foundation established in 1993 while the Museo Salvatore Ferragamo has developed from a permanent retrospective exhibition of the brand into a decorative arts museum where all exhibitions build on themes associated with the history and values of the brand (Ricci, 2015). In particular, the investments of the fashion and textile industries have not only supported the development of fashion studies in Italy, but have directly influenced curatorial approaches as these were devised to address the communication needs of the funding companies and the research aims of the project. The next section delineates the role played by companies and industry associations in the establishment of corporate heritage studies in Italy: although this publication examines the fashion and textile industries, the next section aims to situate their operations within Italian industry at large and to demonstrate that the active role in the preservation and dissemination of corporate heritage in Italy is a preoccupation shared across production fields and a direct consequence of the Italian legal and cultural-economic situation.

2.4 Industry and scholarship

As previously argued, the limited governmental protection of industrial heritage led companies to undertake actions in order to preserve their own corporate heritage. While devising heritage-led projects in order to inscribe them within corporate operations, such as marketing, the process led to the development of scholarship in the field of corporate heritage studies. In the opening remarks of *A Planning Guide for Corporate Museums, Galleries, and Visitor Centers* (1992), Danilov lamented the lack of scholarship in many corporate museums and galleries. His research was circumscribed to the United States and it is necessary to highlight how different the situation was in Italy. Italian publications on the topic (Bonfiglio-Dosio, 2003; Fanfani, 2012) highlight the role of archivists working for corporate institutions in discussing issues related to the preservation of industrial heritage in Italy. From the late 1970s, companies and specialists led many initiatives, from conferences to publications, with the aim of censing corporate archives in Italy and developing the practice around their management and study.

The transportation company Ansaldo was the first major Italian company to establish a corporate archive open to the public in 1980 and was the organizer of a conference on 'beni culturali, ricerca storica e impresa' (cultural heritage, history research and industry) in 1982 in Genoa (Fanfani, 2012). This was the forerunner of a series of conferences promoted by the industry in this field. Exhibitions then became a useful tool to promote corporate history: this resulted in companies commissioning scholars to research their archives and – often – to implement projects of archival reorganization (Fanfani, 2012). The 1985 exhibitions on the shoemaker Salvatore Ferragamo held in Florence was proposed by the Galleria del Costume, the only state-funded institution dedicated to fashion, and its success convinced the company to initiate a ten-year cataloguing and development project which culminated in 1995 with the opening of the Museo Salvatore Ferragamo at Palazzo Spini Feroni in Florence.

These events also allowed an ongoing interaction between professionals in the field of corporate heritage: associations were established to provide platforms for discussion and the identification of common goals and guidelines. Among these is ASSI – Associazione di storia e di studi d'impresa (Association of Company

History and Studies) – established in 1983 to 'encourage and stimulate those who wish to undertake the path of studies, supporting their seriousness and merit'[25] (Amatori, 2004). Franco Amatori, President of ASSI from 1993 to 2004, stressed how the association was based on the voluntary efforts of professionals who then sought support from national and international institutions. He defined ASSI as 'a free association of scholars which provides a space for any cultural orientation, without hesitancy nor limits, if not that of basic fairness in the relations between scholars'[26] (Amatori, 2004). Amatori was also a professor of Business History at Bocconi University in Milan and employed the network of ASSI to establish there a cycle of seminars dedicated to corporate history (*Incontri di storia dell'impresa*) in 1994 which continued for two decades. Another example is provided by CISST – Centro Italiano per lo Studio della Storia del Tessuto (Italian Centre for the Study of Textile History) established in the late 1970s, which favoured the interaction between the textile and fashion history and scholars; the role of CISST is discussed in Chapters 4 and 5.

Companies were also united by a communal effort in liaising with the state to request official recognition and benefits for the private support of industrial heritage. In 1998, Assolombarda organized the first of three conferences (Kaiser, 1998, 1999, 2000) dedicated to corporate museums, which was titled *I musei d'impresa tra comunicazione e politica culturale* (Corporate Museums Between Communication and Cultural Policy). In the opening statement, Benito Benedini (then president of Assolombarda) discussed the manifesto *Pubblico e privato insieme per l'impresa culturale* (Public and private Together for the Culture Industry) which Assolombarda – together with Associazione Bancaria Nazionale (National Bank Association), Associazione Nazionale Imprese Assicuratrici (National Insurance Company Association) and Confindustria – had recently presented to the deputy prime minister Walter Veltroni. They advocated 'the recognition of the fact that an investment of private individuals in the promotion of culture returns to the advantage of those who made it'[27] (Benedini, 1998: 1). The conference was a pivotal moment for the evolution of corporate museums in Italy: by then various archives and other corporate institutions had been founded and this event signalled the beginning of a discourse on corporate museums, where expertise and practice were brought from varied experiences and became the foundations for scholarship in this field. Assolombarda appointed Linda Kaiser to conduct research and lead projects on corporate museums. From the proceedings emerged the need to create shared scholarship on corporate heritage, to then employ in any initiative in the field. This approach was eminently evidenced by the speech given by Carlo Camerana, then Cultural

Heritage Advisor, Assolombarda and president of the Museo Nazionale della Scienza e della Tecnica 'Leonardo da Vinci' (National Museum of Science and Technology in Milan). During the conference, Camerana presented the Assolombarda project for a Centre for Corporate Museums and stressed the interaction they were seeking with existing cultural institutions, especially those thematically closer to them.

> It is not by chance that the location of the future Centre has been identified in a museum context, and in particular in the museum that *par excellence* reflects and 'represents' the culture and heritage of companies on the national soil: the Museum of Science and Technology in Milan … The 'Leonardo da Vinci' Museum will lend not only its own premises, but also and above all its expertise in the fields of conservation, research, interpretation, education and exhibition. (Camerana, 1998: 65)[28]

Given the position held by Camerana at the museum, hosting the future Centre was probably a logistically feasible option, but most importantly the physical proximity to the established institution would have facilitated the exchange between museological scholarship and corporate heritage expertise. Moreover, the museum was the Italian headquarters of ICOM and this operation could be interpreted as the will of the industry for corporate institutions to work to international standards but also to be recognized by official bodies. The mission of the centre was to 'enhance and promote corporate museums in Italy and eventually in Europe'[29] (Camerana, 1998: 66) and one of the objectives was to promote the establishment within ICOM of a committee specifically dedicated to corporate museums (Camerana, 1998). This committee never materialized but its project is proof of the aim of companies to foster exchange between scholarship and industry.

The active role of the industry in developing a practice that combines scholarship and corporate needs is also manifest in the awareness of professionals working for corporate institutions. Most professionals – those with specialist training – strive to apply the highest archival and museological standards possible, driven by professional guidelines, but they also understand the different requirements of the industry (Arezzi Boza, 2007). Francesca Appiani (Museo Alessi, Omegna) took part to the 1999 Assolombarda conference and her speech demonstrates how professionals were aware of the need to adapt their skills to the corporate context.

> We are fortunate to participate in the development of a new form of cultural enhancement; a form that can and must learn from museology and archival

practice, but which, at the same time, can offer an autonomous and original contribution. I think this is one of the most compelling aspects of our work: we are building new realities, potentially free to be structured according to their own intentions, thanks to the indications of a precious methodological tradition. (Appiani, 1999: 116)[30]

Appiani's statement records the understanding of established museological and archival practices as models for the development of a new practice and not as prescriptive guides to follow. Alessandra Arezzi Boza (Fondazione Archivio Emilio Pucci, Florence) also commented on the breadth of skills required for the aforementioned hybridization.

> The approach to the management of a fashion archive must today be very articulated and requires specific skills that are not limited to mere corporate reasons and perspectives, nor to strictly archival or museum ones, but which are able to find a balance between various needs: historical-documentary and conservation, those of critical and cultural readings of the 'visual', iconic, stylistic and creative registers and those of the strategic use of artefacts. (Arezzi Boza, 2012: 148)[31]

The 1999 conference organized by Assolombarda was dedicated to the theme of identity and directions, and in 2000 another conference was held on the management of corporate museums. The long-term outcome of these conferences was the establishment of Museimpresa**,** Associazione Italiana Archivi e Musei d'Impresa (Italian Association of Company Archives and Museums), founded in 2001 in Milan by Assolombarda, Confindustria and fifteen founding companies, including Ferragamo (Museimpresa, 2021). As Martino has pointed out, Museimpresa was established solely for the 'autonomous will of the entrepreneurial world'[32] (Martino, 2013: 109) and now counts more than sixty member companies. It built on previous experiences and effectively implemented enhanced versions of practices shared during the meetings. In November 2001 it launched the first *Settimana della Cultura d'Impresa* (Corporate Culture Week), which had been previously organized by the association ASSI as a biannual event in 1985, 1987, 1989, 1991 and 1993. The Museimpresa Week has since been regularly operating on an annual basis and has grown to include more than sixty events over two weeks (2019 edition). The website operates primarily as a tourist information centre: it has a news feed page that covers events organized by members, national and international conferences as well as foreign institutions, and it proposes itineraries to explore cultural heritage around Italy.

Museimpresa has also worked on promoting corporate heritage to non-specialist audiences and, thanks to its close link with Confindustria, has become the main interlocutor with the Italian State on all issues related to industrial heritage and has advocated the official recognition of corporate institutions by the State. The first recognition came from the field of education: in 2004 an agreement was signed between the Ministry of Education, University and Research, and Museimpresa for the development of educational and exchange programmes for schools by corporate museums and archives. Since then, the Italian State has increased the interaction with private associations, tacitly acknowledging the role and expertise of corporate archivists in particular. In 2008, the Direzione Generale per gli Archivi (General Direction for Archives) of the Ministero per i Beni e le Attività Culturali (Ministry of Cultural Heritage and Activities) stipulated an agreement with the Centro per la Cultura d'Impresa (Centre for Corporate Culture) for the establishment of the Archivio Economico Territoriale (AET, Territorial Economic Archive). Through this agreement, the Centre was appointed to 'acquire, rearrange and make accessible economic archives of considerable historical interest, in collaboration with the local Superintendencies'[33] (Centro per la Cultura d'Impresa, 2014). Then, in 2011, for the 150th anniversary of the Italian Unification, many initiatives took place to celebrate and promote the industrial heritage of Italy. Among these was the *Portale degli Archivi d'Impresa* (Portal of Corporate Archives), an online platform aimed at gathering information and exhibit reproductions of many historical corporate archives, covering more than 1,500 large-, medium- and small-sized businesses (MiBACT, 2011). The project was conceived by the General Direction for Archives of the Ministry for Cultural Heritage and Activities and implemented thanks to numerous partners, two of which are private institutions established by companies: the Commissione Cultura (Culture Commission) of Confindustria and Museimpresa. In December 2017, it finally signed an agreement with the Direttore Generale dei Musei (General Director of Museums), Antonio Lampis, to 'consolidate the relationships of collaboration between the Ministry of Cultural Heritage, Activities and Tourism, and Museimpresa, with the aim to integrate the network of corporate museums in the national museum system'[34] (Museimpresa, 2017).

Through research documented in this chapter, I have established the state of corporate heritage in Italy, the reasons that led Italian companies to manage and preserve their corporate heritage and to implement corporate cultural policies. I have also outlined why companies have increasingly sought control over the cultural events and projects they support, and eventually founded museums to produce their own and stress their contribution to society. The chapter has evidenced how the management of corporate heritage by companies is inevitably combined with marketing, resulting in the combination of corporate and public needs underlying the operations of corporate museums. In order to further the analysis of this phenomenon, in the next chapters, I will focus on the Italian fashion and textile industries to verify the arguments made in this chapter with empirical evidence. In the next chapter, I will focus on corporate institutions and unfold how corporate heritage is managed and interpreted.

3
Corporate heritage and institutions

Literature on corporate institutions is relatively limited and does not provide clear definitions. The term *corporate museums* has been employed as an umbrella term to identify all forms of corporate institutions and facilities, and companies have named these places in a variety of ways, regardless of the specialist meaning of the titles employed (archive, gallery, museum). The first publication on the topic was written in 1943 by Lawrence Veil Coleman, then director of the Association of American Museums, and entitled *Company Museums*, which recorded the facilities set up by American companies to celebrate their history (Coleman, 1943). However, it is the research by Victor J. Danilov, former director and now President Emeritus of the Museum of Science and Industry in Chicago, that became the reference point for subsequent studies. Danilov mapped the northern American panorama with *Corporate Museums, Galleries, and Visitor Centers: A Directory* (1991) and made a list of the 'many things' which can be considered a corporate museum:

> A museum on the history of a company, a collection of artifacts on display, a publicly focused art or science museum, an exhibit on a company's operations and products, a historical corporate building, a memorial or anniversary exhibition, a sizeable lobby display, or even a mobile exhibition. (Danilov, 1991: 9)

In his follow-up publication – *A Planning Guide for Corporate Museums, Galleries, and Visitor Centres* (1992) – Danilov provided a definition of a corporate museum, which he described as a

> corporate facility with tangible objects and/or exhibits, displayed in a museum-like setting, that communicates the history, operations, and/or interests of a company employees, guests, customers, and/or the public. (Danilov, 1992: 4)

He also attempted to create broad categories into which all forms of corporate institutions, cultural spaces and events could be included, however museums were grouped by features that were not mutually exclusive, which prevented a clear identification of the characteristics that differentiate corporate museums. For example, he listed 'collection-based museums' (Danilov, 1992: 13), then 'science centres' (Danilov, 1992: 20) and 'mobile museums and exhibits' (Danilov, 1992: 25). The first group is defined by collecting policy, the second by themes and the third by logistic factors. Subsequent publications contributed to inconsistent categorization: some institutions are grouped by themes or focus, others by display and others by location (Amari, [1997] 2001; Bulegato, 2008; Danilov, 1991, 1992; Negri, 2003).

Various scholars have since built on Danilov's definition and modified it to better suit the angle and findings of their research (Bonti, 2014; Griffiths, 1999; Hollenbeck, Peters and Zinkhan, 2009; Lehman and Byrom, 2007; Livingstone, 2011; Piatkowska, 2014; Stigliani and Ravasi, 2007). Although literature in this field was first established by North American scholars (Coleman, 1943; Danilov, 1991, 1992), Italian literature on this topic is sensibly larger (Amari, [1997] 2001; Negri, 2003; Xu, 2017) and, according to Italian literature, Italy holds the highest number of corporate institutions (Amari, [1997] 2001; Bulegato, 2008; Martino, 2013; Negri, 2003).

The literature does not give a complete picture of corporate institutions. Most texts are academic papers that focus on case studies: Japanese corporate museums (Lehman and Byrom, 2007); Italian companies Alfa, Kartell, and Piaggio (Stigliani and Ravasi, 2007); the World of Coca Cola in Atlanta, the United States (Hollenbeck, Peters and Zinkham, 2008); German manufacturer Porsche, Mercedes and BMW (Piatkowska, 2014); the Museo Salvatore Ferragamo in Florence (Carù, Leone and Ostillio, 2016; Iannone, 2016) and the former Gucci Museo in Florence (Bertoli et al., 2016). Or, there are general surveys and directories (Amari, [1997] 2001; Bulegato, 2008; Baglioni and Del Giudice, 2012; Danilov, 1991, 1992; Martino, 2010; Negri, 2003). Research approaches are primarily exploratory and the fields mostly preoccupied with corporate museums have been marketing and organizational studies, yet two recent publications presented architectural investigations (Messedat, 2013; Xu, 2017). I will endeavour to pinpoint the key features of these institutions and I will use examples dedicated to fashion and textiles.

Corporate institutions have only been briefly discussed in fashion studies. In 2000, Fiona Anderson (then senior curator of Fashion and Textiles, National Museums Scotland, Edinburgh) wrote an essay entitled 'Museums as Fashion Media' dedicated to the relationship of institutions with the contemporary fashion system and their potential as communication media. She did, however, only mention museums dedicated to designers and analysed exhibitions, as opposed to museums as institutions (Anderson, 2000). In 2004, Lou Taylor (professor of Dress and Textile History, University of Brighton) delved more into what she referred to as 'designer museums' in her influential publication *Establishing Dress History* (Taylor, 2004). In 2008, Alexandra Palmer used the provocative expression 'imitation museums' (Palmer, 2008: 34) to discuss the venues in which costume and textile exhibitions were becoming increasingly popular: private galleries, auction houses, department and specialty stores. Palmer did not include corporate museums but her reflection is still relevant as she explored the critical points that emerge when fashion curation is applied beyond the boundaries of traditional museums. In 2010, Berg published a ten-volume *Encyclopaedia of World Dress and Fashion* edited by Joanne B. Eicher (Professor Emerita, University of Minnesota, Minneapolis) and volume ten, dedicated to global perspectives, included a section dedicated to fashion and museums, edited by Amy de la Haye (professor of Dress History and Curatorship, London College of Fashion). Here, the article by British curator and scholar Eleanor Thompson discussed museum collections and the one by Jean Druesedow (director of the Kent State University Museum) discussed exhibitions of dress and fashion and both referred to corporate museums but did not make any significant differentiation.

Therefore, the next sections are dedicated to the differences between foundations (3.1) and museums (3.3) as well as to collecting policies (3.2). This discussion is instrumental to assess the nature of corporate institutions, which combine – to different extents – the preservation and marketing of heritage. This reflection will also provide a theoretical framework within which to review the history of fashion curation in Italy and detect how the heritage operation by fashion brands have impacted on the development of curatorial practices.

3.1 Corporate foundations

The fiscal incentives instituted by the Italian State in 2000 led to an unprecedented growth in the sector of cultural foundations. In 2009, Istat (Italy's National Institute for Statistics) published a report on foundations in Italy which recorded that 'the corporate foundations set up between 1996 and 2005 represent 64.1 per cent of the foundations existing in 2005'[1] (Monteverdi, 2009: 27). This decade was a very important phase in the history of patronage and corporate foundations in Italy for it was also when Italian legislation regulated the operations allowed to a foundation (Paletta, 2009). The Italian legislation decrees the versatility of foundations not only from an organizational perspective, but also in terms of focus: foundations do not necessarily have to deal with the object of production of the parent company but must interact with the local community (Prele, 2008). Nonetheless, the legislation poses limits to foundations, or rather requirements, such as the need to establish in advance which resources (physical or financial) are destined to the foundation. In 1999, Maria Cleme Bartesaghi (then legal representative of Ernst & Young International) wrote that 'the existence of an initial nucleus of assets destined by the founder or founders for the achievement of a specific purpose is essential'[2] (Bartesaghi, 1999: 62).

Foundations are a flexible organizational model, as they come with limited legal requirements. According to the European Foundation Centre (EFC), the defining characteristic of a 'corporate foundation' is its management, that is, the link with the parent company (Bodo and Monteverdi, 2009). No mention is made of the areas or types of operations carried out, but the common practice is named 'organized philanthropy'. Corporate foundations operate a combination of patronage, sponsorship and potential partnership. In Italy, the majority of organized philanthropy focuses on the arts and the nation has a long tradition of bank foundations supporting the arts, starting with the philanthropic activity of the Medici family in the Renaissance (Prele, 2008). The Italian legislation does not provide an explicit definition of a cultural foundation but identifies its main activities: they must engage with 'a significant patrimony, bibliographic, archival, museum, cinematographic, musical, audiovisual publicly available in continuous form'; and they must 'perform and provide services, of ascertained and relevant cultural value, linked to research activities and the held cultural artefacts'[3] (Legge n.534, 1996: art.2). Because these two requirements apply to all cultural institutions, and because corporate foundations are not necessarily related to corporate heritage, foundations are not intrinsically linked with corporate heritage. In fact, in Italy there exist various art foundations established by businesses, which tend to support the arts but do not have a direct connection to their production. These operations are part of the corporate cultural policies and they 'play a crucial role in the artification process, as they not only represent the means for celebrating the brand but also contribute to developing the relationship between the brand and the territory' (Massi and Turrini, 2020: 20). Corporate art foundations are 'still affected by longstanding assumptions prevalent within traditional cultural policy' and focus on core ideas such as the 'artist-genius' as well as the transcendental and public value of art (Hesmondhalgh and Pratt, 2005: 7), as can be assessed by the rhetorical references to the Renaissance and enlightened patrons found in the majority of forewords by sponsors in fashion exhibition catalogues (examples will be provided in the following chapters).

A foundation established by a fashion brand is Fondazione Nicola Trussardi in Milan, which does not have a permanent location and is dedicated to organizing temporary exhibitions by contemporary artists in different venues each time. It is emblematic of the flexibility of the nature of foundations and it has been maintained that a clear separation between foundation and parent company is highly effective because it takes away the stigma of commercial interests and, thus, leads to 'increasing the number of visitors to the contemporary art exhibition and enhancing the resonance and awareness of the non-profit organization' (Rurale and Prestini, 2020:78). Foundations are equally used to preserve the story of the founder and its oeuvre, such as the Fondazione Salvatore Ferragamo: this was created in 2013 for the management of the historical archive, working alongside the existing museum. According to its director Stefania Ricci, the foundation is 'a larger and freer container than the museum, which cannot and must not stray from the corporate mission' (Ricci in Fulco, 2015).[4] Ricci pointed out that the flexibile nature of foundations suits the 'work in progress' nature of corporate cultural policies: 'I believe that the relationship between the museum and the foundation will become clearer over time, since it is a family business everything happens in small steps' (Ricci in Fulco, 2015).[5] This flexibility is crucial for companies who need to adapt their operations to changes in the market as well as in their organizations, for example with a change of creative direction or ownership.

These two examples show that the presence of heritage artefacts is not a requirement for corporate foundations since they are not necessarily tied to the production of the parent company, unlike corporate archives and collections. Given the focus of this book on corporate heritage, the next section looks at the latter to understand the collecting policies of corporate institutions and thus analyse how corporate heritage is interpreted and communicated.

3.2 Collecting corporate heritage

As early as 1992, Danilov observed the difficulty in categorizing these institutions because 'many corporate facilities are combinations with characteristics of museums, galleries, and/or sales showrooms' (Danilov, 1992: 36). The choice of an umbrella term results in a misrepresentation of the phenomenon, especially in Italian literature. Starting from the first publication by Monica Amari ([1997] 2001), Italy was described as the country with the highest number of corporate museums, as the published census included all forms of corporate facilities, with or without permanent displays, with no specific criteria regarding accessibility or curatorial policy. This all-inclusive approach was also adopted by Fiorella Bulegato (associate professor of Industrial Design, IUAV University of Venice) in her 2008 census, which is the most recent to date (Bulegato, 2008). A differentiation between archives, museums and galleries would not diminish the scale of the phenomenon but would introduce the awareness that each facility has specific characteristics. Cecilia Gilodi (manager of the Centro Studi, Confindustria Moda) wrote that:

> Although companies often propose different titles such as 'historical path', 'gallery', 'history gallery', 'museum-workshop', 'documentation centre', 'cultural centre', 'factory house museum', the institution qualifies in any way as museum. (Gilodi, 2002: 7)[6]

She observed that companies name institutions arbitrarily, regardless of the nature associated with specific titles, but she did not state why all these institutions can nevertheless be considered museums. She did, though, state that museums should be defined against archives and collections:

> At the moment, the literature does not provide a shared definition of corporate museums and, therefore, a debate is taking place which prompts to define a corporate museum as different from two other types of similar operations put in place by a company: corporate collections and corporate archives. (Gilodi, 2002:7)[7]

Gilodi suggested a difference between collections, archives and museums but the following classification shows that she did not employ traditional bi/tri-dimensional division between archives and collections. She listed only documents and machinery as the objects that an archive collects, whereas any material related to the production and commercial activity belongs to the corporate collection. She followed on the work of Amari in operating a distinction based on content rather than form: 'a corporate collection is a collection of objects related to the activity and the production of one or more of the companies belonging to the same category of goods' (Amari, [1997] 2001: 72).[8] A more current example coming from a fashion archive is provided by the Benetton Archive. Francesca Ghersetti (Coordinator and Archive Manager at the Documentation Centre of Fondazione Benetton Studi Ricerche) and Greta Gamba (Corporate Communication Manager at Corporate Communication & Public Affairs department of Benetton Group) discussed the structure of their archive and reported that there is,

> a wide range of structured physical archives, both centralised (a 'general archive' and a 'historical archive' run by the general services), and under the supervision of the company's various departments (including the design department archive and the digital archive held in the press office) … Around 70 garments [of the 12,000 held], considered to be the most iconic from the various decades (1960s-1970s-1980s), have been selected by the company's founder, Luciano Benetton, to be permanently kept in the archive and displayed in rotation. When they were transferred to the Archive, these historic garments had to be stored and described according to archive and museum standards. (Ghersetti and Gamba, 2017: 118–19)

Given the inevitability of the presence of three-dimensional objects for a clothing manufacturer, the authors frequently talk about an 'archive' rather than 'a collection' most likely because the garments are kept as a documentary record – a testimony of a fashion company's business – and in fact all other records kept revolve around these garments, their production, promotion and consumption. Corporate heritage professionals tend to adapt terminology in the same way as they adapt their archival or museum skills to suit the needs of a company.

3.2.1 Corporate archives

Companies are legally required to preserve documents for a set number of years for financial purposes, differently according to each national jurisdiction. ICA – the international association established in 1948 by archival professionals – appointed a committee in the 1990s to formulate a shared definition of archive and guidelines on how to establish and operate an archive. In 1993, it published the General International Standard Archival Description, and the definition of archive was adopted in an Italian translation by the official Gazette of State Archives in 1995. Museimpresa (the Italian national association of corporate institutions) employed this definition: 'An archive is a set of documents, regardless of form or support, automatically and organically created and/or accumulated during the activities and functions by a producer'[9] (Museimpresa, 2021). Therefore, according to the ICA, every company has an archive of documents.

Italian legislation does not impose obligations over the preservation of industrial heritage unless the holdings of a corporate archive are declared to have historical interest (Carucci, 2006). Once the declaration is official, 'the private body (i.e. the company) is obliged to preserve the archive and some extraordinary acts such as displacement, transfer to other legal entities, alienation, elimination and rejection, are placed under legal authorization'[10] (Delfiol, 2012: 6). These limiting conditions are among the reasons why companies themselves do not wish to receive the declaration of interest. In fact, Delfiol reported that many companies would discard parts of their archives even without permission, thus creating problems as new managers would not know about the limits imposed on their actions by the declaration of interest. To avoid this, usually only the oldest documents in the archive are declared of interest, so companies can discard the remainder (Delfiol, 2012).

Archival studies in Italy identify three stages in a corporate archive: current archive, deposit archive and historical archive. The current archive is where all documents are kept, almost without selection, while the deposit archive is the intermediate phase of selection and discarding of documents in view of long-term preservation (Fanfani, 2012). Tommaso Fanfani (former director of the Fondazione Piaggio) believed this phase to be the most critical as it called for 'a virtuous combination between the sensitivity of the entrepreneur, the supervision of the appointed institutions (Superintendencies) and researchers'[11] (Fanfani, 2012: 24), and fundamental is scholarship, intended as expertise in archival practice as well as in corporate history. Corporate heritage is then preserved in the historical archive, defined as 'a permanent structure that collects, inventorizes and preserves official and original documents of historical interest produced by a company in the performance of its activities and functions, ensuring its consultation for purposes of study and research'[12] (Martino, 2013: 180). This definition of historical archive by Martino suggests that once a historical archive is established, accessibility and research are, in some way, catered for.

Companies employ archives and their contents in accordance with corporate needs and, as stated by Barbara Costa (archivist at Intesa San Paolo), this process is typical of corporate archives and highly influential with regards to traditional archival practice. Corporate archives 'have shown how an archive can be a source of innovative ideas or become an important actor in corporate marketing and in relationships with customers to increase brand awareness and corporate reputation'[13] (Costa, 2012: 133). This statement by Costa embodies a general attitude of flexibility towards archival practices when implemented within a corporate context. For example, traditionally an archive was understood as a deposit of two-dimensional documents (Costa, 2012) however a survey of proceedings from conferences dedicated to corporate institutions evidences a variety of expressions. Tommaso Fanfani emphasized the variety of artefacts included in an archive – 'extremely heterogeneous in terms of quality and quantity'[14] (Fanfani, 2012: 20–1) – and identified in the addressing of corporate needs the shared characteristic. The archivist Diego Robotti also adopted a similar approach and used the expression 'product archive' to identify documents 'not only written on paper, but also objects, both material and digital and especially hybrids'[15] (Robotti, 2012: 67). Both definitions suggest a preoccupation for the type of objects eligible to be included in an archive, given the traditional assumption that archives should comprise paper documents. This assumption was reiterated by Alessandra Arezzi Boza (former curator of the Fondazione Archivio Emilio Pucci) who differentiates product archives from documentary archives (Arezzi Boza, 2012). She adopted the same perspective as the professionals managing the Benetton Archive and in fact, talked about an *archivio prodotto* (product archive) and an *archivio documenti* (document archive) as the two divisions of the Pucci Archive (Arezzi Boza, 2012: 150). Arezzi Boza stated that the 'scientific project [is applied to] the archives (and the plural is compulsory)' (Arezzi Boza, 2012: 151)[16] though she does not elaborate on the implications of the presence of multiple archives. The testimony of Arezzi Boza is particularly relevant as it records archival practice in a fashion and textile corporate archive.

All authors mentioned in the previous paragraph were published in the same conference proceedings and are established professionals in the field, yet they all provide different definitions of an archive, likely informed by their individual professional experiences and expertise. Contemporary archival practice has moved from the notion of the archive as repository of two-dimensional documents to include three-dimensional and digital material. The archive can remain a separate entity from display spaces – which may be called galleries, visitor centres or museums – where the holdings are shown, or it could be integrated within the museum. For example, the Museo Salvatore Ferragamo, owned by the company, is separated from the archive, which is managed by the independent Fondazione Salvatore Ferragamo. Therefore, to continue analysing corporate heritage, a discussion of collections as groups of three-dimensional objects is undertaken, to assess whether archive and collection can be employed as complimentary terms to describe the complexities of corporate heritage.

3.2.2 Corporate collections

While American literature on corporate institutions did not distinguish archives from collections (Coleman, 1943; Danilov, 1991, 1992), the first Italian publication on the subject presented a differentiation (Amari, [1997] 2001). Amari wrote that 'the collection, which often remains the starting point for a future museum structure, is not to be confused with the archive, which by definition collects only official documents'[17] (Amari, [1997] 2001: 73). This statement can be misleading for Amari does not provide a definition of 'official' and implies that a collection only includes three-dimensional objects; furthermore, her definition of corporate collection – 'materials that can testify to the production and life of the company'[18] (Amari, [1997] 2001: 72) – is similar to 'product archive' (Robotti, 2012: 67). However, in her definition of corporate collection, Amari identified as a characterizing element the conscious effort to gather records of the company's production for testimonial purposes. This may imply Amari's awareness of museological subtleties, a suggestion further evidenced by Amari's recognition that the subject of a collection changes the nature of the collection. Danilov (1991, 1992) had included corporate art in corporate collections, whereas Amari explicitly addressed the difference. Corporate art collections are not necessarily related to the company's heritage, as it is usually 'an expression of personal tastes and artistic tendencies and does not represent the evolution of the company' (Amari, [1997] 2001: 72).[19] Furthermore, while enhancing brand equity and building a positive reputation for the brand, corporate art collections do not affect the understanding of the company's production.

According to Amari, a corporate collection is private, like an art collection, and is not accessible, although 'it can be visited by scholars of the sector and in some cases, it can be used as didactic support for training courses'[20] (Amari, [1997] 2001: 73). Yet, it is this didactic purpose that makes it different from archives: a collection has an underlying idea – 'functional, aesthetic, historical'[21] (Amari, [1997] 2001: 74) – according to which it is organized. The didactic purpose implies the social and cultural relevance of the collection. Building on these observations by Amari, and referencing the work of Russell Belk – whose publication *Collecting in a Consumer Society* (1995) contextualized collection studies within business environments – what differentiates an archive from a collection is the social dimension through which the collection is interpreted, mirroring the difference between individual and institutional collections.

> Our extended selves are affected by institutional collections as well as by our individual collections, except that broader and more aggregate levels of the

extended self are implicated. Instead of the individual or family level of self, it may be the community, regional, or national level of self that is extended by an institutional collection. (Belk, 1995: 102)

This quote by Belk is particularly relevant to the analysis of corporate institutions as it allows to frame the social relevance of their operations: corporate institutions use the material evidence of their history and production to promote their public image, while also highlighting their contribution to society. Corporate collections may be created merely for storage needs, but when their study and presentation to audiences engage with a social dimension, then they can be considered institutional collections. The 'explicit will to assemble and preserve materials that can testify to the production and life of the company' (Amari, [1997] 2001: 72) and its thematic focus are the characterizing elements of a corporate collection. The process of 'active and selective collecting' (Belk, 1995: 67) of the documents testifying to the production of the company takes place in the creation of the historical archive (Bonfiglio-Dosio, 2003; Fanfani, 2012; Martino, 2013), so it can be said that, if agreeing with Amari's definition of collection, the historical archive is the corporate collection, for it is organized according to a precise strategy. Then, the needs of the company and the relevance of the documents for society both influence the selection process and the fruition of the archive, and can be interpreted as an implementation of the corporate cultural policy. I argue that this process is the differentiating factor between an archive as a by-product of the activities of a company and an archive as the corporate institution established to preserve and disseminate the corporate heritage.

The operations of museums respond to a curatorial policy, whether or not they have collections (Desvallées and Mairesse, 2010). This may reflect the 'will' (Amari, [1997] 2001) which has underlined the collecting practice of an individual collector or it could be developed to respond to a variety of collections, in the case of the merging of different collections. In the case of corporate museums, it always responds to a common theme – the company, where it can be devised as the manifestation of the values of a company. What distinguishes a corporate museum from a corporate archive – posit the previously explained technical definition of archive – is what Xu calls the 'interpretative framework to guide people's reflection on that product or fact' (Xu, 2017: 36). Given the centrality of collections to museums (Montemaggi and Severino, 2007), the next section focuses on the nature of corporate museums and their relation with corporate collections and archives.

3.3 Corporate museums

Linda Kaiser (specialist in History and Criticism of Artistic and Environmental Heritage) noted that 'the establishment and enrichment of the historical archive is almost always the basis and the requirement, as well as the initial nucleus, of the corporate museum'[22] (Kaiser, 1998: 4). However, Kaiser differentiates corporate archives from corporate museums for their scope and audience: corporate archives aim for the preservation of corporate heritage primarily for the company but also to the service of scholars, while corporate museums exist to disseminate corporate heritage (Kaiser, 1998). This comment by Kaiser evidences an awareness of the differences between institutions that have not been explored elsewhere in existing literature. Corporate archives are tools by and for the company; they may be open to scholars or to visitors but it is not their main purpose. On the other hand, corporate museums are institutions established purposefully to provide a service to external audiences, while also serving corporate needs. The focus on Italian fashion curation of this publication was chosen to provide the empirical evidence necessary to identify how the coexistence of corporate needs in museums affects curatorial practices, as will be unfolded in the following chapters. Ensuing publications reiterated Kaiser's observation and identified the communication element as the need underlying the establishment of a museum. Robotti wrote that the corporate archive is 'the spontaneous and practical result of the production activity, it has no immediate communicative purpose (with the exception of advertising and part of the samples)' while the corporate museum 'is a structure born for cultural communication'[23] (Robotti, 2012: 68), a division also supported by Martino (2013).

What emerges from existing literature is a complimentary relationship between corporate archives and museums. For example, Robotti wrote that:

> A close relationship must exist between the archive and the museum of the same company: one is the mine of information of the other and the other a powerful disseminating tool for the one … the corporate museum is a powerful apparatus of communication and fruition and can very well be used as an 'introduction' to the archive. (Robotti, 2012: 73)[24]

The presence of a museum does not automatically imply the readiness of archives to welcome visitors: their accessibility is inevitably limited for their very nature of being part of a company, despite offering a public service (Appiani, 1999). At the second conference organized by Assolombarda on corporate museums in

1999, Francesca Appiani, curator of the Museo Alessi in Omegna, advocated for a flexible understanding of public accessibility and clearly stated that despite museums are intended for external audiences, that was not the reason for their creation (Appiani, 1999). The corporate museum was then established to better operate and implement the corporate cultural policy, and usually a triggering event leads to its establishment: 'the decision to design and set up a museum originates from the success of temporary exhibitions relating to the company's historical collections, which are initially conceived and organized as a promotional moment'[25] (Amari, [1997] 2001: 75). Appiani also shed light on how corporate museums understand their nature in relation to traditional museums: she maintains that the differences are only logistic.

> What I would like to insist on is this: in many cases the degree of openness to the public of corporate museums is only 'quantitatively' different from that of traditional museums. Corporate museums are often operating archives, daily used by those who work in companies, allocated in the heart of factories and in tight spaces: all this does not favour public use. This is the case of our museum, and it is the reason why it can only be visited by appointment. In Italy there are many small museums, whose access is regulated in the manner just mentioned, and this does not give rise to particular amazement, as it should not be surprising that access to a company is controlled. (Appiani, 1999: 118)[26]

To paraphrase Appiani, a corporate museum has the operational characteristics of a corporate archive but provides the services of a traditional museum, an interpretation which resonates with Kaiser (1999).

The hybrid nature of corporate institutions is likely the reason that prevented the formulation of suitable categories, together with the belief that corporate museums are different from traditional museums. In fact, the Touring Club Italiano (TCI) – Italy's national tourist association – compiled a public dossier entirely dedicated to corporate museums in 2008, which reads: 'Museums that find the main motivation of their existence in the company and that are therefore the direct emanation of the economic activity of a company, a district or a production tradition of the territory' (TCI, 2008: 27). The TCI, in line with the many papers by specialists previously referenced, identifies the relationship with the parent company as the founding principle of corporate museums (TCI, 2008). The only effective categorization centred around this principle was provided in 2003 by Massimo Negri, director of the European Museum Academy: Negri formulated this description of corporate museums through a precise employment of prepositions to suggest the different degrees of dependence.

> First of all, we can make a distinction between the museum *of* the company and *in* the company, and the museum generated *by* the company. The first category belongs to the classic corporate museum, created by an active company, preferably within one of its offices (generally the main one or the one that is historically most representative). The second belongs to many other museums whose history is inextricably linked to a corporate history from which they have been generated. (Negri, 2003: 18; emphasis in the original)[27]

Negri highlighted the link with the parent company as the defining element: the operations of a corporate museum are moved by corporate needs, and their focus is defined by corporate heritage and the field of production of the company. Museimpresa defines corporate museums and archives as 'exemplary expression of the corporate cultural policy' (Museimpresa, 2021) for this becomes tangible in every aspect of the museums. Every resource is dedicated to the preservation, research and communication of the production (and the field of production) of the company.

3.4 Exhibiting corporate heritage

Having established that these facilities are linked to businesses, we have to assess what they do: all existing definitions, save that of Museimpresa, focus on the display function, or as formulated by Nissley and Casey (2002), *exhibit-based*. Exhibiting is also a purpose of traditional museums: the ICOM definition lists 'acquires, conserves, researches, communicates and exhibits' (ICOM, 2007) as the actions of a museum. Given the precision with which the ICOM definitions are formulated (Desvallées and Mairesse, 2010), it can be assumed that even the order of these actions is important and mirrors the operations within a traditional museum. Bonti recognized two actions – collecting and displaying – yet the addition of *exhibit-based facility* suggests that the main purpose of a corporate museum is to display artefacts preserved in the corporate archives (Bonti, 2014).

The aim of this analysis is to identify which institutional traits corporate museums share with traditional ones. We must then assess whether corporate museums are indeed institutions. In other words, are corporate museums more than just exhibitions or exhibition spaces? In order to provide examples to illustrate this issue and given the focus on fashion curation of this publication, examples are drawn from this field. Due to the increasing popularity of fashion exhibitions since the 1990s, a closer look at fashion curation also allows us to grasp the differences between designer exhibitions at major institutions and exhibitions in corporate museums.

Two exhibitions have been pivotal in the history of both Italian and international fashion curation: *Yves Saint-Laurent* (1983), curated by Diana Vreeland, at the Met in New York; and *Giorgio Armani* (2000), curated by Germano Celant, at the Solomon R. Guggenheim Museum in New York. These displays have become the emblem of the commercialization of museums and of the problematic presence of living designers in traditional museums, however they set a pattern that is now widely employed. Over the last decade, fashion exhibitions have been held in the world's most renowned museums of fine and decorative arts – for an edited list, please refer to Horsley (2014) – often curated by the brands themselves, such as the retrospective *Christian Dior, Couturier Du Rêve*, held at the Musée des Arts Décoratifs in Paris (2017) and at the V&A in London (2019). The display was the most visited exhibition in the history of the Parisian museum, with over 700,000 visitors. These shows are powerful communication tools for brands and can reach many people. Their influence is also extended by touring, which has now become the norm for fashion exhibitions. For example, the retrospective of Salvatore Ferragamo – first held in Florence in 1985 – was subsequently updated and by 2008 had toured to seven other countries. In *Collecting in a Consumer Society* (1995), Russell Belk discussed the exhibitions curated by Diana Vreeland at the MET and stated that 'the benefit of each of these shows to the designers, department stores, and cosmetics firms involved was manifest in the contagion of enhanced image and accelerated sales' (Belk, 1995: 113). This was achieved by 'enshrining and ennobling consumer goods and their producers and purveyors' (Belk, 1995: 113).

The argument that exhibitions may boost sales and enhance corporate image is identified as the primary reason underlying the establishment of corporate institutions in existing literature. There are, however, no quantitative studies that demonstrate such a statement and a comparison with visitor figures paints a different situation. For example, the Museo Salvatore Ferragamo in Florence is visited by 40,000 people on average each year, where eleven-month displays are held, against the 700,000 visitors of a six-month retrospective at a major museum. The Salvatore Ferragamo Museum is also located in the heart of Florence, a ten-minute walk from the Galleria degli Uffizi, which is visited by more than two million people. After the 2017 refurbishment of the Musée Yves Saint Laurent, estimated visitor figures per year are around 100,000, compared to the 34,000 for the two-day exhibition held in 2009 at the Grand Palais in Paris for the Yves Saint Laurent auction. The scale of impact of exhibitions held in corporate museums is but a fraction of their impact at other museums and venues. The exhibitions held in corporate institutions are not comparable to large retrospective exhibitions at popular venues in terms of influence. Nevertheless, they may still be organized by the corporate institutions, which are often established to manage the operations resulting from corporate cultural policies. For example, Alessi set up the museum primarily as an operational centre to better organize exhibitions, which were increasingly becoming important tools of interactions with customers (Appiani, 1999). Since stores have also increasingly become sophisticated platforms of interaction with customers and providers of entertainment (Kozinets et al., 2002) and exhibiting is equally central to retail operations, what is the difference between corporate institutions and stores?

The World of Coca Cola in Atlanta is a prime example of a 'themed flagship brand store' and was described as an 'attraction that charges admission to a theme park-like interactive museum celebrating Coca Cola' (Kozinets et al., 2002: 18). It is an exhibition-based space that celebrates the brand by building on the 'themes of nostalgia, American history, Santa Claus, and globalization' (Kozinets et al., 2002: 18). Although Robert Kozinets (professor of Management, Northwestern University) used the word 'museum', they probably meant an exhibition space with a set narrative-based path, identifying museums with exhibitions as is commonly done in marketing. Interestingly, the World of Coca Cola is listed as a corporate museum in most publications on the topic (Danilov, 1992; Negri, 2003; Hollenbeck, Peters and Zinkhan, 2008). This may also derive from the fact that Coca Cola does not have flagship stores – it is sold via third parties – so a space like the World of Coca Cola, where admission is paid and the Coca Cola drinks are sold together with merchandise, can be viewed as a flagship store. On the other hand, Prada flagship stores are often used as examples of the blurring of boundaries between retail space and art gallery (Ryan, 2007). For instance, Prada opened its New York flagship store in 2001 'on the site of the former Guggenheim Soho Museum' (Ryan, 2007: 17). The store was the first designed by the Office for Metropolitan Architecture (OMA), the architectural firm of Rem Koolhas, and was referred to as 'epicenter': 'an exclusive boutique, a public space, a gallery, a performance space, a laboratory' (OMA, 2018). This store 'was to redefine shopping as cultural entertainment' (Ryan, 2007: 17) and mirrored Koolhas' belief that shopping is 'arguably the last remaining form of public activity' (OMA; 2018: online). The will to make the store a social platform can also be traced in the original plan of a collaboration between Guggenheim and Prada 'so that the museum would host exhibitions and events in the Prada store in return for rent from the fashion brand' (Ryan, 2007: 17). Despite the 'inclusion of art installations and cultural events (Ryan, 2007: 18), the Prada epicenter cannot be classified as a corporate museum, because it served 'private interest' (Ryan, 2007: 18) and mostly because the only products for sale are garments and accessories by Prada, while the rest is an experience complimentary to shopping. Unlike Prada, at the World of Coca Cola the primary product is the experience based on the corporate heritage and complimentary is the merchandise sold at the gift store.

The incorporation of exhibitions in a brand retail space extends the shopping experience and the function of a flagship store but it does not make the space a corporate institution. For example, for the opening of the flagship store on the Champs-Elysées in Paris in 2006, Louis Vuitton commissioned the artist Vanessa Beecroft to create a site-specific work. The installation featured models in different skin tones on the shelves of the store, in poses referencing the monogram and traditional brown–beige colour palette of the brand. This work falls in the category of corporate art, that is, artworks about a company and commissioned by the company. In the Fondation Louis Vuitton in Paris works of corporate art are not exhibited but only those unrelated – from a subject perspective – to the company, which classifies the institution as an operation of corporate patronage. In the publication celebrating thirty years of the Museo Salvatore Ferragamo, the Director Stefania Ricci compiled a list of all the exhibitions held at the museum and the displays of historical artefacts in flagship stores were grouped in a separate list (Ricci, 2015) showing an awareness of the different nature of these operations.

There has been an increasing blurring of boundaries between museums and retail spaces since the 1990s, when Russell Belk observed that 'these stores have also adopted some of the techniques of the museum, including appropriating its prestige and patina status associations' (Belk, 1995: 129). A reflection on these techniques helps towards the discernment between stores and museums. Belk discussed only established institutions and exhibitions focused on fashion designers, as part of a reflection on institutional collecting, though he did not clarify which techniques he referred to. Reference to museum techniques is to be found in later literature on corporate museums, For example, Livingstone implies collecting and researching when she describes the purpose of these institutions 'as documenting, extending and promoting the affiliated corporate brand' (Livingstone, 2011: 18), but her use of the term *technique* is unmistakable: 'the display techniques and terminology they apply draw together museum and merchandising techniques' (Livingstone, 2011: 18). It is worth mentioning that, for what concerns fashion curation, merchandising techniques have long been a core element of displays; for example, the 1971 fashion display curated by Cecil Beaton at the V&A in London was styled by visual merchandisers of London stores (de la Haye et al., 2014). Candice Hollenbeck (professor of Marketing, University of Georgia) did not use the term *technique* but an even broader term, *qualities*: 'by using historical linkages and museum-like qualities combined with an education-driven mission, the brand museum becomes a retailing environment that provides the consumer with a meaningful appreciation of the brand' (Hollenbeck, Peters and Zinkhan, 2008: 352). The expression *historical linkages* is related to the focus of the narrative in these displays: the authors, building on the work of Kozinets (2002), observe the similarities with 'themed flagship brand stores' (Hollenbeck, Peters and Zinkhan, 2008: 334) and state that 'brand museums' are a specific retail environment in which 'the objects of consumption are framed to appear historical and museum-like in display' (Hollenbeck, Peters and Zinkhan, 2008: 336). This definition again suggests an identification between museums and displays. This identification is also present within *Fashion Theory*, where curator Alexandra Palmer used the expression 'imitation museums' (Palmer, 2008: 34) to discuss the venues in which costume and textile exhibitions were becoming increasingly popular: private galleries, auction houses, department and specialty stores. While more judgemental in tone, the expression *imitation museum* is comparable to *museum-like* and Palmer's preoccupation lied in the ability of visitors to differentiate these spaces from 'bona fide museum settings' (Palmer, 2008: 34), especially as established art institutions were also mounting fashion displays (Palmer specifically referenced the 2000 Armani display at the Guggenheim in New York). What Palmer calls 'bona fide' museum settings are what I refer to as traditional museums, that is, those who follow the ICOM definitions. If we are to use the term museum to indicate institutions that follow the ICOM definition, they would also have research and education programmes as core activities, differentiating them from other corporate exhibit-based facilities. As Xu pointed out, less than 40 per cent of a museum surface is usually dedicated to display (Xu, 2017), making this association misleading. Indeed, the definition of corporate museums and archives by Museimpresa does not include the term 'exhibit', but instead states that corporate museums are the manifestation of the corporate cultural policy. To conclude, exhibitions are an essential element of corporate institutions but they are not their only purpose.

3.5 Researching corporate heritage

Corporate exhibition-based facilities have been identified as museums primarily because of formal attributes – the display techniques – rather than as a result of an analysis of curatorial approaches. In addition, in the case of fashion curation, the intertwined history of museographic and merchandising techniques, as well as the debated inclusion of fashion in established museums, hinder a clear demarcation between corporate museums, traditional museums, stores and other display spaces. One clue is provided by Luca Marchetti (professor of Fashion Studies, Geneva University of Art and Design) who observed that stores do not develop 'the conceptual density of fashion as their main vocation' as exhibitions do, but the 'enhancement of the aesthetic significance of brands'[28] (Marchetti, 2017: 87). While not discerning between museum and non-museum exhibitions, Marchetti identified in critical analysis the core element of exhibitions (Marchetti, 2017). However sophisticated, store displays are not aimed at presenting or stimulating an analysis of fashion. On the other hand, by simply tracing *historical linkages*, displays in corporate spaces can suggest cause–effect or inspiration–creation relationships. As noted previously, according to ICOM the actions that characterize the operations of a museums are: acquisition, conservation, research, communication and exhibition. If we take the original formulation in French, the definition centred around the expression '*faire des recherches*' (to undertake research), from which all other operations stem (Desvallées and Mairesse, 2010). Research is instrumental for analysis and is what differentiates commercial displays from narrative-based exhibitions.

Commissioning research into corporate history is an established practice (Section 2.4) but it has now become a common tool for the enhancement of brand equity: 'a properly researched historical background thus makes a critical contribution to the credibility of a company and its brand(s)' (Ehle and Hauser, 2013: 39). The institution of a research centre dedicated to corporate monographs in Italy attests the growth of the field. In 2010, Mario Magagnino (professor of Corporate Communication at the University of Verona) established the Osservatorio Monografie d'Impresa (Observatory Corporate Monographs) to analyse the increasing employment of publications as tools for heritage management and communication by companies. In 2013 it launched a yearly award to identify best practices and by 2018 the archive of OMI gathered more than a thousand Italian monographs. Research is essential to undertake the critical analysis of a company's heritage and operations, however the results of the analysis provide tools for development and heritage management enhances a company's competitiveness (Messedat, 2013). For this reason, and for the confidential nature of corporate archives, critical analyses may be undertaken by companies but not shared with visitors, who are presented with edited content.

When discussing the Ford Museum in Dearborn, Michigan, Russell Belk lamented its 'celebratory tone' and the absence of ethnographic research of drivers or engagement with problems such as pollution and road deaths (Belk, 1995: 120). Belk's account of the fashion exhibitions at the MET also denounced a lack of criticism and the issues associated with sponsorship. This is inevitable given the corporate needs these operations attend to, and this is even more emphasized in corporate institutions, which 'must provide an interpretation of a product that is given from the aspect of a company' (Xu, 2017: 2). Corporate museums and exhibitions must promote an interpretation of the company's heritage and products advantageous for the company, but they can nevertheless produce academically rigorous research: the presence of corporate needs does not deny the objectivity of the interpretation *per se*, but should be understood as limiting the areas in which this interpretation is publicly discussed. Exhibitions of contemporary fashion are inevitably bound to commercial interests but, as I will later demonstrate, these do not limit the industry's contribution to scholarship and the development of curatorial practices.

The results of researching corporate heritage are communicated through exhibitions and publications but also employed by the company for internal revision and development. Convenors at the 2015 ICA conference on corporate archives agreed that a fundamental justification for investment in the management of corporate heritage is its value as an operational resource (Pino, 2017). Corporate museums should then be identified as those 'originated in various ways by a company whose heritage is closely related to the *specific* activity of the business' (Negri, 2003: 19).[29] This distinction is fundamental as it inevitably influences the curatorial approach of the museum: 'Due to the marked parallels, corporate art museums and public art museums are more closely related than those which deal with cultural historical phenomena' (Warnecke, 2013: 33), that is museums that provide a cultural–historical interpretation of corporate heritage. Corporate cultural policy may include forms of patronage and sponsorships however, as the field of sponsorship (art exhibition) is different from the field of production – even if a company owns a corporate collection or museum – the link with the company is only contextual. The research and discussion on the value of the exhibits does not include or affect the production, while research into corporate heritage is viewed as a key contributor for heritage brands since their differentiating factor is precisely corporate heritage.

3.6 Interpreting corporate heritage

A corporate museum is 'not just about archiving and exhibiting the inheritance, but also about working actively with it' (Messedat, 2013: 9). It is an institution in which the 'interpretative framework' (Xu, 2017: 36) is not only applied in the development of narratives for exhibitions, but also in educational policies (e.g. training courses) and in research and dissemination (commissions of corporate monographs and publications). The interpretative framework also informs the choices of corporate archives, particularly in the definition of corporate museums and archives by Museimpresa, which states that they 'derive from an economic activity' (Museimpresa in Negri, 2003: 36).[30] The expression covers both the documentary recording of corporate operations and collecting activities, and while being open to interpretation, stresses the cause–effect relationship with the company. According to the definition, the corporate cultural policy is manifest in the various operations of archives and museums, which are implementations of the interpretative framework. Museimpresa's definition groups together corporate museums and archives for they are driven, though to different extents, by the interpretative framework. They 'report on the origin of product and the development of production methods as well as about social change' (Messedat, 2013: 8), therefore interpreting their heritage from a collective perspective and associating it with the 'more broader levels of self' (Belk, 1995).

While it is correct that to state that corporate institutions have a bias towards the interests of parent companies as 'there is often little room for an oppositional version of a company's glorious history' (Xu, 2017: 80), it is also true that, in traditional museums, curators must attend to the needs of sponsors, and fashion exhibitions have been particularly criticized for their evident commercial, marketing value. What has emerged in existing literature is that fashion exhibitions inevitably have a marketing value if a company is still operating. I argue that the distinction between traditional and corporate museums is located precisely in the coexistence of marketing needs and socially relevant research and in their declaration to the audience. The purpose of the adjective *corporate* is indeed necessary to declare the commercial nature of these institutions and the word museum declares their public dimension.

The audience of corporate institutions has only been discussed from a marketing perspective, where it has been studied as a manifestation of brand communities. The term 'community' can be understood as describing a nucleus of society, as included in the ICOM definition of museums, especially considering the local and regional connotation which literature has established a recurring trait of corporate institutions. Xu stated that 'the corporate museum is a place that benefits both civic needs and company profits' (Xu, 2017: 46). For what concerns company profits, further explanation as to how corporate institutions can benefit company profits was provided by Belk who stated that 'an institution involved in collecting can affect the marketplace [and] legitimize and sacralise certain objects as being worthy to be collected' (Belk, 1995: 102). Belk was describing institutional public collecting and not corporate collecting, so this statement becomes even more relevant when discussing 'institutional collections' that are communicated and promoted following the marketing policies of a company. Yet there is another aspect of institutional collections that has not been investigated, due to the marketing focus of previous studies.

Jan-Christian Warnecke (exhibition planning, German Museum Association) observed that corporate museums are considered to belong to a parallel sphere to public institutions, as their 'more goal oriented approach' is perceived to be in contrast with 'the more idealistic approach of a public museum' and this 'makes it more difficult for a consciousness to develop that both are working for the same thing' (Warnecke, 2013: 33). Granted that companies find their prime purpose in profit – not merely financial but in the broader sense of benefits to the company - I have already argued that they also work for research and that this serves civic needs. Existing literature has identified the social engagement in the spatial, public dimension of the corporate museum: 'People experience the museum as a brand place that facilitates a sense of community' (Xu, 2017: 18). Yet, what discerns a community of customers to community as a small unit of society – responding to the ICOM definition – depends on how the collection is interpreted. The ability of a museum to engage with a sense of community was addressed by Belk (1995) in his discussion of institutional collections, as discussed above.

I maintain that what classifies corporate exhibition facilities as institutions is the active engagement with these broader levels of the extended self. The celebratory tone denounced by Belk can often be detected in corporate museums and is the result of the immediate response to corporate needs. However, it can also be accompanied by a reflection of the historical, social and cultural relevance of the history of the designer, the company founder and the products. For example, the Museo Salvatore Ferragamo in Florence actively engages with the community: the shoemaker Salvatore Ferragamo is one element of the narrative which focuses around the local, regional or national community. Salvatore Ferragamo was presented as one of the many early-twentieth-century Italian immigrants in the exhibition *1927. The Return to Italy* (Sisi and Ricci, 2017) and the history of the medieval palace where the company headquarters are located was the narrative thread linking a celebration of the history of Florence in *A Palace and the City* (Ricci and Spinelli, 2015).

To conclude, I argue that when a corporate space presents a display that focuses on the products, the company positions visitors in the role of customers or appreciators of the brand. Instead, when a corporate space presents a display that focuses on the social relevance of products and contextualizes them within a broader culture, the company positions visitors as part of the society discussed by the exhibition and therefore attends to the collective levels of the extended self like traditional museums. In the latter case, I propose that the exhibition facility can be described as a corporate museum. With reference to the benefits to society, corporate archives and collections have the potential to be interpreted from a collective perspective as companies are producers of material culture, the analysis of which is inevitably linked to society. The choice of focus on the founder as opposed to the contexts of production and its users manifests the approach of the company. Xu recognized that corporate museums are repositories of indigenous culture (Xu, 2017), yet it depends on the curatorial approaches – on the interpretative framework – whether the indigenous culture is, indeed, researched and communicated through the operations of the corporate museum. In the next chapter, I will present a chronological critical review of fashion curation in Italy to highlight how the industry impacted the way fashion heritage has been interpreted and exhibited, which will allow to trace connections between corporate aims and curatorial approaches in Chapter 5.

4

A history of fashion curation in Italy

The structure of this chapter was modelled on the contribution made by Akiko Fukai to the *Berg Encyclopedia of World Dress and Fashion*, edited by Joanne B. Eicher in 2010. In Volume 10 (*Global Perspectives*), Part 5 (*Dress and Fashion Resources Worldwide*), Amy de la Haye edited a section dedicated to 'dress and fashion in the context of the museum' (2010: 285), in which Fukai analysed 'dress and fashion museums' (2010: 288) and attempted to divide the history of fashion curation into eras mirroring a change in theoretical approaches.

> The earliest period, prior to 1970, was characterized by a general approach to collecting dress and fashion. In the second period, from about 1970 to 1990, museums tended to develop a specialized focus on some aspects of dress and fashion. Museums of the third period, the twenty-first century, seem to move their focus away from Paris to other fashion centers that have been developing around the globe. (Fukai, 2010: 288)

The only proposed timeframe in Italian literature is by Maria Giuseppina Muzzarelli who associated each era to a different scholar: the first one with Rosa Genoni (early 1900s), the second one with Rosita Levi Pisetzky (1930s to 1960s) and the third one with Grazietta Butazzi (from 1970s). Muzzarelli's focus was the development of fashion studies, therefore she centred her account on scholars. As this account focuses on curation, I propose a different timeframe which centres instead on exhibitions, although they equally trace the development of discourses around fashion. While Genoni and Pisetzky had a limited impact on curation, Butazzi took part in pioneering projects and her centrality is here recognized. Grazietta Butazzi had a similar impact in Italy to James Laver's influence in the UK, that is developing a social, anthropological and semiotic approach to the study of dress, a multifaceted approach now identified as cultural studies (Muzzarelli, 2016). As emerged during the proceedings of the 2014 conference dedicated to her held at Fondazione Antonio Ratti, Butazzi's methodology is still widely employed by leading scholars (Morini, Rizzini and Rosina, 2016) and the article dedicated to the biography of Butazzi (Rizzini, 2016) proved fundamental for the compilation of the chronological account here presented.

The account does not aim to be a comprehensive history of fashion curation in Italy: it is a substantial reconstruction from a broad range of sources to unfold how Italian fashion and textile manufacturers and trade associations contributed to the development of curatorial practices. In order to organize the timeframe of the account, I first identified pivotal events that mirror the approach I associate with each era. In 1951, the Italian textile manufacturer SNIA Viscosa established the Centro Internazionale delle Arti e del Costume (International Centre of the Arts and Costume) in Venice, which promoted research on historical textiles and dress as well as international debates through an extensive programme of publications, exhibitions and conferences. In 1978 CISST, Centro Italiano per lo Studio della Storia del Tessuto (Italian Centre for the Study of the History of Textiles) was created, gathering textile and dress scholars across Italy. In 1980, the first exhibition solely dedicated to twentieth-century fashion opened at the Poldi Pezzoli Museum in Milan and in 1981 the first conference dedicated to the discussion around a possible fashion museum was funded by trade associations and organized by the national association of textile and dress scholars. In 1992, the exhibition *La Sala Bianca: The Birth of Italian Fashion* was commissioned by Pitti Immagine and Centro di Firenze per la Moda Italiana and opened a prolific season of events promoted by the corporate cultural policies of these trade associations, including the 1996 Biennale di Firenze, a citywide series of events and exhibitions that aimed at highlighting fashion as a contemporary visual language. In 2000, the monographic exhibition dedicated to the Italian fashion designer Giorgio Armani opened at the Guggenheim Museum in New York and triggered debates around the presence of fashion in museums. In 2001, two important exhibitions were organized by corporate institutions: *Silk: The 1900s in Como* by the Fondazione Antonio Ratti in Como and *Uniform: Order and Disorder* by the Fondazione Pitti Immagine Discovery in Florence. In light of this, and of the fact that events cannot be used as precise separation lines between eras, I propose three phases, each associated with a characterizing approach:

1. 1950s to 1970s: scholarship focused on the study of historical textiles and fashion;
2. 1980s to 1990s: increased interaction across scholars and exchange with the industry, and study of twentieth century fashion;

3. 2000s to 2010s: corporate institutions as key players of Italian fashion curation.

These sections are preceded by a brief discussion of fashion exhibitions in the early twentieth century.

4.1 The beginnings (1900s–1940s)

Many international exhibitions organized in the second half of the nineteenth century and in the early twentieth century included displays of textiles and clothes, as they were promoting contemporary productions. These exhibitions were a chance for countries to present their industries internationally and Italy, who had only been a unified country since 1861, was adamant to compete with other established European countries. Textiles were particularly important as they held 'a central, symbolically charged place in the universe of commodities, so much so that the textile sector was viewed as a key indicator of a modern nation state's ability to project its power at home and abroad' (Schnapp, 1997: 196). Turin was the Italian city with a history in the industrial production of clothing and hosted two exhibitions in 1902 and 1911 with 'entire pavilions devoted to illustrating the relationships between fashion and industry' (Merlo and Perugini, 2020: 325). The exhibition most frequently discussed in Italian fashion history is however the one held in 1906 in Milan, where the Milanese couturiere Rosa Genoni won the first prize for her clothes, which she had created as a manifesto for Italian fashion – previously discussed in Chapter 1.

In the accompanying booklet, titled *Al visitatore* (To the Visitor), Genoni was quite judgemental towards Parisian fashion, which she wrote was 'more flashy than luxurious, more titillating than aesthetic, more scenographic than refined, more impressive than harmonious' (Genoni, 1906: 3).[1] Genoni was advocating for an authentic Italian style and urged women, artists and seamstresses to 'collaborate in the fruitful effort to overcome misoneism and the habit of slavishly copying the model of Paris; and so also in this branch of art, Italy will be able to assert itself in an original way, as it is about to do so victoriously in all the other fields of the Decorative Art' (Genoni, 1906: 4).[2] In order to achieve this, Genoni created dresses inspired by famous Italian artworks and explained the rationale underlying the models exhibited

> The ball gown is inspired by Botticelli's Primavera, which can be admired in the Uffizi Gallery in Florence. Trying to preserve the freshness and lightness of the

Figure 4.1 The display of Italian fashions by Rosa Genoni at the International Exhibition of Milan in 1906, winner of the Grand Prix. Courtesy *Archivio Genoni Podreider Milano*.

model for the dress, the exhibitor has replaced the usual fluffy muslin with an artistic scalloping of fabric, as can be seen in the painting itself. She then wanted, with the utmost naturalness, to reproduce in embroidery the wildflowers in their varied range of designs, in their inexhaustible palette of colors, partly fallen, partly torn, partly peeled, partly blown by the wind; and thus symbolically stick to the theme of the Primavera itself. (Genoni, 1906: 6)[3]

Genoni was meticulous in all descriptions, not only of garments but also of the display design. She first criticized the overuse of wax models in exhibitions and stores and then explained why she chose less garish models in order to produce an effect 'more refined, more ideal, more mystical, more Italian' (Genoni, 1906: 8).[4] She even commented on the colour of the edges of the vitrine: everything was studied to look timeless, *classico*. The detailed descriptions were likely intended by Genoni as guidelines, as she wanted others to follow her on the quest for Italian fashion.

Genoni's vehemence was a result of her patriotic and feminist activism, which she chiefly articulated through her writings. In 1908, she gave a speech at the *Congresso Nazionale delle Donne Italiane* (National Congress of Italian Women), which was attended by 1,400 women. She criticized French fashion and declared it unsuitable for 'our ethnic and historical character, our artistic traditions, our body type, our newly-found national life' (1908: 9).[5] She analysed the garments she had created for the 1906 Milan exhibition and suggested other themes, such as local, traditional costumes, for further inspiration. Genoni was effectively proposing a form of heritage marketing, promoting a continuity with an artistic past that was internationally recognized to be an excellence. Her method was to 'adapt these classic models to the needs of the modern costume and of our time, while retaining all the diffused nobility of style and the flavor of the classic memory' (Genoni, 1908: 10).[6]

From 1908 to the 1928, Genoni continued to promote Italian fashion and wrote articles for newspapers, which have been recently digitized by the Università di Bologna.[7] She also published two collections of slides and sketches on the history of costume (Genoni, 1909 and 1918), as well as articles on newspapers. For this reason, she has been framed as the initiator of fashion studies in Italy (Paulicelli, 2015a). Muzzarelli wrote that 'Genoni played a pioneering role using the history of fashion to read the society of her time and more generally through time and also to contribute to the construction of a new society'[8] (Muzzarelli, 2016: 74). While the attempt is undeniable, the impact of Genoni's work was limited and her publication *La Storia della Moda attraverso i secoli* (*The History of Fashion Across the Centuries*, 1925) was likely a didactic tool employed by Genoni in her classes of costume history at the Humanitarian School in Milan (this affiliation appears on the cover of the book). There is no evidence of subsequent scholars referencing this text as a key source. Genoni was an interesting yet isolated case; nevertheless, she was a pioneer in articulating Italianness through fashion and in the strategic use of the past in this field.

Exhibitions played a central role for the establishment of the Italian textile industry, especially for artificial fibres in the 1920s and 1930s. The fascist regime strongly promoted the development of the fashion industry and created organizations for this purpose. In 1932, the Ente Autonomo per la Mostra Permanente Nazionale della Moda (Autonomous Body for the Permanent National Fashion Exhibition) was established in Turin, where it oversaw the production of two biannual exhibitions and fashion shows, the first one taking place in April 1933 (Merlo and Perugini, 2020). In 1937, a grand exhibition was held at the Circus Maximus in Rome dedicated to all national textiles. The Mostra del Tessile Nazionale (National Textile Exhibition) was aimed at 'boosting clothing manufacturers' confidence in the Italian textile sector' (Collicelli Cagol, 2013: 157) and especially promoted artificial fibres, which represented Italy's ability to thrive under the self-sufficiency scheme. As noted by Schnapp (1997) and Collicelli Cagol (2013), there was a juxtaposition of scenes from the past, represented by agriculture and symbolled by the Ancient roman location, and from the future, represented by the machinery on display and the rationalist exhibition design. The central pavilion also included a catwalk where fashion shows were held to demonstrate the versatility of Italian textiles and promote Italian fashion (Collicelli Cagol, 2013).

Exhibitions were systematically employed to promote textile and clothing production and this practice would be reprised after the Second World War. In the late 1940s and early 1950s, regional and national bodies were created in various cities – Turin, Milan, Rome, Florence and, to a lesser extent, Venice – which were competing to become the centre of Italian fashion (Pinchera and Rinallo, 2017; Scarpellini, 2019). This domestic 'war' has been documented, with a particular focus on Florence where the heritage strategies put in place by the industry can be considered the most effective, as discussed in Chapter 1. What I will now analyse is how exhibitions were created and supported by the industry to promote the study of historical textiles and dress, with the understanding that marketing the cultural and social relevance of these productions would be beneficial to the industry.

4.2 The study of historical textiles and fashion (1950s–1970s)

The start of the first phase of fashion curation in Italy can be identified with the Centro Internazionale delle Arti e del Costume (CIAC) (International Centre of the Arts and Costume), which opened in 1951 in Venice.

4.2.1 CIAC, the International Centre of the Arts and Costume

The CIAC was founded by Franco Marinotti, owner of the Italian textile manufacture SNIA (Società Nazionale Industria Applicazioni) Viscosa, which was producing artificial fibres and in the 1920s and 1930s was the world's second producer (and largest exporter) of rayon. Marinotti had started supporting scholarship in textile and dress history in the late 1940s (Rizzini, 2016) and followed the customary approach of the time, when industrialists provided financial support through sponsorship but, even when establishing private foundations, they did not directly promote their products.

The CIAC was located at Palazzo Grassi, a prominent historical palace on the Canal Grande in Venice; it was directed by Marinotti and responded to the SNIA Viscosa marketing strategy to promote its products through philanthropic activities (Collicelli Cagol, 2015). From its opening, it organized and promoted exhibitions and conferences dedicated to the history of costume. For the inauguration of the institution, the exhibition *Mostra del Costume nel Tempo. Momenti di arte e di vita dall'età ellenica al romanticismo* (Exhibition of Costume Over Time. Moments of Art and Life from the Hellenic era to Romanticism) was held from 25 August to 14 October 1951. It started from Ancient Greece and Rome and gathered exhibits over three floors to illustrate a history of costume and textiles up until the nineteenth century. Artefacts on display were on loan from Venetian, national and international museums, as well as those of the collection which Marinotti had endowed to the Centre. The catalogue featured the exhibition's itinerary, the list of all exhibits with relevant images and detailed captions. The final room of the exhibition was dedicated to another display entitled *Mostra di libri d'arte sul costume* (Exhibition of Art Books on Costume), where rare editions and illustrations were exhibited. This display promoted the library which had been created for the Centre with the aim to increase the prestige of this newly formed institution. It held more than eight thousand specialist publications 'on costume, fashion, economy and art that the Centre acquired from all over the world … The CIAC library became a prime meeting and study point for all researchers interested in exploring the theme of costume and fashion'[9] (MUVE, 2021).

The exhibition was intended as 'a concise presentation of the themes that the Centro Internazionale delle Arti e del Costume intends to address and unfold in the exhibitions of the coming years' as well as 'a demonstration of the importance of costume over time and the vastness of the subject'[10] (CIAC, 1951: 3). The exhibition design featured a technique which had been first employed for exhibitions under the fascist regime: covering the walls with the materials studied in the display. This is the visual manifestation of the corporate interests underlying the operation, that is, the promotion of SNIA Viscosa fabrics, as well as conveying 'in the minds of visitors the awareness that the past belongs to the present, and that through the present it had to be rethought' (Collicelli Cagol, 2013: 183).[11] The plan for the centre was to play a central role in the international marketing strategy of SNIA Viscosa:

> The CIAC set up a series of national committees in various countries such as Brazil or the United Kingdom (often strategic locations for the SNIA Viscosa businesses) that, depending on their proposals, could either present exhibitions

at the Palazzo Grassi or organise events in their own countries with the collaboration of the CIAC. (Collicelli Cagol, 2013: 184)

By touring exhibitions, SNIA Viscosa could broaden the pool of networks while also promoting the cultural relevance of textiles and Italy's centrality in this history. This strategy was not successful but it nevertheless attests the clarity with which corporate needs were addressed.

4.2.2 Textiles and fashion at CIAC

After the introductory exhibition of 1951 which served as a manifesto of interests, in 1952 CIAC focused on textiles with the display *La leggenda del filo d'oro, le vie della seta* (The legend of the golden thread, the silk routes) (18 August–19 October 1952). It covered the history of silk from its Chinese origin to the contemporary alternatives provided by artificial fibres. The last two rooms were called *I Ricercatori* (The Researchers) and *Miracolo della Scienza* (The Miracle of Science). As shown in Figure 4.2, both presented display installations aimed at evoking the progress of science and technology and conveyed a futuristic atmosphere, thus positioning artificial fibres as part of a historical narrative of the history of textiles of dress and had a marked international breadth, which 'was part of Franco's strategy to distance artificial fibres from the previous propaganda narrative that related them to a nationalistic discourse' (Collicelli Cagol, 2013: 185). This approach to exhibitions was defined by Cagol as an 'historic event, capable of helping the individual to understand him or herself' (2013: 191), facilitating sense-making experiences to visitors whilst also promoting a company and its industrial field at large.

The CIAC provided a platform for international exchange among scholars: it was not only Italians who were benefitting from the funds made available by SNIA Viscosa, but also a vast pool of renowned foreign scholars, who all took part in the international conference organized in 1952 (CIAC, 1952). In conjunction with the exhibition on silk, the conference took place in the Renaissance Palazzo Vendramin-Calergi and focused mainly on seventeenth- and eighteenth-century costume. It ran for eight days (31 August–7 September 1952) and scholars, collectors and curators from fourteen countries took part. The conference was organized by Marinotti and his son, Paolo, who were praised by Giuseppe Segati, then president of CIAC, for their contribution to the history of costume. Segati in particular mentioned the plans for 'a museum intended to receive and preserve the documents concerning the past of costume'[12] (Segati, 1952: 18). There are

Figure 4.2 The last room of the exhibition *La leggenda del filo d'oro, Le vie della seta* (*The Legend of the Golden Thread, the Silk Routes*) dedicated to technological developments in textile production, titled *Il Miracolo della Scienza* (*The Miracle of Science*), Centro Internazionale delle Arti e del Costume, Palazzo Grassi, Venice, 1952. Courtesy *Fondazione Musei Civici Venezia*.

no further traces of Marinotti's plan, however the efforts were acknowledged by all the speakers of the congress, starting from James Laver (then Keeper of Prints, Drawings and Paintings at the V&A), who had been appointed as the president of the congress (Laver, 1952). Another speaker was Doris Langley Moore, described in the proceedings as the 'Director of the Museum of Costume of London'. She discussed her proposal for the establishment of a museum and reflected on the various types of institutions dealing with costume. In her analysis, Langley Moore singled out CIAC as 'the first organization with international perspectives – in my opinion the only correct conception with regards to fashion'[13] (Langley-Moore, 1952: 214). Langley Moore's statement confirms that textile and fashion companies played an active role in supporting research and institutions.

The congress was organized to 'give the newly established CIAC a central role in the international research on the history of fashion'[14] (Rizzini, 2016: 17). Butazzi later highlighted the importance of this event for the development of the discipline in Italy (Butazzi, 2008) and Rizzini recorded how Butazzi referenced the proceedings, directly and indirectly, numerous times in her publications (Rizzini, 2016). Among the convenors was François Boucher, then Honorary Curator at the Musée Carnavalet in Paris. Boucher had founded in 1948 the Union Française des Arts du Costume (UFAC) – in the same year that he retired from his post at the Musée Carnavalet (Taylor, 2004) – together with members of the fashion and textile industries, including the couturier Lucien Lelong, who had been the head of the Chambre Syndacale de la Haute Couture between 1937 and 1947. Boucher chaired the fourth (of the five) study sessions during the congress, dedicated to *Documentation. Inventaire des collections, classification, bibliographie, photothèques, fiches internationals, etc.* (Documentation. Inventory of collections, classification, bibliography, photo libraries, international records, etc). Boucher is now considered a pivotal figure in the history of costume for his detailed 1965 publication *Histoire du Costume (en Occident de l'Antiquité à nos jours)* [*History of Costume (in the West from Antiquity to Today)*] (Boucher, 1965). Interestingly, while Boucher's publication enjoyed multiple re-editions and international recognition, a coeval publication by the Italian dress historian Rosita Levi Pisetzky has never been employed by foreign scholars (possibly for its focus on Italian costume and most likely for being published in Italian), despite its presence in many major public libraries across Europe (Levi Pisetzky and Butazzi, 1995).

Rosita Levi Pisetzky (1898–1985) was the only Italian speaker at the congress, where she presented a paper on colour in Italian dress. She was 'a self-taught scholar who loved studying clothes but also collecting them'[15] (Muzzarelli, 2016: 75). Levi Pisetzky championed a research methodology which combined artefacts with literary and iconographic sources and started her career in the 1930s with studies published in women's magazines and journals. She is renowned for the articles on dress in the sixteen volumes of the *Storia di Milano* (*History of Milan*), published by Treccani – Italy's prime encyclopaedic publisher – between 1953 and 1962. Treccani later commissioned Levi Pisetzky to write the five-volume *Storia del Costume in Italia* (*History of Costume in Italy*), published between 1964 and 1968. In the 1970s, the publisher Einaudi commissioned two shorter publications in which the existing research on costume was integrated with history of fashion and aimed at a broader audience: *Moda e Costume* (Levi Pisetzky, 1973) (*Fashion and Costume*) and *Il Costume e la Moda nella Società Italiana* (Levi Pisetzky, 1978) (*Costume and Fashion in Italian Society*). These books are similar in structure and methodology to the highly referenced *Costume and Fashion: A Concise History* by James Laver (1969) which was later republished by Thames and Hudson who invited Amy de la Haye, a fashion historian and V&A curator of the new generation to update the book (Laver and de la Haye, 1995). In the same way, Einaudi asked Grazietta Butazzi to introduce the 1995 re-edition of Levi Pisetzky's 1978 book with a critical analysis of her work (Levi Pisetzky and Butazzi, 1995).

While the 1952 exhibition on silk only touched upon artificial fibres towards the end, maintaining a distance between corporate institution and parent company, in 1954 CIAC organized a display which openly celebrated the interests of SNIA Viscosa. *I Tessili dell'Avvenire* (Textiles of the Future) only lasted ten days (22 May–1 June 1954) being even closer to trade exhibitions than museum displays and sensibly shorter than displays from previous years. During the first two days, fashion shows were held to present the potential of man-made fibres and more than a hundred garments were presented. This was the first fashion show held at CIAC and signalled the beginning of an increasing focus on fashion.

In 1951, SNIA Viscosa had sponsored the fashion shows organized in Florence by Giorgini (Scarpellini, 2019) and Marinotti had wanted to create an international centre for fashion in Milan for the promotion of this industry (Collicelli Cagol, 2013). The Milan centre was not established but yearly fashion shows were organized from 1956, when the centre inaugurated the *Prima rassegna internazionale dell'abbigliamento* (First International Clothing Festival), attended by couturiers from eight countries: Italy, Germany, the UK, Japan, the United States , Ireland, Spain and India (Colaiacomo and Caratozzolo, 2010).

More than a hundred labels presented their creations produced with man-made fibres (Collicelli Cagol, 2013). SNIA Viscosa was using these events to improve the reputation of man-made fibres as suitable for fashion textiles and, at the same time investing in Venice as one of the centres of Italian fashion. These events would become grander and grander and the CIAC would continue to be used as an operational centre for cultural marketing in the fields of corporate interests. In 1969, Paolo Marinotti described CIAC as 'a useful means of information for those who must promptly orient the public in the field of fashion, and therefore a tool intended for the service of the market to support the decisive choices that transform fashion into costume'[16] (Marinotti in Archivio Luce, 1969), and with costume Marinotti intended the cultural and social dimensions of clothing.

It was not only an introductory project, which served as a manifesto of the interests of the institution, but it also opened a series of events directed at the definition of costume, with each project highlighting different aspects. For example, in the same year the CIAC organized the *Festival dell'Alta Moda e del Costume nel Film* (Festival of Haute Couture and Costume in Film) and theatrical costume would be addressed through exhibitions and conferences (CIAC, 1954). Ethnic dress was also discussed, notably in 1956 with *Arte Tessile e Costumi dell'India* (Textile Arts and Costumes of India).

4.2.3 CIAC in the 1960s

After the 1952 conference, CIAC continued to organize events on costume and textiles, as well as cultural activities such as theatre plays and ballet performances (Collicelli Cagol, 2015). In 1956, a symposium was dedicated to exploring the definitions of costumes. With *Termine e Concetto di Costume* (Definitions and Concepts of Costume), the CIAC declared an awareness of its potential contribution to the studies in this field and plans were announced to support a university tenure centred on costume (CIAC, 1957). The plan was never achieved and CIAC actually stopped organizing exhibitions on the history of textiles and costumes after 1956 as a new direction towards contemporary art was the result of the increasing leadership of Paolo's son, Franco Marinotti (Collicelli Cagol, 2013).

When he took over the direction of CIAC in 1959, an exhibition signalled this change. *Vitalità nell'arte* (Vitality in Art) was co-curated by Paolo Marinotti and Willem Sandberg, director of the Stedelijk Museum, Amsterdam. The display was first held at CIAC in Venice, travelled to Amsterdam in 1960 and toured to two other European venues, the Kunsthalle in Recklinghausen, Germany, and the Louisiana Museum, Copenhagen. Marinotti was aiming to 'break with the CIAC's previous program and with the SNIA Viscosa agenda pushed by his father' (Collicelli Cagol, 2015). In order to loosen its marketing ties without losing the funding (SNIA Viscosa sponsored exhibition and tour), 'Marinotti still had to guarantee his father the presence of artificial textiles within the rooms of Palazzo Grassi' (Collicelli Cagol, 2015). The resulting display, which ran from August until October 1959 at Palazzo Grassi, presented subtler references to SNIA Viscosa and effectively developed a more complex model of sponsorship, which included commissions and interaction with the sponsor's products. The Dutch artist Karel Appel created an installation using textiles by SNIA Viscosa: it is telling that the installation did not travel to the Stedelijk Museum, which was significantly less tied to the sponsoring company than CIAC. Furthermore, the Italian architect Carlo Scarpa, well known for leading a new approach in museum displays, was commissioned to create the display for the exhibition. Scarpa 'took full advantage of the SNIA Viscosa's connection with CIAC' and used 'meters of colored textiles to cover parts of ceilings, walls, and plinths, and concealing and reframing portions of rooms and interrupting sight lines': as Collicelli Cagol put it, 'the whole exhibition screamed textile' (2015).

SNIA Viscosa effectively implemented a diversified corporate cultural policy: its corporate institution, CIAC, managed allocated resources to generate research and cultural events that were directly and indirectly related to the production of the company, and mirrored the values promoted by the company through its marketing strategy. From its inception, CIAC used publications as channels to disseminate specialist knowledge, although its initiatives seem to have been short lived. In 1952, it published two issues of the journal *Arti e costume: rassegna semestrale del Centro internazionale delle arti e del costume, in Venezia a Palazzo Grassi* (*Arts and Costume: Biannual Bulletin of the International Centre of the Arts and Costume, in Venice at Palazzo Grassi*) but no following issues are recorded nor have survived. In 1964 and 1965, two issues of *Notizie* (*Newsletter*) were published but, again, were discontinued. From 1960 onwards, CIAC adopted a different sponsoring model by inviting artists to use SNIA Viscosa fabrics for their works. However, Franco Marinotti was committed to continue promoting research on costume – especially given the outstanding collection he had donated to the centre – and commissioned a publication dedicated to dress and textiles collections around the world, edited by Grazietta Butazzi.

In 1963, Butazzi was appointed the External Relation officer of the Ufficio Studi (Study Bureau) of the CIAC operational centre in Milan (Rizzini, 2016). She contributed to the first two issues of *Notizie* (1964, 1965) and, from 1963 to 1970, undertook extensive research to identify public collections of costume and textiles worldwide. While she is not credited as the author – CIAC is, as was customary at the time (Rizzini, 2016) – she is credited for 'raccolta del materiale e redazione' (research and editing) in the acknowledgements (CIAC, 1970). The book was entitled *Guida internazionale ai musei e alle collezioni pubbliche di costumi e di tessuti* (*International Guide to Public Museums and Collections of Costumes and Textiles*) and was tri-lingual (Italian, French and English): it surveyed 736 institutions, of which collection contents, history and general information were reported. The introduction opens with a statement, likely written by Butazzi, of acknowledgement of the support of SNIA Viscosa who made the publication possible (CIAC, 1970). In the one-page introductory text, the methodology for the compilation of the guide is explained, as well as its aim, 'to establish a productive base for its work needs [CIAC] and a source of precise and up-to-date information for those who are interested in these studies in the broader sector of Costume understood in its human and social meaning'[17] (CIAC, 1970: 5). The scale of this publication remains unparalleled, however in my research I have only found it mentioned in three international publications (Jackson Jowers, 2013 Yarwood, 1978; Sterlacci and Arbuckle, 2007).

The CIAC slowly decreased its activity, due to limited funding, and ceased its operations in 1978, although its location, Palazzo Grassi, has since remained a cultural institution. It was first sold to a group of Venetian industrialists and transformed into an institute that 'continued the cultural activities and the organizational structure used by CIAC for a few years' (MUVE, 2021). It was then purchased by the car manufacturer FIAT in 1984, so the Municipality of Venice bought the former collections and library of CIAC from FIAT. In 1985 the Fondazione dei Musei Civici di Venezia (Foundation of Civic Museums of Venice) established the Centro Studi di Storia del Tessuto e del Costume (Study Centre of the History of Textile and Costume) at Palazzo Mocenigo and incorporated the materials of CIAC.

4.2.4 Fashion studies in Milan in the 1970s

While the activity of CIAC was slowly decreasing in the 1970s, Milan was enjoying a particularly thriving moment for fashion (Rizzini, 2016). On the one hand it was establishing itself as the Italian centre of ready-to-wear and it was witnessing the rise to prominence of the role of freelance designer, known in Italian as *stilista* (Stanfill, 2014); on the other hand, two institutions – the Civiche Raccolte d'Arte Applicata (Civic Collections of Applied Art) and the Museo

Poldi Pezzoli – initiated many projects dedicated to research and exhibitions on the history of dress and textiles.

In 1972, Rosita Levi Pisetzky donated her collection of garments and accessories (dating from mid-1800s to 1950s) to the Civiche Raccolte d'Arte Applicata (Civic Collections of Applied Art), located in the Castello Sforzesco in Milan, as well as a large portion of her vast library to the Civica Raccolta delle Stampe Achille Bertarelli (the Achille Bertarelli Civic Collection of Prints) (Rizzini, 2016), located in the same institution; the remainder of the library was acquired from Levi Pisetzky's heirs after her death. In the same year, Grazietta Butazzi was appointed by Clelia Alberici (then director of the Civiche Raccolte) to catalogue the dress and textiles collections. Butazzi later took part in the course *Storia della moda in Italia dal Rinascimento all'Ottocento* (History of Fashion in Italy from Renaissance to the Eighteenth Century), held at the Museo Poldi Pezzoli and strongly supported by its director, Alessandra Mottola Molfino. The course was run by Maria Teresa Binaghi Olivari, then an officer of the Soprintendenza ai Monumenti e alle Gallerie di Milano (Superintendence of Museums and Galleries of Milan).

In 1976, the results of Butazzi's work on the Raccolte Civiche was presented to the public with the exhibition *Costumi dei secoli XVIII e XIX* (Costumes of the XVIII and XIX Centuries) held at the Rotonda della Besana in Milan; Butazzi curated the selection of exhibits and edited the catalogue (Butazzi, 1976). The display had also been made possible thanks to the collecting policy of Alberici who, at the time, was encouraging donations as well as managing acquisitions for the collections (Rizzini, 2016). The exhibition also signalled the beginning of Alberici's campaign for the establishment of a costume museum. The project was very ambitious and in the exhibition's introduction, Alberici was urging *maisons* to send their creations in order to gather both antique and contemporary artefacts. This exhibition also established what was to become a future pattern: the use of displays to trigger discussions on museums of costume. The 1951 opening exhibition of CIAC had already been used as a manifesto for the curatorial policy of the Centre. In 1979 the historical dress exhibition at Palazzo Pitti in Florence led to the opening of the Galleria del Costume (Gallery of Costume) in 1983, also housed in Palazzo Pitti. In 1980 the exhibition dedicated to Italian Fascist fashion at the Museo Poldi Pezzoli was linked to a conference dedicated to the establishment of a costume museum in Milan. The 1985 exhibition dedicated to Salvatore Ferragamo at Palazzo Strozzi in Florence initiated the works on the Ferragamo archives which led to the opening of the Museo Salvatore Ferragamo in 1995, and the 2000 Armani exhibition at the Guggenheim Museum in New York served as the foundation for the permanent display at the Armani/Silos inaugurated in Milan in 2015. The CIAC was a fundamental step in the development of fashion studies and curation in Italy. Together with its legacy found in the Study Centre now held at Palazzo Mocenigo, it provided a successful model for a corporate institution with a diversified programme. With its closing, Milan first, and later Florence, became the centres of fashion studies. The activities were led by independent scholars and public institutions, but the industry increasingly supported interest in corporate archives and contemporary fashion, as it mirrored its preoccupations.

4.3 Moving towards contemporary fashion (1980s–1990s)

In the 1970s, the institutional landscape in Italy was fragmented: most collections of textiles and historical dresses were managed by local Superintendencies, often governed by complex procedures. A large portion of what are now publicly accessible collections were private, many of them belonging to textile manufacturers or fashion professionals, such as the collection of the fashion journalist Silvana Bernasconi now held part of the Civiche Raccolte in Milan (Morini and Rosina, 2005). Despite this fragmentation, in the 1980s and 1990s many links were created between companies, collectors and scholars, establishing the foundation of a network that still operates today.

Without the presence of a centralizing institution – such as the V&A in London or the Palais Galliera in Paris – providing models for cataloguing, curation and management, fashion curation developed in Italy in a capillary way, in which small institutions operated around the regional centres of Milan, Venice and Florence. This resulted in the lack of an identifiable curatorial direction, which could be detected in London and Paris, for each initiative responded to the needs and resources of the associated institution. On the other hand, these limitations led to the maturation of what I argue is the distinctive trait of fashion studies in Italy, that is a close-knit collaboration between scholarship and industry. Companies did not only sponsor projects related to their own heritage, they also provided access to their archives as well as employing established curators and historians for the management of these archives, allowing for an open exchange between scholarship and industry, in which both parties addressed their needs while also facilitating the other's fulfilments. In this phase, the role of associations was pivotal: a national association of dress and textiles scholars united independent professionals and public employees and favoured the identification and development of common procedures, guidelines and best practices; the trade associations focused on building the cultural profile of the industry they were representing and engaged with scholars for the creation of cultural initiatives.

4.3.1 CISST, the Italian Centre for the Study of the History of Textiles

In February and March 1978, Alessandra Mottola Molfino organized at the Museo Poldi Pezzoli a course on the history of textiles, which was part of a series of lectures dedicated to the history of applied arts. This course was held by the Roman costume historian and conservator Lucia Portoghese, which most Milan-based scholars attended (Rizzini, 2016). On this occasion, Portoghese likely discussed with other scholars the possibility to establish a specialist association that would favour the exchange between the growing number of scholars interested in costume and textiles, along the lines of the Lyon-based CIETA, Centre International d'Etude des Textiles Anciens([International Centre for the Study of Ancient Textiles). On 5 April 1978, CISST, Centro Italiano per lo Studio della Storia del Tessuto (Italian Centre for the Study of the History of Textiles) was registered in Rome. There were twenty-six founding members, 'Italian historians of applied arts, and in particular of textile, costume and lace [which were moved by] the need to build an organism that united the efforts of individuals in an attempt to affect the current situation of the Italian textile heritage'[18] (CISST, 1980: 3). The members adhered to the association as independent scholars or 'for the institutional roles that they held in museums, research centres and superintendencies, institutions already sensitive at that time to the problem of the conservation of the Italian textile heritage, the least considered of the already little studied decorative arts'[19] (Rizzini, 2016: 26). The statute was discussed in two meetings held in Milan on 3 October and 21 November.

During this developmental stage of Italian fashion studies, courses provided the chance to discuss and develop a shared methodology. Another course on textile techniques was held in September 1978 at the Museo Civico di Modena. Rizzini viewed this course as a response to the need to train professionals dealing with the cataloguing of textile artefacts with specialist skills and specific terminology, following the general methodology devised by the Istituto Centrale per il Catalogo (Central Institute for Cataloguing) in 1975. The course was run by Donata Devoti, an applied art historian based at the University of Pisa and member of the CIETA. Devoti had published a seminal work in

1974, *L'arte del Tessuto in Europa. Dal XII al XX Secolo* (*The Art of Textiles in Europe. From XII to XX Century*). There were twenty participants including Alessandra Mottola Molfino, Maria Teresa Binaghi Olivari, Grazietta Butazzi as well as the conservator Francesco Pertagato – who would later collaborate on many occasions with Mottola Molfino and Butazzi in Milan – and Chiara Buss, who would become the first director of the textile museum of the Fondazione Antonio Ratti and develop its innovative digital catalogue in the 1990s.

From January to September 1979, the exhibition *Curiosità di una reggia. Vicende della guardaroba di Palazzo Pitti* (Curiosities of a Palace. Affairs of the Wardrobe of Palazzo Pitti) was held at Palazzo Pitti in Florence (Aschengreen Piacenti and Pinto, 1979). It displayed artefacts that had never been shown before and also served to test the public interest. The positive feedback encouraged Kirsten Aschengreen Piacenti, who curated the exhibition with Sandra Pinto, to develop a plan for the establishment of a costume museum in the palace. At the time, Aschengreen Piacenti was the director of the Museo degli Argenti (Museum of Silverware) and Sandra Pinto was the director of the Galleria Moderna (Gallery of Modern Art), both located in Palazzo Pitti. Rizzini pointed out how this exhibition was an important moment for collective research (Rizzini, 2016) and many scholars continued to gravitate around Pitti. The role of Pitti became even more central as an organizer of projects and a collection centre after the Galleria del Costume (Gallery of Costume) was established in 1983, with Kirsten Aschengreen Piacenti as its director. Grazietta Butazzi described the Galleria del Costume as 'the first Italian state museum dedicated entirely to the preservation and study of fashion, clothes and accessories for costume and textiles'[20] (Butazzi in Rizzini, 2016: 28). Initially, the collection of the institution was very small but the director undertook many efforts to raise funds for acquisitions and to build relationships with designers, private collectors and manufacturers to encourage donations, such as those from the costumier Umberto Tirelli, the designer Gianfranco Ferré or the collector Cecilia Matteucci Lavarini (Chiarelli, 2009). The operations of the museum in recent years are analysed in the following section, and will demonstrate how the increasing influence of the fashion industry will not only shape curatorial approaches, but will also lead to the renaming of the Galleria del Costume in the Museo della Moda e del Costume (Museum of Fashion and Costume) in 2017.

The first general assembly of CISST was held in Rome at the oratory of the church Santa Maria dell'Orto on 26 February 1979: 110 members were present and organized into 5 regional sections (Lombardia, Liguria, Emilia, Toscana e

Figure 4.3 The Sala Bianca of Palazzo Pitti was set as a procession of bishops, with mannequins wearing liturgical vestments from the eighteenth and nineteenth centuries, for the exhibition *Curiosità di una reggia. Vicende della guardaroba di Palazzo Pitti* (*Curiosities of a Palace. Affairs of the Wardrobe of Palazzo Pitti*), Florence, 1979. Courtesy *Gallerie degli Uffizi*.

Lazio). The CISST board identified national guidelines, yet each regional section also held independent meetings, built relationships with local authorities and companies, and established close groups of collaborators. The assemblies became an important tool for the identification of themes of investigation: over the following twelve years, CISST organized seven conferences on various issues related to the study and conservation of textiles and costumes, attended by prominent international scholars – such as the British dress historian Janet Arnold – both as speakers and attendees. Only one was dedicated to fashion, in 1990, and will be later discussed as it best epitomizes the synergies between scholarship and industry that characterized the 1980s and planted the seeds for subsequent initiatives.

4.3.2 The 1980 exhibition at the Museo Poldi Pezzoli in Milan

At the same time as Aschengreen Piacenti was working on the project for the Galleria del Costume, Alessandra Mottola Molfino was turning the Museo Poldi Pezzoli in Milan from a historic house into an innovative institution that promoted research and discussion on fashion. She coordinated an exhibition in 1980 which is still seen today as the single event that founded fashion studies in Italy (Morini, Rizzini and Rosina, 2016): *1922–1943 Vent'anni di Moda in Italia. Proposta per un museo della moda a Milano.* [1922–1943: Twenty Years of Fashion in Italy. Proposal for a Museum of Fashion in Milan], ran from 5 December 1980 to 25 March 1981. The exhibition was curated by Grazietta Butazzi and in committee with Clelia Alberici, Carlo Bertelli, Rosita Levi Pisetzky, Roberto Monoelli and Alessandra Mottola Molfino (Butazzi, 1980). This committee can be viewed as the transition between two generations, as it gathered scholars that characterized the previous phase and those who would shape the forthcoming years. The exhibition focused on fashion under the fascist rule in Italy, a brave experiment that used fashion as an indirect focus to discuss the fascist era, still a challenging topic in 1980. It featured garments and accessories displayed around the rooms of the museum, as well as magazines and illustrations. The exhibits belonged mainly to the Civic Collections of Milan, which lacked a location for displays, and Mottola Molfino was adamant to use the museum she directed to bring this issue to the public, together with presenting the first exhibition solely dedicated to twentieth-century fashion. The intention to establish a fashion museum was so closely connected to the exhibition that it was declared in its title; the display was conceived as 'a proposal for a fashion museum in Milan'[21] (dell'Acqua, 1980: 9) but also a chance to involve the public in its development by stimulating donations. The Milanese department store La Rinascente was acknowledged in the list of exhibition supporters together with three trade associations:

1. Assomoda, Associazione italiana rappresentanti moda (Italian Association Fashion Salesmen);
2. Associazione italiana degli industriali dell'abbigliamento (Italian Association of Clothing Industrialists);

3. Associazione italiana produttori maglierie e calzetterie (Italian Association of Knitwear and Hosiery Manufacturers).

The exhibition addressed a problematic era in Italian history, yet the support of the industry can be interpreted as the strong will to promote both fashion scholarship and the establishment of a museum, further evidence in support of the argument of is this book. In fact, these companies also financed a conference organized after the closing of the exhibition, on 27 March 1981 at the Fiera di Milano, entitled *Prima conferenza internazionale per un Museo della Moda* (First International Conference for a Museum of Fashion). Designers and manufacturers attended and they were adamant that there should also be a school associated with the museum and, soon after, a commission was formed by the city government to develop the project (CISST, 1981). Among the speakers were Levi Pisetzky, Alberici and Butazzi, as well as international museum professionals such as Penelope Byrde (Fashion Museum, Bath, UK), Madeleine Delpierre (Palais Galliera, Paris, France), Jun Kanai (Kyoto Costume Institute, Kyoto, Japan), Stella Blum (Costume Institute, Met Museum, New York, United States), and Valerie Mendes (Victoria and Albert Museum, London, UK). Speakers reported on the histories of their collections and on curatorial practices: it was a discussion between museums 'to identify shareable guidelines and practices, with the common awareness of the need for an active and efficient museal reflection on fashion' (Monti, 2019: 69).[22] Similar to the 1952 conference at CIAC, this event initiated a debate and, as Rizzini stated, 'it was the official beginning of a long and tormented path that would involve many people and public and private institutions'[23] (Rizzini, 2016: 30). The museum did not materialize but triggered 'a great development of studies and research, through exhibitions, conferences, establishment of museums, projects and publications now part of the history of the studies on fashion and textile in Italy'[24] (Rizzini, 2016: 30).

The debate around a museum of fashion was also being covered in publications outside the specialist circle of costume scholars. The architect Alessandro Mendini, who had been editor-in-chief of the architecture and design magazine *Domus* since 1979, started to include fashion in the May 1980 issue but, mostly importantly, created the supplement *Domus Moda*, published twice in 1981 but immediately discontinued (Maddaluno, 2015). Mendini authored the opening editorial in both issues and dedicated the second (October 1981) to the study of fashion; it was entitled 'Musei della moda? Considerazioni teoriche a proposito di un museo della moda per Milano' (Museums of Fashion? Theoretical Considerations Regarding a Museum of Fashion for Milan). In the article, Mendini reflected on the relevance of fashion in society and how its study would favour a better understanding of ideals of beauty and their consumption by the masses (Mendini, 1981). Butazzi was actually teaching fashion history in the 1980s at the Domus Academy, the postgraduate institution aimed at training architects and designers, founded by the magazine *Domus*. The circulation of ideas across fields, from museums to industry and to magazines, would characterize the development of fashion studies in the following decades. What Mendini was describing was a cultural approach to the study of fashion history that mirrored the works of contemporaneous scholars such as Butazzi, whose 1981 publication *Moda: arte, storia, società* (*Fashion: Art, History, Society*) became the manifesto for a new methodology for the study of fashion history, which might be likened for approach and influence to the book *Adorned in Dreams: Fashion and Modernity* by leading British fashion historian Elizabeth Wilson (1985). For Butazzi, fashion,

> became a set of signs, each of which had different implications and meanings (cultural, artistic, social, psychological, psychoanalytic, etc.) that could be analysed only by resorting to different sources (fashion press, but also literature, diaries, dance manuals, etiquette, monographic texts, and so on). The images were part of this multiplicity of sources, but not as a simple confirmation or illustration of what was documented elsewhere. (Morini, 2016: 82)[25]

Another key publication was *La Moda Italiana* (*Italian Fashion*), written in 1985 by Butazzi, Mottola Molfino and the art historian Arturo Carlo Quintavalle. Quintavalle was a professor in History of Art at the University of Parma and, together with being an internationally established scholar of Medieval Art, he greatly focused on contemporary culture: in 1968 he had founded the Centro Studio e Archivio della Comunicazione (Study Centre and Archive of Communication). The CSAC was originally built on the idea that *disegno* (drawing) is the core testimony of artistic and design production and it originally collected only bidimensional artefacts, although it has now heterogeneous collections. This approach was likely due to Quintavalle's expertise which led to the favouring of the drawing over the object. Nevertheless, Quintavalle recognized the cultural and historical importance of drawings and sketches when no one else paid attention to these sources and between the late 1970s and the early 1980s he gathered an astonishing number of documents by contacting manufacturers and designers and asking for donation. The archive was divided early on in five sections: *arte* (art), *fotografia* (photography), *media*, *moda* (fashion), *progetto* (industrial design). It now gathers more than 12 million artefacts and documents including 70,000 fashion illustrations (CSAC, 2021).

Exhibitions and catalogues were regularly produced to disseminate the results of the research undertaken at the CSAC. Gloria Bianchino started collaborating with the centre in the early 1980s, where she catalogued the fashion collections and published three accurate catalogues on the work of the Sorelle Fontana (Bianchino, 1984), on the work of the designer Walter Albini (Bianchino, 1988) and a retrospective of fashion illustrations in Italy from 1945 and 1980 (Bianchino, 1987). In 1984, CSAC promoted a conference dedicated to fashion, attended by leading scholars such as Rossana Bossaglia, and the round table *L'archivio di Parma e il progetto di moda* (The Archive in Parma and Fashion Design) attended by members of the industry including Krizia, Missoni and Moschino (CSAC, 1990). In 1989 Bianchino became the director of the CSAC, a post she held until 2015. In 2007 the centre moved to the Abbey of Valserena near Parma and in 2015 a museum was opened on the premises to provide a permanent space for displays. The collecting activity has sensibly decreased, especially due to the importance companies now grant to their own heritage, which they are unwilling to donate, yet the CSAC[26] remains a model to follow for archival management and scientific research and they also provide consultancy services (Fava and Soldi, 2018).

The 1985 publication analysed the history of post-war Italian fashion up until contemporary times and was divided in two volumes: *Le origini dell'alta moda e la maglieria* (The *Origins of High Fashion and Knitwear*) (Butazzi, Mottola Molfino and Quintavalle, 1985), and *Dall'antimoda allo stilismo* (From Antifashion to Freelance Designers) (Butazzi and Molfino, 1986). As happened in most projects at the time, 'they involved academic lecturers, but also early-career scholars from all over the nation'[27] (Rizzini, 2016: 31). By interacting with other professionals, Butazzi allowed for a common method to be developed and shared. This was confirmed three decades later in 2014 during the conference dedicated to her legacy at the Fondazione Antonio Ratti (Morini, Rizzini and Rosina, 2016), which was attended by the leading Italian textile, dress and fashion scholars. From the proceedings of the conference emerged the unanimous belief that Butazzi led generations of scholars into this field of research and that her publications were meticulously studied not only for their contents but as methodological models, supporting Rizzini's statement that the 1985 publication 'was probably the beginning of the Italian studies on contemporary fashion'[28] (Rizzini, 2016: 31).

Butazzi became the reference point not only for the community of scholars engaged in the study of fashion, but also for the industry which sought to support research in fashion and in their heritage, as will be later demonstrated by the commission of the clothing manufacture Gruppo Finanziario Tessile (GFT) to

Butazzi to undertake a research project on the history of fashion manufacturing. The influence of the industry on the evolution of fashion studies and curation in Italy was not only achieved through the active engagement of companies, but most importantly through the mutual interaction between industry and scholarship.

4.3.3 The 1985 retrospective on Salvatore Ferragamo

Many exhibitions were organized throughout the 1980s and touched upon textiles, dress and fashion. For example, *Conseguenze impreviste. Arte, moda, design: ipotesi di nuove creatività in Italia* (Unexpected Consequences. Art, Fashion, Design: Hypotheses of New Creativities in Italy] was held in Prato and organized by the local council for culture (18 December 1982–28 February 1983). Displays took over buildings in the old town, with sections identified by differently coloured neon lights. The section on fashion was held in the same building: a collective display where designers had their individual installations and presented their latest work. The exhibition has been analysed by Monti who noted that it was 'a spectacle of ideas, of inventions, of objects which aimed at being perceived as an event deeply rooted into contemporaneity' (2019: 70).[29]

In 1983, an exhibition was curated by Butazzi, Mottola Molfino and Pia Soli, the latter an established fashion journalist, on one living designer: the display *Gianni Versace: dieci anni di creatività* (Gianni Versace: Ten Years of Creativity) was held in Verona at the contemporary gallery Studio La Città (Butazzi, Mottola Molfino and Soli, 1983). In the following year, Pia Soli curated the industry-wide retrospective entitled *Il genio antipatico. Creatività e tecnologia della moda Italiana 1951–1983* (The Troublesome Genius. Creativity and Technology of Italian fashion 1951–1983), first held in Rome and later in Genoa (Soli, 1984). The project had the support of the industry, with the board largely made up of representatives from different sectors, from brands to textile and clothing manufacturers. Because of Pia Soli's position and connections, the exhibition centred on the 'sensitivity and insight of the insider' (Monti, 2019: 75).[30]

In 1985, Fendi organized an exhibition with the Galleria d'Arte Moderna (Gallery of Modern Art) in Rome to celebrate two decades of collaboration between the brand and the designer Karl Lagerfeld. It was entitled *Un percorso di lavoro* (A Journey of Work) and was curated by Ida Panicelli, director of the museum. It included 180 sketches from 1966 to 1985 as well as garments exhibited alongside the works of art present in the museum. One section was called *retrobottega* (back shop) which represented production phases from sketches to patterns, showing the stretching and nailing of skins before the finished product. The last room was instead dedicated to the spectacle of fashion: visitors could sit on steps that had been installed while watching a fashion show of moving mechanical mannequins (Laurenzi, 1985). As discussed in Chapter 1, this project was criticized in the contemporary press and even during a Senate session. Though the catwalk and workshop sections of the exhibitions have become staples in recent fashion exhibitions, the exhibition has been almost absent from existing discussion of fashion curation in Italy, and it is likely that it was not an influential experimentation despite of its innovations.

The late 1970s and the early 1980s have been considered pivotal for the development of fashion curation because of the exhibitions associated with Diana Vreeland's appointment as special consultant to the Costume Institute at the Metropolitan Museum of Art in New York. In 1983, Vreeland curated an exhibition on the French designer Yves Saint Laurent (Saint Laurent and Vreeland, 1983). This exhibition led to great criticism given fashion's commercial nature and the belief, at the time, that museums should not entertain commercial operations (Silverman, 1986). It is not clear whether and how exhibitions in Italy might have been influenced by Vreeland's exhibitions and a reconstruction of a detailed exhibition chronology in Italy as well as of the exchange between curators and scholars internationally could provide precious insights to survey curatorial interests and approaches. There is, however, one exhibition which connects Italian fashion studies to English (American and British) fashion studies and evidences the differences: the 1985 retrospective on Salvatore Ferragamo in Florence.

According to the testimony of Stefania Ricci, now Director of the Museo Salvatore Ferragamo, the Vreeland exhibition suggested a similar operation to the director of the newly found Galleria del Costume in Florence (Ricci, 2015a). Since the opening of the museum, Aschengreen Piacenti worked on developing ties with companies to encourage donations to populate the relatively limited collection of the museum (likely a few hundred artefacts, while it now amounts to six thousand). One of these connections led to the first major solo exhibition dedicated to a designer in Italy: from 4 May to 30 June 1985, the display *I protagonisti della moda. Salvatore Ferragamo (1898–1960)* [Leaders of Fashion. Salvatore Ferragamo (1898–1960)] was held at the Palazzo Strozzi in Florence. The exhibition was organized by the Centro Mostre di Firenze (Florence Exhibitions Centre) in collaboration with the Galleria del Costume and the curators credited were Aschengreen Piacenti, Guido Vergani (journalist and fashion scholar) and Stefania Ricci. The latter was a young art historian who was introduced to the Ferragamo family by Aschengreen Piacenti with the task to 'study and organize the extremely rich collection of documents, photographs, videos and shoes of the founder of the company, Salvatore Ferragamo'[31] (Ricci, 2016b: 47) in view of the exhibition. Ricci would continue to work on the archive after the exhibition and manage subsequent stagings of the display, a constantly updated retrospective that toured until the late 2000s; Ricci would also develop the project for the corporate museum and has been its director since its opening in 1995 (Ricci, 1995).

There are two differences with the 1983 Yves Saint Laurent exhibition by Vreeland. Firstly, the narrative presented in Florence was a 'completed history' as it focused solely on the work of Salvatore Ferragamo, even though his daughter successfully continued the work of the company – following the request of the family (Ricci, 2015a). Secondly, the catalogue was conceived as a tool to demonstrate the cultural relevance of the topic and the academic rigour of the research. In the introduction to the catalogue, Sergio Salvi (then director of the Centro Mostre di Firenze) anticipated potential criticism and

Figure 4.4 A vitrine of the exhibition *I protagonisti della moda. Salvatore Ferragamo (1898–1960)* [*Leaders of Fashion. Salvatore Ferragamo (1898–1960)*], displaying shoes by Salvatore Ferragamo alongside advertising artworks by the Futurist Lucio Venna. Palazzo Strozzi, Florence, 1985. Courtesy *Museo Salvatore Ferragamo*.

stressed the rigour of the project. He even used the adjective scientific, if tentatively, and underlined the fact that Salvatore Ferragamo was deceased, almost as a justification. The text is here quoted at length as it captures the caution with which fashion exhibitions were approached in 1985, the opposite approach to the theatrical operation devised by Vreeland in New York (Silverman, 1986).

> With this exhibition on the figure, but especially on the work, of Salvatore Ferragamo, the Florence Exhibitions Centre also produces an exhibition dedicated to a truly fashionable subject, as the recent exhibitions in Milan and Venice, respectively dedicated to theatrical costume and to evening dress, demonstrate: and nothing seems to be more fashionable today, as an exhibition, than an exhibition precisely on fashion. Of course, Florence has the advantage of having been able to establish first – among all the Italian cities that have long held the legitimate desire – its own fashion museum, that is the prestigious Costume Gallery of Palazzo Pitti: and it can thus enjoy the comfort of a serious structure and a team of trained and meticulous specialists. And since the Ferragamo exhibition was born in collaboration with the Costume Gallery, it appears, as well as seductive for the exhibited objects, also philologically impeccable, as demonstrated by the truly beautiful catalogue that accompanies it ... This 'cut', which we can define even 'scientific' (with all due respect to physics, chemistry and mathematics) is undoubtedly favoured by the fact that the figure of Ferragamo is now completed and entirely incorporated in history, so that the exhibition, without abdicating its own contemporaneity, can be called an anthological retrospective, thus free from close ties to a present too close (although it appears very useful as an eminent example for the present and even for the future).[32]

(Salvi, 1985: 8)To dedicate space in an exhibition catalogue to methodology, as well as a glossary of technical terms relating to shoes, was unprecedented. The catalogue entries were modelled upon those developed by June Swann, former Keeper of the Boot and Shoe Collection of the Northampton Museum in the UK, in her article *Proposed Scheme for Cataloguing Shoes*, published in *Costume, The Journal of Costume Society* in 1977. It had already been used by Grazietta Butazzi to catalogue the eighteenth-century footwear collection at the Castello Sforzesco in Milan. The curators of the Ferragamo exhibition also explained how the model had been modified 'to adapt a cataloguing system devised originally for antique footwear to models produced more recently and with very different techniques' (Aschengreen Piacenti, Ricci and Vergani, 1985: 44).

4.3.4 The 1990 conference on ready-to-wear history

Over the next two decades, applying scientific rigour to cataloguing and involving independent scholars became an established practice for corporate institutions (Arezzi Boza, 2012). An example of how the industry actively promoted research is provided by Antonio Ratti, owner of the Ratti textile manufacture. Ratti sponsored exhibitions in Milan and Venice (Chiara, 2013) and the 1985 exhibition *The Costumes of Royal India* at the MET. He then continued to sponsor the American museum and in 1995 provided the majority of funds to build the Antonio Ratti Textile Center. Ratti had himself been collecting ancient and modern textiles since the 1960s, used as a source of inspiration for his work.

Ratti implemented a similar operation to Marinotti when he founded CIAC in 1951. In 1985 he founded the Fondazione Antonio Ratti with the aim to promote historical and cultural research in textiles as well as to support and organize exhibitions and lectures. In 1993 he endowed the foundation with his collection (Chiara, 2013) and five subsequent exhibitions were organized to present the scale of this collection. Ratti appointed experts to undertake the research on the collection and to edit themed catalogues: *Silk, Gold and Silver* (Buss, 1992), *Qibti* (Donadoni Roveri, 1993, *Cravates: Women's Acessories in the 19th Century* (Peter-Muller, 1994), *Cachemire* (Lévi-Strauss, 1995), *Velvets* (Buss, 1996) and *Silk and Colour* (Buss, 1997). In 1998 the Fondazione Antonio Ratti became accessible to the public with the opening of the Museo Tessile (Textile Museum), later renamed Museo Studio del Tessuto (Textile Study Museum) and Chiara Buss, a textile historian who had been part of CISST since its inception, was appointed director.

From 26 to 28 February 1990, CISST organized its fifth international conference, this time dedicated to ready-to-wear clothing. The three-day conference did not only look at contemporary fashion but traced its origins back to sixteenth-century dress. It was sponsored by the manufacturer Gruppo Finanziario Tessile (GFT) and the theme had developed out of the research conducted on the archive of GFT in the 1980s. Elsa Golzio Aimone (then manager of the GFT archive) also presented the work of the corporate archive at the conference. Every attendant received a copy of the publication on the history of GFT and its archive, which had been published in 1989 by the company itself (Berta, 1989). Another representative of the corporate culture was Fiammetta Roditi, then director of the specialist library on clothing manufacture and knitwear which had been founded by the industrialist Attilio Tremelloni in 1983 in Milan. This conference was possibly the most inclusive of all organized by CISST as it covered an extremely broad variety of topics and eras, and combined artefact-based research with theoretical discussions and reflections on research methodologies. It also gathered an impressive number of internationally renowned scholars, all invited by Butazzi who organized the programme, such as the British dress historians Janet Arnold and Aileen Ribeiro and the American curators Jean Druesedow and Richard Martin, and Canadian curator Alexandra Palmer.

The proceedings were published – each paper in its original language – in 1992 by Edifir, the publishing house established in 1985 by Centro di Firenze per la Moda Italiana (Centre of Florence of Italian Fashion) for 'the production and diffusion of books, magazines and publications related to fashion (it edits the catalogues of the Pitti fairs)'[33] (CFMI, 2021). The Centro di Firenze per la Moda Italiana is an association founded in 1954 to organize the fashion shows in Florence, which had started in 1951. In 1972 it organized the first edition of Pitti Uomo, which is currently the world's leading trade fair for menswear. In 1983 the Centro created a company specifically to manage the organization of all Pitti fairs, which had by then expanded to Pitti Donna (womenswear), Pitti Filati (textiles), Pitti Maglia (knitwear) and Pitti Bimbo (childrenswear), originally called Centro Moda Firenze s. r. l. and in 1988 renamed Pitti Immagine s. r. l., which is still the name in use.

Pitti Immagine financed the publishing of the CISST proceedings and was also linked to the sponsoring of the conference, for Marco Rivetti was the president of both GFT and Pitti Immagine. In the preface, Rivetti stated that its activities were directed at fashion and textile professionals but were also relevant to a wider public, and that the initiatives supported and organized by Pitti Immagine aimed at providing 'numerous opportunities for cultural analysis and stimuli to critically analyse its past, present and future'[34] (Rivetti, 1992: xi). Although the focus of the conference was historical, Rivetti stressed the value of knowing the history of the industry, as it suggests 'causes for reflections about current problems'[35] (Rivetti, 1992: xi) and highlighted the continuity in the commission of statistics-based and history-based research for the aims of Pitti Immagine. The relationship between Pitti Immagine and CISST was extensive: Pitti Immagine is referenced as a financial contributor to four of the five issues (1990, 1991a, 1992, 1993, 1994) of the annual journal of CISST, *Arte Tessile* (*Textile Art*), published by Edifir, effectively another indirect support of the work of the scholarly association by Centro di Firenze per la Moda Italiana.

4.3.5 The relaunch of Florence as a fashion capital

Throughout the 1990s, Pitti Immagine implemented a diverse range of operations centred around fashion that aimed at the cultural revival of Florence, building on its 'leading role in reflection of the cultural history of Italian fashion' (Desiderio, 2015: 14). Florence had lost its leading position within the Italian fashion system in the 1980s (Stanfill, 2014) and Marco Rivetti, since his appointment as president of Pitti Immagine in 1988, sought to relaunch the image of the city. Pitti Immagine operated in conjunction with its founding association, the Centro di Firenze per la Moda Italiana (CFMI). The aim of its president Vittorio Rimbotti, appointed in 1989, was to explore a variety of communication platforms and the Centro sought direct control in all these fields (SAN, 2010), including publishing (Edifir) and the training of future professionals through a higher-education institution (Polimoda), founded in 1986. Rivetti and Rimbotti devised a strategy centred around events to locate nationally and internationally Florence as a fashion hub. For this purpose, Luigi Settembrini, a New York-based Italian entrepreneur, was appointed as creative consultant to Pitti Immagine with the aim to devise exhibitions that would complement the programme of fairs. This was the starting point of a corporate cultural policy through which Pitti aimed at becoming a producer of cultural events; through it, 'the dialogue between the fair and the city's cultural context grew closer' (Flaccavento, 2015: 134).

The exhibition *La Sala Bianca: Nascita della moda italiana* opened in June 1992, in conjuction with Pitti Uomo. The display – discussed in Section 1.4 – was a successful attempt at establishing a historical narrative in which Florence is the birthplace and fashion so the foundations thus laid could be used to build a contemporaneous image of Florence (Malossi, 1992). This exhibition was held in a Renaissance building, Palazzo Strozzi and the change can also be detected in the chosen location for 1993. Stazione Leopolda was a former train station which was then used for storage. This space would reconfigure the approach from heritage centred to contemporary: having established its past, Pitti communicated its agency in the present and, in order to stress the cultural relevance of the fair itself and the products sold, they supported a series of exhibitions which discussed fashion as contemporary visual language. Giannino Malossi would be the key figure in this phase as the curator devising a variety of projects spanning from subcultures to masculinity and objectification – often focusing on men and menswear as that was the core business of the Pitti Immagine fair. A company was established to manage Stazione Leopolda and organize the staging of events (PleaseDisturbNow, 2013). The first exhibition was

Supermarket of Style, dedicated to street style, curated by Malossi with designer Italo Lupi in collaboration with Ted Polhemus. It opened in conjunction with Pitti Filati in January 1993. Later in June 1993, in conjunction with Pitti Uomo, opened the exhibition *La Regola Estrosa: Cento anni di eleganza maschile italiana* (La Regola Estrosa: One Hundred Years of Italian Male Elegance), curated by Settembrini. This exhibition aimed at presenting an Italianness articulated through menswear and elegance (Malossi, 1993), another historicizing process to grant cultural relevance to the products sold at the fairs.

From this moment, Stazione Leopolda would become a key place over the following fifteen years and through which Pitti Immagine and CFMI articulated their corporate cultural policy and redefined both the image of Florence and the use of exhibitions as promotional tools. Over time, these displays became a form of cultural commentaries of themes connected to current trends and preoccupations in fashion studies. In fact, Malossi confirmed that there was awareness of the development of this field and that exhibitions were intended as introductory platforms to research and debates, putting fashion in relation with other contemporary creative languages such as music, cinema, design and

Figure 4.5 The exhibition *La Sala Bianca: The Birth of Italian Fashion* was commissioned by Pitti Immagine to celebrate the fortieth anniversary of the first show in the iconic room of Palazzo Pitti. The installation was designed by architect Gae Aulenti and theatre director Luca Ronconi. Palazzo Strozzi, Florence, 1992. Courtesy Pitti Immagine.

photography.[36] There was a limited time to prepare each exhibition, between six to twelve months, therefore limited time could be dedicated to research. For this purpose, national and international specialists were asked to collaborate on projects and this approach would become systematic with the establishment of the Fashion Engineering Unit (FEU) in 1997. The FEU was a working group, led by Malossi, tasked with the organization of cultural events, complimentary with the fair programming. In 1998, the first exhibition of FEU was inaugurated during Pitti Uomo. *Il motore della moda* (The Style Engine), held at Stazione Leopolda, was intended as a manifesto of interests for the FEU and Pitti, a way of presenting a layered understanding of fashion as industry but also as cultural and social practice, and the starting point of an exploration across disciplinary fields (Malossi, 1998) This became even more evident in 1999, with the exhibition *Volare: The Icon of Italy in Global Pop Culture*, which initiated an analysis of Made in Italy and the catalogue (Malossi, 1999) is a useful resource – referenced in Chapter 1 – which frames Italianness as an extra-national concept. This catalogue in particular and its many references in subsequent Italian and foreign publications evidence the impact of a systematic strategy, which also included the appointment of a US-based publisher to ensure extensive distribution.[37] The last exhibition organized by FEU was *Uomo oggetto. Mitologie, spettacolo e mode della maschilità* (Material Man. Masculinity, Sexuality, Style) in 2000 (Malossi, 2000) and FEU stopped operating with the establishment of the Fondazione Pitti Immagine Discovery.

4.3.6 The 1996 Biennale di Firenze

In the mid-1990s, there is one event, organized by Luigi Settembrini with the support of Florentine fashion trade associations and representative of the industry at large, which has attained a mythical stature for its monumental scale as well as its almost immediate death. In 1996, Florence hosted the first edition of the Biennale di Firenze, which was intended to become a biannual festival dedicated to fashion and the arts, on the model of contemporary arts, design and film festivals. Settembrini formulated the initial idea and curated the Biennale with Germano Celant (a famous Italian contemporary art curator) and Ingrid Sischy (American editor and critic). The Biennale was a large-scale series of events that took over the city of Florence for three months. It was the first major event organized independently by the industry and in which established institutions were partners. It situated the Florentine fashion industry as one of the main cultural producers of the city, a position it still holds, as will be

Figure 4.6 The exhibion *Il motore della moda* (*The Style Engine*) is the first display organized by the Fashion Engineering Unit for Pitti Immagine. Stazione Leopolda, Florence, 1998. Courtesy Pitti Immagine.

evident in the next section of this chapter. Vittorio Rimbotti, in the foreword to the general catalogue of the Biennale, traced a link between fashion studies and the fashion system, highlighting not only a symbiotic relationship but also a contemporaneous evolution: 'that an initiative of this kind has been conceived and held in Italy, however, is the sign that in this country the reflection on fashion goes hand in hand with the international establishment of its companies and its famous designers'[38] (Rimbotti, 1996: xiv). Rimbotti also stressed – as all other contributors to the catalogue – that the aim of the Biennale was to 'investigate the relationships between fashion and the other contemporary creative languages'[39] (Rimbotti, 1996: xiv). The idea of fashion as one of the prominent languages of contemporaneity underlies the catalogue introduction by Settembrini, entitled *La Biennale di Firenze: un progetto culturale sulla contemporaneità* (The Biennale of Florence: A Cultural Project on Contemporaneity). Settembrini argued that this aspect of fashion should be promoted and could be achieved by displaying fashion together with other manifestations of contemporaneity (Settembrini, 1996). The title of the Biennale was indeed *Il Tempo e la Moda* (Time and Fashion). The Biennale ran from 20 September 1996 to 25 January 1997 and was based on the model of the Biennale d'Arte of Venice: six exhibitions took place all over the city, together with site-specific installations by twenty designers in existing institutions and famous landmarks. The aim of these displays, in particular the *Visitors* installations, was to reflect on the museum as an institution, and its perceived sacredness. De la Haye described it as 'a seminal point at which fashion and dress were situated in art practice with a series of citywide installations, which generated international publicity and broader debate about fashion as a medium within museums and galleries' (de la Haye, 2010: 286).

These installations and exhibitions, and in particular the display *Art/Fashion* which was dedicated to the artists who addressed or employed fashion in their works, were developed to highlight connections and differences amongst artworks. A different approach was used for to the catalogue (Celant et al., 1996), where each exhibition was presented with an introductory essay and illustrated with minimally captioned images. It was unlike previous catalogues such as the one for the 1985 Ferragamo retrospective, which had featured detailed object-specific captions and explanatory essays, underlied by the need to demonstrate the cultural relevance of the exhibits and the academic rigour of the research. Celant took for granted that fashion was serious – to use an expression later employed by exhibition maker Judith Clark to describe her own work:

> I think that a lot of curators felt and still feel that depth is the point; that if you research something in enough detail then it sort of legitimizes itself. It becomes academically acceptable. I have always been interested in trying to take for granted that dress is serious and interesting, and so it frees me to try to look at it from different perspectives just as you would as a contemporary historian or curator of anything else. (Clark in Stevenson, 2008: 226–7)

What Celant stimulated was the interaction between visual languages, presented without any preconceived hierarchy. Clark particularly identified the installation of Gianfranco Ferré in the Cappelle Medicee during the Biennale as an inspiration that informed her practice (Stevenson, 2008).

The purpose of the Biennale was to demonstrate, through visual dialogues, the ability of fashion to converse with languages considered more complex and less superficial (Celant, Settembrini and Sischy, 1996). Although the Biennale is traditionally associated with art, it is actually an event model rather than a curatorial model, and it is applied to the most different topics, from art to dance, from cinema to theatre. In fact, in 1998 a second Biennale di Firenze was held and it was dedicated to the dialogue between fashion and cinema. It was built on the same model, with exhibitions and site-specific installations but with an entirely different curatorial team, chaired by Leonardo Mondadori, a prominent Italian publisher, and on a smaller scale than the previous edition. In

Figure 4.7 The installation of Gianfranco Ferré for the Biennale della Moda involved larger-than-life crinolines floating in mid-air in the Cappelle Medicee. Photograph by Paola De Pietri. Florence, 1996. Courtesy Archivio Fondazione Gianfranco Ferré.

1997, Mondadori had been appointed president of the Biennale Internazionale d'Arte Contemporanea di Firenze (International Biennale of Contemporary Art of Florence), now only referred to as Florence Biennale, which is still ongoing. The same institutional and civic bodies supported both biennales, further proof that this operation was intended as a series of events inscribed into a policy for the relaunch of the city, previously discussed.

In 2001, Pitti Immagine was awarded the Premio Guggenheim – Cultura & Impresa – discussed in Section 2.3.4 – a recognition of the work done throughout the decade and in particular in the late 1990s with FEU. Although Pitti Immagine events are organized for industry professionals and press, these exhibitions were opened to visitors to 'strengthen the relationship between Florence and those consumers who love fashion and culture' (Aiello et al., 2016: 159). I would argue that these exhibitions were projects of interpretation: specialist professionals such as Malossi – who had experience in bridging culture, research and industry since the 1970s with Fiorucci Dxing – were able to detect the layered consumption of fashion, which was becoming an increasingly culture-intensive industry in those years, and organize events that would address both corporate needs as well as consumption needs. They were commodifying culture and cultural experiences became part of the consumption of fashion but at the same time these exhibitions, to different extents, were addressing broader levels of the self (Belk, 1995), making visitors more than consumers but members of cultural communities. The cultural marketing of fashion was not a novelty, for it had been part of the Florentine fashion system since the 1950s (Stanfill, 2014). The difference now was in the breakdown of a hierarchy between the arts, and fashion being presented at the same level as other visual media.

4.4 The lead of corporate institutions (2000s–2010s)

The third phase of Italian fashion studies is characterized by the active agency of corporate institutions. The beginning of the 2000s was marked by major exhibitions which became models for the curatorial practices of the following two decades: in 2000 the retrospective *Giorgio Armani* opened at the Guggenheim Museum in New York; in 2001, *Silk. The 1900s in Como* was organized by the Fondazione Antonio Ratti in Como and *Uniform. Order and Disorder* was organized by the Fondazione Pitti Immagine Discovery at the Stazione Leopolda in Florence.

From 2000 to 2001, the Solomon R. Guggenheim Museum in New York held an exhibition dedicated to the work of the Italian fashion designer Giorgio Armani (Celant and Koda, 2000). It was curated by Germano Celant, senior curator of contemporary art of the hosting institution, with Harold Koda, then director of the Costume Institute of New York, and designed by the artist, designer and theatre director Robert Wilson. It was structured as a retrospective solo show, with artefacts grouped by themes and presented with general introductions. The show was heavily criticized for the scarcity of information provided (Taylor, 2005) and subsequently became an eminent example of the problematic relationship between fashion, museums and commerce (Palmer, 2008; Steele, 2008), also due to the conspicuous donation of $15 million from the Armani Group to the museum, which could have been interpreted as a payment for the inclusion of Armani's work by the renowned cultural institution though the exhibition was sponsored by the magazine *InStyle*. This operation was different from the Armani installation at the 1996 Biennale di Firenze, where his clothes were exhibited in a gallery of the Uffizi: while the earlier display claimed fashion's right to dialogue with art, the later one implied the recognition of Giorgio Armani as an artist. The 1983 exhibition of Yves Saint Laurent at the MET had received similar criticism (Silverman, 1986). Despite these issues, monographic exhibitions on fashion designers have become a popular genre and have been widely staged since (Horsley, 2014).

Another exhibition held in 2001 was *Seta. Il Novecento a Como* (Silk. The 1900s in Como), held at Villa Olmo in Como, which investigated the Como silk industry throughout the twentieth century. It was organized by the Fondazione Antonio Ratti and curated by Chiara Buss with contributions from many scholars, all belonging to the now dissolved CISST association. Catalogues were published both in Italian and English, and surveyed all the companies working in the silk industry and featured a number of fashionable garments. The academic approach and historical focus – which had characterized CISST – were employed for the study of corporate archives. The industry links of the foundation allowed access to the archives of many manufacturers of the Como silk district. The introduction to the catalogue by Chiara Buss is quoted here at length as a testimony of the thorough knowledge on corporate archive and their study, the result of the two-decade work of CISST and its regular exchanges with the industry.

> After two years of hard work along these lines, and in spite of the generous welcome which we received from many firms to look in their archives, the history

of Como production can not yet be sketched in its entirety for two reasons. It is too late and it is also too soon. It is too late because there are some highly important archives that were destroyed, such as those belonging to Dolara or Bernasconi, or so broken up, like those of Edoardo Stucchi, that they are of little significance for an historical reconstruction. It is too soon because, as production is still going on, there are firms which will not allow their own archives or those of others, acquired over time, to be seen, since they consider them to be precious, and therefore confidential, working tools. It is too late in the fairly frequent cases where firms that are still active have reorganised several decades of archives 'by theme', thus destroying the time-sequence and therefore the possibility of dating the production and of following the technical and decorative development – an essential element for those who want to recognise historical cycles in the past and so recognise those in the present. It is too soon for some converters who have achieved great fame over the course of the last few decades to reveal the names of their suppliers. In this fragmentary panorama, although it is very rich in discoveries, it is really quite easy to become enthusiastic about the presence of a nucleus of production that has reached us, complete and documented, and to devote a chapter of Como history to it, as has been done in the past, without being able to compare it with all the other production going on at the same time. (Buss, 2001: 12)

The rigorous methodology would serve as a model for many subsequent exhibitions organized and held by corporate institutions, making these the most fruitful hubs for research in fashion and textile history in Italy, especially when focusing on production techniques. Further discussion on this is provided in Section 5.3.

4.4.1 The Fondazione Pitti Immagine Discovery

The year 2001 was also the year of the first major fashion exhibition organized by Pitti Immagine Discovery, a programme of events created in 1999 by Pitti Immagine to promote the cultural nature of fashion. An exhibition space was opened in the headquarters of Pitti Immagine, which was 'neither a gallery, nor a museum or even a collection' but instead 'an ongoing workshop where the capacity of a company to affect a city and its cultural life is experimented' (Pitti Immagine, 2021). It was a continuation of the curatorial experiments of Pitti Immagine during the 1990s and Pitti Immagine Discovery signalled the institutionalization of these experiments. In 2002 Pitti Immagine partnered with Centro di Firenze per la Moda Italiana to establish the Fondazione Pitti Immagine Discovery, a legally recognized foundation 'with the aim to grant more institutional relevance to the activities of the Group linked to contemporaneity'[40] (Pitti Immagine, 2021). The mission of the foundation is to promote and enhance 'cultural research and artistic productions, analysing those areas where fashion finds its creative inspirations and forms of experimentation' (Pitti Discovery, 2021) by strengthening the links across contemporary visual languages.

In 1999, Francesco Bonami, Senior Curator at the Museum of Contemporary Art in Chicago, was appointed director of Pitti Immagine Discovery and coordinator of artistic projects for Pitti Immagine. As it had done in 1996 for the Biennale, Pitti Immagine chose an internationally renowned Italian curator of contemporary art to develop exhibitions and projects, which can be divided into two main themes: fashion and its relation with other cultural languages; and contemporary art. The first major exhibition was held at the Stazione Leopolda, from 11 January to 18 February 2001: *Uniforme. Ordine e Disordine* (Uniform. Order and Disorder). Bonami co-curated it with Maria Luisa Frisa and Stefano Tonchi. Frisa and Tonchi had collaborated in 1984 and 1985 with Pitti Immagine in the development of Pitti Trend (the fair dedicated to trend forecasting) and had been founders and editors of the magazine *Westuff* from 1984 to 1987. *Westuff* would late inform the format of the *Emporio Armani Magazine* in 1988 and run until 1997, with Frisa as the sole editor-in-chief. Tonchi moved on to *L'Uomo Vogue, Self, Esquire, The Sunday Times Magazine*; in 2004 created and became editor-in-chief of *T: The New York Times Style Magazine* and in 2010 was appointed editor-in-chief of *W* magazine. In addition to her work on the *Emporio Armani Magazine*, Frisa also worked as consultant to Giorgio Armani for communication and artistic events until 2003 and in 2004 became the director of the newly established course on fashion design at IUAV, Istituto Universitario di Architettura Venezia, a post founded by the Marzotto company. Throughout her career, Frisa has also regularly contributed to Italian newspapers and magazines discussing fashion and visual arts. Frisa and Tonchi have since been regularly co-curating exhibitions in Italy, include two large retrospectives on Italian fashion: *Bellissima. L'Italia dell'Alta Moda 1945–1968* (Bellissima. Italy and High Fashion 1945–1968) at MAXXXI, Rome, in 2014, and *Italiana. L'Italia vista dalla moda 1971–2001* (Italiana. Italy Through the Lens of Fashion 1971–2001) at Palazzo Reale, Milan, in 2018.

The exhibition *Uniform. Order and Disorder* opened in conjunction with the Pitti Uomo fair and presented garments and accessories alongside videos, magazines and other visual artefacts, investigating the concept of uniformity in fashion (Bonami, Frisa and Tonchi, 2000). As Frisa later reflected on her curatorial approach, she stated that it aimed at keeping 'intact the relationship

Figure 4.8 A view of the exhibition *Uniforme. Ordine e Disordine* (*Uniform. Order and Disorder*), held at the Stazione Leopolda, in conjunction with the trade fair Pitti Immagine Uomo 59. Photograph by Carlo Fei. Florence, 2001. Courtesy Pitti Immagine.

between fashion and the world' in order to 'offer new points of view in looking at fashion' (Frisa, 2008: 172). Unlike the historical research that had characterized the work of CISST, Frisa's approach was 'not an effort to achieve historical fidelity to fashion, but rather a critical exercise' that would unfold 'the relationships between fashion and other disciplines' (Frisa, 2008: 172). Frisa was the only Italian curator to contribute to the 2008 *Fashion Theory* volume dedicated to fashion curation (McNeil, 2008), where she compared her work to 'fashion prediction (using the kind of skills that identify trends and style directions) rather than formal academic research' (Frisa, 2008: 173). The parallel with trend forecasting can link Frisa's statement to her previous work for Pitti and provides a key to understand her visual approach, in which text is presented as complimentary to the fruition of the results of her 'critical exercise' (Frisa, 2008: 173). The books published in conjunction with exhibitions are, in fact, not created as accompanying catalogues but are independent from the display, even in terms of design. Her stress on this point is likely due to her experience in magazines, which led her to conceive publications as linked yet separate projects through which to articulate – in a different way – the same theme of the exhibition.[41] Nonetheless, these two elements, publication and exhibition, are built on the same process: they both present images taken from a variety of sources and are 'brought together without any kind of hierarchy' in order to highlight 'analogies and contrasts' (Frisa, 2008: 174). It could be argued that Frisa is more interested in the suggestive nature of these artefacts than in artefacts as testimonies to a history constructed through the exhibition: the unguided presentation of various artefacts is conceived to trigger discussions, as opposed to the dissemination of the results of historical research. Moreover, as noted by Eugenia Paulicelli, the study of fashion was being reconfigured from a linear historical evolution to 'a malleable collage in which different temporalities and spaces coexist' (Paulicelli, 2014: 159), making Frisa's approach effective at communicating this aspect.

In 2011, Frisa authored a book, *Italian Fashion Now*, aimed at surveying the contemporary state of the Italian fashion system. She quoted the journalist Silvia Giacomoni to state her ambition 'to offer the protagonists of this world a critical contribution on their activity, setting aside the laudatory tradition of journalism specializing in the sector' (Frisa, 2011: 11). Frisa identifies her role as the provider of a critical reflection on the Italian fashion system from a cultural perspective (Frisa, 2011), situating herself as an industry commentator rather than a historian, an interpretation. She indeed recognizes that her work is not primarily directed at the general public but to 'those who, like me, are interested in reflecting on fashion, keeping alive the debate for fashion's many audiences and embracing the many forms which fashion uses to express itself' (Frisa, 2008: 177).

Frisa, with Bonami and Tonchi, championed a new form of fashion curation centred on criticism rather than explanation, in which exhibition designs borrow more from contemporary art installations than from the museographic tradition of costume and textiles. This was in line with the interests of Pitti Immagine and CFMI, whose 1990s corporate cultural policies first repositioned Florence as the birthplace of Italian fashion and later shifted the narrative from a heritage *locus* to a contemporary creative hub. The direct engagement with contemporary art was fundamental in this process, which comes to the fore in the early 2000s with the work of Bonami and Frisa. Furthermore, because of an increasing interest in contemporary art in the 1990s, the marketing value of this practice had increased and the fashion industry promptly engaged with this potential. 'Pitti's operation was simple: to advertise through Barney and Juergen Teller, Pipilotti Rist, Susan Ciancolo, Shirin Neshat, in short, the art world, instead of investing in advertising pages'[42] (Frisa in Tozzi, 2015). Rather than presenting fashion using established channels, Pitti used contemporary art to frame a new understanding on fashion and established artists were asked to interact with it and offer new perspectives.

4.4.2 Exhibitions as promotional tools

The use of exhibitions as promotional tools was not a new practice. In 1985, Versace was invited to host a fashion show at the V&A and give a talk to students. In the same year, in conjunction with the launch of the fragrance *Versace l'Homme*, a contemporary art exhibition was held in Paris, presenting the works of artists in relation with Versace's fashion and in 1986 the Musée de la Mode de Paris held *Gianni Versace, dialogues de mode: des photographes autour d'une creation* (Gianni Versace, Dialogues of Fashion: Photographs Around a Creation) a display presenting photographs of Versace's creations by the leading photographers Richard Avedon, Gian Paolo Barbieri, Helmut Newton, Giovanni Gastel, Bruce Weber, Irving Penn (Palais Galliera, 1986). In 1989 the Castello Sforzesco in Milan held a retrospective of twenty-five years of Versace's work, entitled *L'abito per Pensare* (Dress for Thought). This exhibition was curated by Nicoletta Bocca with Chiara Buss and unfolded Versace's creative process (Bocca and Buss, 1989). This exhibition was praised for the critical approach – later discussed in Section 5.3 – as well as for the mannequins, which were purposefully designed by Gianni Versace in the style of classical busts (Monti, 2019). This exhibition would be integrated in 1992 for the display *Versace Signatures* held at the Museum at the Fashion Institute of Technology and toured to the Kunstgewerbemuseum in Berlin in 1994 in conjunction with the opening of a new flagship store in the German capital. Versace's use of exhibitions for marketing had become, by then, an established practice and in 1997 he co-curated the display *Beauty Icons* with the Galleria d'Arte Moderna in Bologna and there he presented the new Versace cosmetic line, in conjuction with the thirtieth edition of Cosmoprof, the international beauty fair held yearly in Bologna. Versace also used traditional sponsorship as a marketing tool and in 1995 financed the exhibition *Richard Avedon 1944–1994* at Palazzo Reale in Milan, which incidentally included photographs of Versace's clothes by Richard Avedon. In 1996 the link became even clearer when he sponsored the exhibition *Weber Vietnam Versace Viaggi Vogue*, also at Palazzo Reale in Milan. In December 1997, a few months after Versace's death, Richard Martin curated an exhibition on Versace at the MET and, in 1998, Martin updated it into a two-venue display in Como organized by the Fondazione Antonio Ratti, with its museum director Chiara Buss as head curator. It was later re-edited for the Museum of Modern

Art of Miami in 1999 and in 2002 Buss served as co-curator for the then largest retrospective the V&A had held on a designer (Wilcox, Mendes and Buss, 2002), which was well-received by the critics and scholars, unlike the 2000 Armani retrospective, and was praised for the technical information presented in the display (Mason, 2005).

One of the key areas of criticism to the Armani exhibition and the 1992 Salvatore Ferragamo retrospective at the Los Angeles County Museum of Art (Belk, 1995), was the celebratory tone, unsupported by information to contextualize the work of the designers, which resulted in the exhibitions being perceived as commercial operations. Nonetheless, this exhibition model continued to be employed by designers and the 2007 display *Valentino a Roma: 45 Years of Style,* which had a similar approach, did not trigger the same negative feedback. This exhibition marked the retirement of the Italian designer Valentino Garavani and was installed around the Ara Pacis, one of Rome's most iconic monuments of the Ancient Roman era. The theatre designer Patrick Kinmonth conceived the display as a visual spectacle. Criticism might have been restrained due to the particular moment of Valentino's career. A documentary entitled *Valentino: The Last Emperor* was shot during the preparation of these retirement-related events, produced and directed by Matt Tyrnauer and released in 2008. Valentino's retirement campaign was structured to build the cultural and historical value of the individual designer to ensure the subsequent survival of the brand and in 2011 Valentino launched the *Valentino Garavani Museum*, a digital, 3-D permanent display of Valentino's work: although still accessible and sporadically updated, this project has not proved successful – probably due to the fast-changing world of digital and virtual environments – and has remained an isolated experiment. With hindsight, Valentino's retirement and its associated projects signalled a turning point in the fashion industry, in which marketing shifted its focus from the relationship between fashion and art to heritage, affecting the themes addressed by fashion curation.

4.4.3 The increasing importance of fashion heritage

The 2008 financial crisis affected global economy, including luxury fashion, where heritage became not only a differentiating factor but a key guarantor for the stability of heritage brands. As a result, more companies started to engage strategically with their heritage. This phenomenon, together with the increasing success that fashion exhibitions had been enjoying since the 1990s, resulted in their widespread presence and popularity, as testified by the list compiled

Figure 4.9 The exhibition *L'abito per Pensare* (*Dress for Thought*) displayed custom-made mannequins designed by Gianni Versace and inspired by classical busts, Castello Sforzesco, Milan, 1989. Photograph by Beppe Caggi.

by Jeffrey Horsley in the publication *Exhibiting Fashion: Before and After 1971* (Clark and de la Haye, 2014).

In 2008 Ferragamo updated its retrospective display and entitled it *Salvatore Ferragamo. Evolving Legend 1928–2008*. The exhibition was held at the Museum of Contemporary Art in Shanghai during the spring and toured to the Triennale

Figure 4.10 A view of the section *Woven pattern*, dedicated to figured textiles in the exhibition *Gianni Versace. La reinvenzione della materia* (*Gianni Versace. The Reinvention of Matter*). Fondazione Antonio Ratti, Como, 1998. Photograph by Giorgio Pizzi.

Design Museum in Milan during the fall. The narrative contrasted the original 1985 retrospective: curators no longer counterbalanced the commercial aspect of such an event by stressing the historical and scientific approach to the analysis of a designer from the past (Salvi, 1985), but they included contemporary models. The exhibition is not conceived as the retrospective of a completed *oeuvre* but as the investigation of the roots of a brand in order to explain the present and serve as a guarantee for the future of the company. The focus is no longer on the past but on 'contemporaneity' and these displays are constructed to demonstrate the continuation of original artistic and artisanal values into the present (Ricci,

2008). This exhibition also introduced a visual manifestation of the key trait of Italianness, that is, the roots in Renaissance workshops and craftsmanship, through a tableau vivant: 'A colourful reconstruction of a clean model workshop, full of leather scraps, hides and tools, in which two shoemakers make shoes by hand "as they used to", wearing white aprons and spectacles perched on their noses' (Segre Reinach, 2010: 208).

Further signs of change could be detected in Florence. Pitti Immagine and the Fondazione Pitti Immagine Discovery, after a decade of exhibitions focused on the relations between fashion and other visual media as elements of the contemporary reality, held their first display at the Galleria del Costume inside Palazzo Pitti in 2008, still inaugurated as customary during the opening of the Pitti Uomo trade fair (73rd edition). *Simonetta. La Prima Donna della Moda Italiana* (Simonetta. The First Lady of Italian Fashion) was a retrospective on Donna Simonetta Colonna di Cesarò, an Italian aristocrat and couturiére who worked in the post-war era, curated by Maria Luisa Frisa, exhibition maker Judith Clark and fashion historian Vittoria Caterina Caratozzolo (Caratozzolo, Clark and Frisa, 2008). Another event that took place in Florence was the first

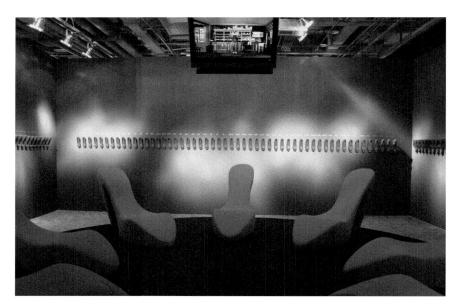

Figure 4.11 The exhibition *Salvatore Ferragamo. Evolving Legend 1928–2008* was an updated version of the 1985 retrospective on the shoe designer. This edition marked the eightieth birthday of the founder and aimed at promoting the heritage of the brand as well as contemporary production. Museum of Contemporary Art, Shangai, 2008. Courtesy *Museo Salvatore Ferragamo*.

edition of the *Costume Colloquium* conference, organized by the Associazione Amici della Galleria del Costume (Association Friends of the Gallery of Costume) and the non-profit cultural institution Fondazione Romualdo Del Bianco, both based in Florence. The conference ran from 6 to 9 November 2008 and it investigated various aspects of costume, intended as textiles and dress, as well as fashion. It was dedicated to Janet Arnold, the influential British scholar of historical dress. The attendees and speakers were mostly European but the conference presented an international breadth of perspectives comparable to the 1990 CISST conference on ready-made fashion; in fact, many speakers from the 1990 conference convened at the 2008 *Costume Colloquium*, including Grazietta Butazzi who was a member of the honorary committee and there presented the paper 'Studi e Ricerca sul tema Moda e Costume: la situazione in Italia' ("Fashion and Costume Research and Study: The Situation in Italy") (Butazzi, 2008). Unlike the CISST precedent, the 2008 *Costume Colloquium* event was not financed by members of the fashion industry yet companies were represented in a session dedicated to 'Florence, Historic Italian Fashion Centre: Future Prospects', where all convenors worked for corporate institutions. They included: Alessandra Arezzi Boza, then curator of the Fondazione Archivio Emilio Pucci, Florence; Enrico Minio, director of the Fondazione Roberto Capucci, Florence; Laura Fiesoli, manager of the contemporary department of the Fondazione Museo del Tessuto, Prato; and Stefania Ricci, director of the Museo Salvatore Ferragamo, Florence.

In 2011, for the 150th anniversary of the Italian unification, the royal palace of Venaria in Turin organized the exhibition *Moda in Italia. 150 anni di eleganza* (Fashion in Italy. 150 Years of Elegance). The display mainly featured the collection of the Roman costumier Tirelli with additional loans from fashion brands and was divided into two sections. (Goria and Merlotti, 2011). The first part covered the years from the unification to the establishment of the Italian fashion industry and was curated by the costume designer Gabriella Pescucci. The second part looked at contemporary fashion from the 1970s and was curated by the then editor of *Vogue Italia*, Franca Sozzani. This exhibition opened a season of displays which looked at the collective history of Italian fashion.

In 2014, *The Glamour of Italian Fashion, 1945–2014* opened at the V&A in London. The curator Sonnet Stanfill delineated an overview of the diverse and fragmented Italian fashion industry, dedicating one of the three sections to industrial and artisanal manufacturing, exploring the variety of production methods. Stanfill worked closely with corporate museums and archives, and scholars from these institutions were asked to contribute to the publication

(Stanfill, 2014). Later in the year, the exhibition *Bellissima. L'Italia e l'alta moda 1945–1968* (Bellissima. Italy and High Fashion 1945–1968) was held at the contemporary arts museum MAXXI in Rome, curated by the MAXXI director Anna Mattirolo, Maria Luisa Frisa and Stefano Tonchi. The display was an extensive exploration of the first years of Italian fashion history, centring the narrative on high fashion and granting Rome pride of place as it was and still is considered the national capital of high fashion. Bulgari was the main sponsor and another partnership was with Altaroma. This company is responsible for the organization of fashion shows and exhibitions in Rome as well as the promotion of emerging talents: it is self-defined as 'the driving force of Italian emerging fashion' (ALTAROMA, 2021). *Bellissima* had the marketing value of re-establishing the position of Rome as the incubator of high-quality, traditional yet innovative, fashion production. Frisa and Tonchi later curated an exhibition that charters the years following those covered by *Italiana. L'Italia vista dalla moda 1971 2001* (Italiana. Italy through the lens of fashion 1971–2001), which was held in 2018 at Palazzo Reale in Milan and produced by the Comune di Milano and the Camera Nazionale della Moda Italiana (National Chamber of Italian Fashion). The display focused on Italian ready-to-wear and industrial production, unfolding the fruitful exchanges between fashion designers with textile and clothing manufacturers. This phase of Italian history is associated with Milan becoming the main Italian fashion week in the 1970s, still organized by the Camera Nazionale which is headquartered in Milan. Similar to the 1992 *Sala Bianca* exhibition promoted by Pitti Immagine and CFMI, *Bellissima* and *Italiana* can be framed as strategic historicizing exhibitions promoted by trade associations to strengthen the position of the local fashion system represented by those associations.

Another exhibition sponsored by the Camera Nazionale was *Il Nuovo Vocabolario della Moda Italiana* (The New Vocabulary of Italian Fashion), held in 2015 at the Triennale in Milan and curated by Paola Bertola and Vittorio Linfante, respectively Professors of Fashion Design and Graphic Design at the Politecnico University of Milan. It surveyed the post-Prada generation of Italian fashion designers, that is after 1998, to identify which traits are still characterizing Italian fashion production (Bertola and Linfante, 2015). The Triennale exhibition of Milan was originally established as a design trade exhibition in the 1930s, therefore the focus on contemporaneity of *Vocabolario* was in line with the Triennale history. The institution had previously hosted many touring exhibitions, such as the retrospectives on Giorgio Armani (the Guggenheim one) in 2007 and on Salvatore Ferragamo in 2008. However in

Figure 4.12 *Italiana. L'Italia vista dalla moda 1971–2001* (*Italiana. Italy Through the Lens of Fashion 1971–2001*) was a retrospective display of the golden age of Italian fashion production. It was produced by the City of Milan (Cultura – Politiche del Lavoro, Attività produttive, Moda e Design – Palazzo Reale) and the Camera Nazionale della Moda Italiana. Palazzo Reale, Milan, 2018. Photograph by Francesco de Luca. Courtesy *Camera Nazionale della Moda Italiana*.

the late 2010s it reconfigured itself, at least in relation to fashion, as a space for designers to articulate their imageries through exhibitions, that is, artist installations rather than fashion exhibitions. In 2016, *Antonio Marras: Nulla dies sine linea* was a display of garments, sketches and mixed-media artworks reworked into installations by the Italian designer. In the following year, a similar process was undertaken for *Subhuman Inhuman Superhuman*, an exhibition on the work of Rick Owens. It was presented as a retrospective covering two decades, with exhibits ranging from clothes to furniture selected by the designer himself, who also conceived the exhibition design. Both displays are a hybrid between retrospective and creative installation, thus allowing designers to reorganize existing elements into a visual output that matches the current vision, effectively proposing another approach to heritage communication. Over the 2010s the consumption of fashion heritage diversified and witnessed a boom in digital consumption.

Figure 4.13 The exhibition *Il Nuovo Vocabolario della Moda Italiana* (*The New Vocabolary of Italian Fashion*) presented an overview of Italian fashion in the twenty-first century. Photograph by Agostino Osio. Triennale Design Museum, Milan, 2015. Courtesy ©*Triennale Milano – Archivi*.

4.4.4 Online archives

The relevance of fashion heritage was acknowledged by the Italian state in 2010, when the SAN, Sistema Archivi Nazionale (National Archival System) launched the portal *Archivi della Moda del Novecento* (Archives of Twentieth-Century Fashion). It aimed 'to discover, enhance and make available a wide range of sources, so far unexplored, of the archival, bibliographical, iconographic, audiovisual heritage related to Italian fashion'[43] (SAN, 2010). This project was supported by state bodies and subscribed by more than two hundred public and private institutions, archives and collections. Among these, six private archives stipulated a convention for the cataloguing and the digitization of their heritage, and to make it publicly accessible through the portal: Fondazione Emilio Pucci, Fondazione Gianfranco Ferré, Fondazione Micol Fontana, Fondazione Roberto Capucci, Gattinoni and the Museo Salvatore Ferragamo. The initiative was presented during the 75th edition of Pitti Uomo. Although the portal was financed by public funds and supported by individual members of the industry through their corporate archives, the trade fair Pitti Uomo was selected as the

Figure 4.14 The exhibition *Antonio Marras: nulla dies sine linea. Vita, diari e appunti di un uomo irrequieto* (*Antonio Marras: Never a Day Without a Line. Life, Diaries and Notes of a Restless Man*) was an unusual retrospective of the Sardinian designer, who reworked his clothes, artworks and notes into installations. Photograph by Daniela Zedda. Triennale Design Museum, Milan, 2016. Courtesy ©*Triennale Milano – Archivi*.

ideal occasion for its launch, stressing once again the links between research and industry.

Digitization is another example of how operations developed to address internal needs of companies can also be employed for external operations and fulfil needs of scholarship. In the phase signalled by heritage marketing, the operational optimization of corporate archives became necessary to develop and implement marketing campaigns; it also enhanced the usage for design teams, who regularly interact with corporate archives in heritage brands. The participation to the national digital platform evidences the willingness of companies to share the results of internal operations. There are limitations though, and these are represented by the confidential information preserved in corporate archives. External access is restricted to historical and iconic artefacts and is mostly devoid of technical descriptions, the disclosure of which does not hinder or reduce the competitiveness of the company.

The relevance of corporate archives was also recognized by the two international digital portals *Europeana Fashion* (2013) and *We Wear Culture* (2017). *Europeana Fashion* was co-founded by the European Union and was the third thematic collection launched by the Europeana Foundation, after Europeana Art and Europeana Music. The initiative aimed at creating an online platform where the digital reproductions of artefacts – more than 700,000 – held in 22 European institutions would be available to anyone with access to the Internet. It was coordinated by Fondazione per il Rinascimento Digitale (Foundation for the Digital Renaissance) established in 2011 in Florence to support the promotion and diffusion of the heritage of the Renaissance through digital tools. Alessandra Arezzi Boza of the Fondazione Archivio Emilio Pucci was among the founders of the Europeana Fashion International Association, the body especially created for the management of the platform, and its communication and content manager. The Museo Salvatore Ferragamo would also be among the leading partners of another digital initiative organized by the Google Cultural Institute: in 2017, Google Arts & Culture launched the platform *We Wear Culture*, where digital content belonging to almost two hundred institutions is presented and curated. The Museo Salvatore Ferragamo was one of the key institutions featured in the promotional campaign, most likely due to the mass appeal of one of their holdings: a pair of stiletto shoes, created by Salvatore Ferragamo and worn by Marilyn Monroe in the film *Bus Stop* (1956). In 2021, Gucci inaugurated its new corporate archive at Palazzo Settimanni in Florence, calling it Gucci Archivio. This is an operational structure to the service of the company that will likely provide occasional access to the general public, though what was made readily available is a virtual tour with the function of 'backstage access' to the history of the brand.

The international prominence acquired by corporate archives is probably a result of the lack of a national institution with a major collection of dress and fashion in Italy, but I argue it is mostly a consequence of the consistent resources invested by companies to research and promote their heritage and make it accessible. The influence of companies in the evolution of fashion curation in Italy is not solely linked to curatorial narratives and the employment of exhibitions as communication tools. It can also be detected in the increasing importance gained by corporate archives first in the Italian national institutional landscape, and later in the international landscape.

4.4.5 Recent developments

The relationship between industry and scholars is twofold: on the one hand the industry supports research, on the other scholars employ approaches to highlight the relevance of research for the industry. This is eminently represented by MISA, the Associazione Italiana degli Studi di Moda (Italian Association of Fashion Studies), founded by Maria Luisa Frisa in Venice in 2013. Frisa had developed her curatorial method directed at the industry in the 2000s, and she now formulated it as a guideline for a scholarly association, which 'must reflect the great changes that have taken place in the fashion system … the Association therefore aims to be an effective tool not only for the promotion of research and cultural activities'[44] (MISA, 2013). The association aimed to bring together the various approaches to the study of fashion (semiotic, psychologic, artistic, historical, etc.) and open to scholars, professionals and students. The first meeting was held on 2 February 2013 where the election by the fifty-eight founding members appointed Maria Luisa Frisa as president and five fashion historians and scholars as board members: Patrizia Calefato, Paola Colaiacomo, Enrica Morini, Bruna Niccoli and Simona Segre Reinach. The first event organized by MISA was a two-day conference on 22 and 23 November 2013: *Insegnare la moda. Modelli e politiche culturali tra formazione e industria* (Teaching Fashion. Cultural Models and Policies Between Education and Industry), supported by the Camera Nazionale della Moda Italiana. There were no speakers associated with the previous phase of Italian fashion studies but a large number of industry professionals, notably manufacturers and journalists. This may be read as a sign of the new model of synergy between scholarship and industry, which I argue characterizes this phase of Italian fashion studies. The website of MISA is currently inaccessible and there are no traces of operations after 2014; however, despite its short-lived experience, MISA highlighted one preoccupation shared by scholars and companies: training. In 2015, the Fondazione Fashion Research Italy (FRI) was established by the former patron of La Perla, Alberto Masotti, as 'a didactic exhibition center' (FRI, 2021). FRI holds three archives (Fondo Brandone, Fondo Schvili, Fashion Photography Archive), though research on these is yet to be published. The activity they have been mostly pursuing is training as they have organized courses at various levels and held the first course in Italy on the management of fashion archives in November 2017. It was a two-week course with scholars and archivists from both the previous and current phase of Italian fashion studies, and it has since been running.

Since the end of the 2010s, the interest and support of the Italian state to the preservation of fashion heritage has also increased, and I argue that it is the results of the efforts by and collaboration between industry and scholarship. The first study day on this topic, organized by the regional government of Lombardy in collaboration with Federmoda – the largest Italian trade association of fashion manufacturers and retailers – was held on 20 March 2018 in Milan: *Fashion Cultural Heritage. Cultura, formazione e nuove progettualità del Sistema Moda. Giornata di studio sulla valorizzazione degli archivi della moda come motore di sviluppo per il Made in Italy* (Fashion Cultural Heritage. Culture, Education and New Design Practices of the Fashion System. Study Day on the Valorisation of Fashion Archives as Triggers for the Development of Made in Italy). Further governmental support was provided in 2018 by Alberto Bonisoli, Minister of Cultural Heritage and Activities, through the institution of a 'Commissione di studio per politiche pubbliche a favore della moda italiana' (Study Committee for Public Policies Supporting Italian Fashion). Of the thirteen members of the committee, six are corporate heritage professionals or have extensively collaborated with companies or industry associations:

1. Rita Airaghi, (then) Director of the Fondazione Gianfranco Ferré;
2. Lapo Cianchi, Director of Event Communication at Pitti Immagine;
3. Raffaele Curi, Artistic Director of the Fondazione Alda Fendi;
4. Maria Luisa Frisa, independent curator;
5. Stefania Ricci, Director of the Museo Salvatore Ferragamo;
6. Margherita Rosina, former Director of the textile museum of the Fondazione Antonio Ratti.

No tangible outcomes resulted from the work of the committee but a newly found interest in institutionalizing fashion heritage can be detected, though the end results are still to be seen. Further evidence of this interest is attested by the exhibition *MEMOS. A proposito della moda di questo millennio* (MEMOS. On Fashion in this Millennium) which opened in 2020 at Museo Poldi Pezzoli in Milan. The exhibition was curated by Maria Luisa Frisa, designed by Judith Clark and produced by the Camera Nazionale della Moda Italiana. It was a reflection triggered by Italo Calvino's *American Lessons*, articulated through the display of garments across the museum, as well as a tribute to the 1980 exhibition *1922–1943: Vent'anni di moda italiana,* also held at Museo Poldi Pezzoli, discussed in Section 4.3.2. This could be interpreted as the will to review four decades of fashion curation in Italy and reflect on future directions.

This account has provided the evidence that the perspectives developed in Italian fashion curation are closely connected to the industry. Chapter 5 will now provide a critical commentary on how the Italian fashion and textile industries have developed a complex system of curatorial and communication tools aimed at the cultural presentation of fashion, which combines independently organized projects, corporate cultural policies, and the interaction and mutual exchange between industry and scholarship.

5

Industry and curation: A critical commentary

As emerged from the previous chapter, the fashion and textile industries played a fundamental role in the history of fashion curation in Italy. Employing different forms of support, such as patronage and sponsorship, as well as devising their own events, these industries engaged with curatorial practices to address corporate needs: they promoted their work by highlighting the cultural and social dimensions of their products, thus inscribing their operations in collective, local and national narratives.

In this chapter, I build on the empirical evidence presented in Chapter 4 and on the theoretical framework devised in the previous chapters to provide a critical commentary on the relationship between industry and curation. The next sections examine how companies increasingly became more active in cultural production, with their role shifting from sponsors (Section 5.1) to producers (Section 5.2). I will then assess the impact on curatorial approaches that I argue are the result of the corporate cultural policies of the fashion and textile industries (Section 5.3) and I will conclude with a reflection on how corporate institutions are able to manage commercial and academic interests (Section 5.4) and, despite their corporate bias, I will make a case for their contribution to fashion studies and curatorial practices.

5.1 Companies as sponsors

A reflection on sponsorship in relation to fashion exhibitions was provided by curator Melissa Taylor, who used the expression 'cultural sponsorship' to describe the process,

> in which the consumer or visitor would accept and unknowingly acknowledge the attachment of the revered status of the cultural institution to the nature of

the brand. As such, the brand is projected into the context of, and therefore confers upon itself, the value system of high culture. (Taylor, 2005: 455)

As sponsorship is a generic term, Taylor likely used the word 'cultural' to define the field within which it takes place. She explained the choice of established institutions as the locations for fashion exhibitions with the desire of companies to have the 'revered status' of the museums associated with the brand. More specifically, this type of sponsorship aims at building the cultural status of fashion artefacts by associating them with artefacts usually exhibited in the museum or gallery, the status of which is established, be them fine or decorative arts. The subject of this type of exhibition can be an individual designer or a generation or national group. For example, in 2015 La Triennale di Milano held the exhibition *Il Nuovo Vocabolario della Moda Italiana* (The New Vocabolary of Italian Fashion), curated by Paola Bertola and Vittorio Linfante, respectively professors of Fashion Design and Graphic Design at the Politecnico University di Milano (Figure 4.13). It surveyed the post-Prada generation of Italian fashion designers, that is after 1998 (Bertola and Linfante, 2015). Entirely focused on contemporaneity – in line with the history of the Triennale, an international design and art exhibition recurring every three years created in 1923 – it identified the common traits of current designers in the Italian artistic and craft traditions, and analysed the recent exhibits through paradigms that had characterized Italian high fashion and *moda boutique* in the 1950s and 1960s (Bertola and Linfante, 2015). The display was sponsored by the Camera Nazionale della Moda Italiana (National Chamber of Italian Fashion) and the Confederazione Nazionale dell'Artigianato e della Piccola e Media Industria (CNA) (National Confederation of Crafts and Small and Medium Industries). In the catalogue Raffaello Napoleone, then president of Pitti Immagine, stated that the exhibition was 'an ambassador in a role very similar to that of Pitti Immagine'[1] (Napoleone, 2015: 9). As evidenced in Chapter 4, what has characterized the corporate cultural policy of Pitti Immagine since the 1990s is the transparency with which they declare the marketing and promotional purposes of these exhibitions.

Another type of sponsorship aims at creating a 'revered status' (Taylor, 2005: 455) for the companies, as opposed to their products. This is achieved through the financial support of exhibitions and projects on fields unrelated to their production, either curated externally or by their own corporate institutions. This approach found its lineage in the artistic patronage of Renaissance rulers. In fact, the rhetoric of the Renaissance patron can still be found in prefaces authored by CEOs in the catalogues of exhibitions sponsored by their companies. For example, in the opening remarks of the catalogue to the second edition of the Biennale di Firenze (1998), the lead curator Leonardo Mondadori wrote that 'fashion designers have entered our global market and today are the equivalent of the great patrons of the Renaissance, curious, willing and aware of the various influences that fashion generates and attracts' (Mondadori, 1998: 21). Some of them actually engage with patronage (Section 2.3.1), with corporate institutions dedicated to host the personal collections of the designers or through the commission of new works of arts. All these operations, when framed with the Renaissance lens, can then contribute to strengthening the main historical narrative associated with Italian fashion and centred around the Renaissance, as explained in Chapter 1.

To further ensure that the status of a company is revered (Taylor, 2005), a company can support or establish an institution that develops and promotes research on the field of the company, yet not directly addressing the corporate production. This is the case of CIAC, Centro Internazionale delle Arti e del Costume (International Centre of the Arts and Costume), funded by the SNIA Viscosa textile manufacturer in 1951 as a 'multidisciplinary private center dedicated to art and costume' (Collicelli Cagol, 2015). As reported in Chapter 4, CIAC produced exhibitions and publications on the history of textiles and dress and organized international conferences. The programme was devised and implemented by specialist scholars, nevertheless it 'responded to the SNIA Viscosa marketing strategy to promote its products through a philanthropic enterprise' (Collicelli Cagol, 2015). Establishing their own institution allowed SNIA Viscosa more control over the projects and ensured that these responded to the values and interests of the company and its communication policies. The corporate cultural policy of SNIA Viscosa addressed two aims: it financed research on textile and costume studies, triggering developments in scholarship, and it promoted the cultural relevance of their field of production, fulfilling marketing requirements. Even after 1958, when the CIAC President Paolo Marinotti decided to shift the focus of the institution from textile history to contemporary art, the communication policy of the parent company was still addressed. Since an exhibition of contemporary art would not have directly increased the value of textiles as research on the history of textiles would have done, he conceived a way to include textiles in the display without incorporating them in the curatorial narrative, thus loosening and disguising 'the marketing ties with the funding company' (Collicelli Cagol, 2015). He commissioned artworks to be produced using fabrics by SNIA Viscosa and the architect Carlo Scarpa created an exhibition design which heavily employed fabrics. Though textiles had been used for scenographic displays since the 1930s and in the 1950s exhibitions of CIAC dedicated to textiles and costume, this operation can also be understood as a less overt inclusion of corporate products into a sponsored exhibition.

Sponsorship must not, however, be solely viewed as a tool used by the industry to enhance its cultural status, but also as a support actively sought and encouraged by scholarship. The CISST, Centro Italiano per lo Studio della Storia del Tessuto (Italian Centre for the Study of the History of Textiles), was an independent association of textile and costumes scholars, curators and connoisseurs created in 1979. While retaining autonomy in the development of research projects, exhibitions and publications, CISST established close collaborations with textile and fashion manufacturers, not only as financial sponsors but also as owners of resources, namely their archives. For their part, companies commissioned research on their heritage: they were not directly influencing the outcomes, but were increasingly becoming part of the curatorial narratives. For instance, in the 1980s, the Gruppo Finanziario Tessile (GFT) commissioned research on the origins of ready-to-wear (Rizzini, 2016) in conjuction with the compilation of their corporate history and appointed the fashion historian Grazietta Butazzi as consultant. The research did not lead to any significant observations but prompted further investigation into the field and Grazietta Butazzi organized a whole conference on this topic for CISST in 1990. The three-day symposium aimed at surveying existing research by international scholars on the various topics related to this field. The CISST worked independently but GFT sponsored the conference and used the occasion to present a publication with the results of the research on their corporate history (Berta, 1989), given to all the attendees. Elsa Golzio Aimone, manager of the GFT archive, was also a speaker at the conference, where she presented the methodology employed for the running of the corporate archive. The collaboration between scholarship and industry then went beyond financial support of the industry using museums and public collections for inspiration (Anderson, 2000). In the CISST annual journal *Arte Tessile*, published between 1990 and 1995, there are recurrent references to the active collaboration with the industry. In the first issue, Alessandra Mottola Molfino, then President of CISST, wrote:

> The members, the national board of directors, the regional secretariats, the president of CISST, while aiming above all to the knowledge of ancient textiles, for reasons of survival of these, have however always held contacts of mutual exchange even with the contemporary production of fabrics and fashion and with its operators. (Mottola Molfino, 1990: 2)[2]

Mottola Molfino was transparent in her declaration of the reason that initially led them to approach companies, the high costs for the preservation of ancient textiles, and she referred to them as patrons ('mecenati'). Yet, she also viewed them as collaborators with whom to develop projects. 'In the future, with the support of our patrons (including also manufacturing companies which are increasingly interested in the history of textiles) we would like to start some targeted research'[3] (Mottola Molfino, 1991: 2). The CISST was modelled on CIETA but the ability to diversify their operations and open to contemporary fashion led to a synergy with the industry. It was also noted by fashion historian Enrica Morini and textile historian Margherita Rosina, both members of CISST, that the Italian fashion industry boomed in the 1980s and companies were welcoming projects that could contribute to the promotion of fashion and its cultural relevance.[4] Most importantly, companies were very profitable in those years and they had financial resources to support these projects. Further proof of the mutual exchange between industry and scholarship lies in the papers of Grazietta Butazzi. After her death in 2014, her family donated these, together with Butazzi's personal library, to a corporate institution, the Fondazione Antonio Ratti in Como, who organized a one-day conference to celebrate the legacy of the fashion historian (Morini, Rizzini and Rosina, 2016).

Despite this mutual exchange between industry and scholarship, CISST remained an independent association, whose work was unmistakably identified as separate from the operations of companies. This separation clearly emerges from the introduction to the proceedings of the 1990 CISST conference by Marco Rivetti, president of Pitti Immagine and GFT. Rivetti stated that the aim of Pitti Immagine was to offer 'to operators in the sector (but also to an ever-wider public) numerous opportunities for cultural analysis and stimuli to critically analyse its past, present and future'[5] (Rivetti, 1992: xi). He then presented the two areas in which Pitti Immagine commissioned research: contemporary social economy and marketing, and textile and fashion history. Pitti Immagine's contribution to both fields can also be traced in the work of Edifir, the publishing house they established in the late 1980s (with Centro di Firenze per la Moda Italiana) to manage the publication of the catalogues of the fairs and events organized by Pitti Immagine. Together with catalogues, Edifir also supported scholarship in textile and fashion studies, as proved by their publishing of the proceedings of the 1990 CISST conference and all the issues of the CISST journal *Arte Tessile* (1990–5), though the latter was paid for by the CISST. The connection between past and present is provided by the employment of the results of these distinct research projects commissioned by Pitti, rather than the merging of the two fields in the research projects – which would instead characterize the curatorship of Maria Luisa Frisa at the Fondazione Pitti Immagine Discovery ten years later.

To sum up, the fashion and textile industries sought interaction with cultural institutions and scholarships and employed forms of sponsorship in order to both support research in their field and employ the results for the cultural communication of fashion – which became of increasing importance in the 1990s. While sponsorship is a form of support still employed today, since the 1990s fashion and textile companies have also engaged in the active organization of cultural events and in the establishment of institutions, with the aim to directly address their commercial and communication needs. The next section focuses on companies as cultural producers and specifically analyses the corporate cultural policy of Pitti Immagine and its integration of marketing and historical research.

5.2 Companies as cultural producers

Sponsorship is characterized by the clear separation between sponsors and sponsees. Notwithstanding the expansion of the points of interaction between scholarship (institutions and professionals) and industry, up until the 1990s their roles in Italy remained divided and defined by their temporal focus: scholarship attended to history while the industry attended to contemporaneity. The exhibition on the 1950s Florentine fashion shows held in 1992 at Palazzo Pitti was the first overt attempt at the historicization of Italian fashion with marketing purposes. It was organized by Pitti Immagine and curated by Giannino Malossi, while the scholars from Galleria del Costume were engaged for the historical research. The display was designed by archistar Gae Aulenti and theatre director Luca Ronconi. As explained in Chapter 1, this project was strategically commissioned to relaunch Florence as the cultural centre of Italian fashion so it employed the association of Italianness with the Renaissance to claim the right of Florence to be placed back at the centre of the Italian fashion system. This was part of a broad campaign promoted by Carlo Rivetti since his appointment as president of Pitti in 1987 which involved educational, editorial, curatorial and promotional projects.

The independent curator Giannino Malossi collaborated with Pitti from the late 1980s to the 1990s and the exhibitions explored fashion from a contemporary cultural perspective.[6] Malossi's approach can be inscribed in cultural studies and moved away from historical fashion and dress studies which had characterized scholarship in the previous decades. Cultural studies were initially developed in the UK and featured prominently in English literature. I would argue that these operations were successful for they employed an international approach which suited the interests and audience of Pitti Immagine. Though there was a regular exchange between scholars of different countries, as shown by the work of CIAC and CISST, we can detect an international nature of the projects devised by Malossi. For example, in 1994 he curated the exhibition *Supermarket of Style* at Stazione Leopolda in Florence (in conjunction with an edition of the Pitti Immagine fair) in collaboration with Ted Polhemus, who curated in the same year the exhibition *Street Style* at the Victoria and Albert Museum in London, both dedicated to subcultures.

Malossi had directed Fiorucci DXing from 1976 to 1980, an in-house interdisciplinary centre which combined cultural and creative research, producing publications, exhibitions and contributing to the artistic direction of the brand Fiorucci. He sat between scholarship and industry: as a cultural industry, fashion required products (such as books) and experiences (such as exhibitions) which could provide complimentary consumption of fashion from a more markedly cultural angle. This meant that projects were devised in response to the companies commissioning these cultural products. For example, the Pitti fair has editions dedicated to different product categories but is mainly associated with menswear. Though exhibitions on menswear are not remotely comparable in popularity and frequency to those on womenswear, Malossi curated *Latin Lover* in 1996 and *Material Man* in 2000, both held at Stazione Leopolda in conjunction with fairs.

Exhibitions became cultural commentaries presented alongside trade fairs, an effective strategy to promote the cultural and social relevance of fashion and, thus, its consumption. As these displays became a regular feature of the Pitti offer, in 1996 Malossi created the Fashion Engineering Unit, a working group dedicated to fashion supported by Pitti, to have an efficient team of exhibition making since there was only six months to one year to prepare each display.[7] As Malossi stated in an interview, there was research available to be employed for the production of exhibitions so the Fashion Engineering Unit (FEU) had the task to scout and work with what was available and interpret it through angles in line with corporate interests. He recognized that the exhibitions could not go in depth to a level of an academic monograph for the lack of time allowed and so the displays were intended as an introduction to themes, thus also changing the idea of 'exhibition as dissemination of findings' which had been the approach of CISST. This was exhibition-making at the service of the industry for the engagement with the public.

The systematic approach to exhibition making would later be institutionalized with the establishment of the Fondazione Pitti Immagine Discovery which had Francesco Bonami as director. Although the output was diverse throughout the 2000s, ranging from cultural and sociological reflections on uniforms and 1980s to solo exhibitions of artists to historical retrospectives on Italian designers and photographers, the team was more aligned to contemporary art than to cultural studies. The shift towards contemporary art can be traced back to the first edition of the Biennale di Firenze, organized in 1996, which initiated a process wherein these divisions were broken and led to a revision of roles. Pitti Immagine organized the whole event and asked museums and institutions to take part, but Pitti retained the lead. The first trace of this process can be detected in a change of narrative: before the Biennale, cultural events on fashion were constructed from a historical perspective, and the aim of research was to provide authority and justification to that inclusion of fashion within a history of the arts. At the Biennale, instead, fashion was presented as an expression of contemporaneity, whose past is used as a key to understand the present. This approach was already present in the work of Malossi; the monumental scale of the Biennale, the tour of one of its displays *Art/Fashion* to the Guggenheim Museum SoHo in New York in 1997, and the attention it generated internationally made this experiment more impactful.

In the introduction to the Biennale catalogue, the three curators repeatedly stressed the wish to create an event that would explore the nature of fashion as contemporary culture. They acknowledged that the fashion industry, unlike art, already had a 'complex system for its diffusion: collections, companies, boutiques, advertising, magazines, attention of the mass media' (Celant, Settembrini and Sischy, 1996: xxxi). However, they compared fashion to other visual languages and pointed out the absence of cultural initiatives – such as the Biennales – that are established practices for art, architecture and cinema. They interpreted it as a consequence of the absence of official recognition of fashion 'as being part of *true* culture' despite its 'huge influence on our culture'[8] (Celant, Settembrini and Sischy, 1996: xxxi).

The emphasis on the contemporaneity of fashion mirrored the evolving preoccupations of fashion studies in the 1990s, both in Italy (Chapter 4) and in the UK and the United States (Cumming, 2004; Taylor, 2002). Most importantly to assess the agenda of the industry, this emphasis was a consequence of the corporate cultural policy. While Germano Celant was appointed chief curator of the Biennale, the catalogue credits the origin of the idea to Luigi Settembrini, who declared that the project was conceived within the Centro di Firenze per la Moda Italiana (Settembrini, 1996). The association was a representational body managing institutional relationships and the cultural communication of the Florentine fashion district, and actively worked to relaunch the city of Florence as a centre of contemporary artistic production. Florence was a city inevitably associated with its Renaissance history, architecturally imposing over the urban landscape, and the inescapability of its history was addressed by juxtaposing contemporary and historical artefacts. The series of installations of fashion designs in the city's museums, *Visitors*, was an attempt to build a bridge across eras.

Only a decade before, in the 1985 retrospective on Salvatore Ferragamo organized at Palazzo Strozzi, the separation between the historical figure of Ferragamo and the contemporaneity of the brand was heavily marked throughout the catalogue (Aschengreen Piacenti, Ricci and Vergani, 1985). Indeed, the curators were adamant to assert academic rigour and viewed temporal distance as a way to ensure objectivity. In contrast, one decade after the Biennale, Frisa openly declared in *Fashion Theory* her free employment of history and a non-hierarchical presentation of references (Frisa, 2008). Frisa's curatorial practice was rooted in journalism and art criticism and was likely freed from the specific boundaries posited by academic scholarship. Furthermore, by being developed within a corporate institution – the Fondazione Pitti Immagine Discovery – projects were not primarily aimed at the dissemination of scholarly research, but instead at the demonstration of the continuity between past and present of the Florentine and Italian fashion industry. This change was the result of the corporate cultural policy that Pitti Immagine had implemented during the 1990s. In the introduction to the 1996 Biennale catalogue, Settembrini wrote that 'investing in culture therefore means continuing to maintain the contents, ways and forms of a past productive for contemporaneity, as this past would otherwise be destined to lose its value, making the present posthumous'[9] (Settembrini, 1996: 8). The expression 'investment', as examined in Chapter 2, testifies the existence of expectations that companies have on their financial contribution to cultural initiative. It also testifies the intentions and awareness of Pitti Immagine and Centro di Firenze per la Moda Italiana, as well as the long-term aims of their corporate cultural policy, which presented a clear structure: the foundation developed its own cultural projects to be held in conjuction with the events of the parent company as well as manage the external cultural operations supported by the parent company.

The Fondazione Pitti Immagine Discovery was established in 2002 with the 'objective of giving continuity and prominence to the activities of promotion of the contemporary and innovation' (Desiderio, 2015: 14). While the 1996 Biennale was rooted in contemporary art and in the curatorial model of the arts festival associated with it, the curatorship of Malossi, the Fashion Engineering Unit and the Fondazione Pitti Immagine Discovery presented a new approach. After four decades of increasing collaboration with scholarship, the fashion industry borrowed research and curatorial tools to apply them entirely to its needs. However, because the marketing of Italian fashion has employed history since the 1950s (Chapter 1), the research on and engagement with fashion history are considered a shared need by the industry. In fact, the Centro di Firenze per la Moda Italiana and Pitti Immagine implemented their corporate cultural policies to establish Florence 'as the city able to play a leading role in reflection on the cultural history of Italian fashion' (Desiderio, 2015: 14). On this premise, Maria Luisa Frisa, with the regular collaboration of Stefano Tonchi and Francesco Bonami, developed a model of 'exhibition as a mechanism of construction, a device that uses present and past, personal and public materials to suggest new interpretations of current developments' (Flaccavento, 2015: 135). Exhibitions were not intended as dissemination of research for a general or specialist audience – which is often the main preoccupation of academic scholarship – but as a critical exercise for industry professionals, 'offered to all intents and purposes as an appendix to the seasonal reflection on trends' (Flaccavento, 2015: 135).

The awareness and importance placed by Centro di Firenze per la Moda Italiana on their cultural policy is testified by their publication, *Firenze Fashion Atlas* which the President Stefano Ricci intended 'not so much a retrospective, as a manifesto for the future' (Ricci, 2015b: 9). The text was not a chronology of the association but a list of events organized by location, conceived to mark the sixtieth anniversary of the association. It was edited by Frisa, in line with her non-historical approach, and the geographical focus was used to explore the concept of heritage, intended as the legacy of the past into the present (Frisa, 2015). Further evidence of this approach is given by the role ascribed to the Galleria del Costume in Palazzo Pitti. In the publication, Ricci defined it as the 'fashion headquarters' (Ricci, 2015b: 10) of Florence. While organizing its own events, the CFMI also sought close collaboration with the national institution – considered the repository of collective heritage – to enhance the continuity between past and present. In 2016, the Gallerie degli Uffizi (the institutional group of which the Galleria del Costume is part of) and the Fondazione Pitti Immagine Discovery signed an agreement for a three-year programme of 'exhibitions on contemporary fashion culture to be held at Palazzo Pitti' (Cavicchi, 2017: 14). The institution became so closely integrated within the fashion system that in 2017 it changed its name from Galleria del Costume (Gallery of Costume) – what was likely perceived as a dated title – to Museo della Moda e del Costume (Museum of Fashion and Costume). The exhibition *The Ephemeral Museum of Fashion*, curated by Olivier Saillard, inaugurated the exhibition programme with the new name. The president of Pitti Immagine, Claudio Marenzi, stated that 'it is an extraordinary moment, one in which cultural institutions, the business world and the government are at last working together to obtain the common objective of promoting Italian quality and projecting it forcefully at an international level' (Marenzi, 2017: 17). While continuing to operate as a centre for the preservation of historical dress, the museum is now openly positioned as a part of the fashion industry and its curatorial programme is devised in collaboration with the industry.

Evidence of the awareness of the shift from sponsors to producers comes from three corporate institutions. They all stressed their role as producers through publications in which they highlighted their contribution to the cultural understanding of fashion. In 2007, the Museo del Tessuto in Prato authored the book *Thirty Years of Donations* (Museo del Tessuto, 2007). It was a guide to the collections of the museums which presented textile artefacts by era and time but also discussed the role of donors – mainly entrepreneurs–collectors and companies – recognizing the support of the industry in the history of the museum. In 2012, the Fondazione Antonio Ratti marked the tenth anniversary of the death of its founder with a two-day conference, *Collecting Textile*. The first paper was given by Francina Chiara, then textile curator of the foundation, who traced the history of Antonio Ratti as collector, entrepreneur, patron and, ultimately, founder of a cultural institution (Chiara, 2013). Other speakers included Thomas Campbell (then director of the MET), Maximilien Durand (director of the Musée des Tissus in Lyon) and Sonnet Stanfill (Victoria and Albert Museum, fashion curator). A corporate institution placed itself on the same level as international established institutions, which endorsed its activity and recognized its contribution to the field (Rosina, 2013). As previously underlined, corporate institutions actively sought interaction with and validation from traditional institutions: I argue that this can be interpreted as evidence that companies supported and valued the scholarly contributions of their corporate institutions. In 2015, the Museo Salvatore Ferragamo celebrated the thirtieth anniversary since the first retrospective and the establishment of the archive, and the twentieth anniversary of the opening of the museum. In the book *Museo*

Figure 5.1 *Il museo effimero della moda (The Ephemeral Museum of Fashion)* was the first exhibition inaugurating the programme of the Galleria del Costume with its new name, Museo della Moda e del Costume (Museum of Fashion and Costume). Photograph by Alessandro Ciampi. Florence, 2017. Courtesy Pitti Immagine.

Salvatore Ferragamo. I nostri primi trent'anni (*Museum Salvatore Ferragamo. Our First Thirty Years*), the Director Stefania Ricci reflected on the history of the institution, its evolution and future trajectories (Ricci, 2015a). Antonio Paolucci, former director general for Cultural Heritage in Tuscany and now director of the Vatican Museums, recognized how 'the mutation of the corporate philosophy, from an exclusively economic subject to one that is also cultural, is always tricky, risky and yet full of possibilities for the future'[10] (Paolucci, 2015: 9). The museum is described by Paolucci as a cultural producer, regardless of the motivations underlying the production: the Museo Salvatore Ferragamo is no longer a display space where the brand presents its heritage, but it is a branch of the brand. It is a museal institution run according to the values and heritage of the brand. It is not a facility that merely presents displays about the brand but a brand that provides cultural services.

The legacy of the cultural policies of Pitti Immagine, CFMI and corporate institutions is to have merged past and contemporary narratives into a new form of curation, in which they present corporate history and current production together and the connecting thread is provided by the values that emerge across the eras. This operation works from a critical perspective, in which the past is used to analyse the present (a prerogative of scholarship), but also from an organizational perspective in which heritage research is a tool for innovation (a prerogative of the industry). Showing continuity with the past has defined the Italian fashion industry since the 1950s; however, the elements involved have changed. When the Italian buyer Giovanni Battista Giorgini launched the collective shows of Italian fashion in 1951, he sought to demonstrate the artistic value of Italian fashion by constructing a continuity with the artistic past of Florence (Stanfill, 2014; Malossi, 1992). Now, the fashion industry seeks continuity with its own past and promotes research on its heritage, to then present it alongside new trends, as pioneered by Pitti Immagine. The industry has actively changed the role of museums and its relation with scholarship: both are understood to be working for the same aim but in different ways, and the interactions are openly declared. In the next section, further evidence of this phenomenon is sought in the curatorial narratives which have been influenced by corporate cultural policies.

5.3 Curating corporate heritage

The influence of the fashion industry can also be detected through an analysis of curatorial approaches. The technical knowledge and resources available to corporate archives and museums have permitted to explore and illustrate the manufacturing side of the fashion industry in depth. One example of the technical narrative in exhibitions is provided by displays on Versace. The 1989 exhibition *L'Abito per Pensare* (Dress for Thought) held the Castello Sforzesco in Milan was praised for the critical analysis it operated of Versace's work. As noted by Monti, the curator Chiara Buss, through her research on the materials used by Versace, contextualized fashion design within the Italian textile tradition, thus showing the exhibited *dress* 'not as an absolute object, but as the outcome of a long design project' (Monti, 2019: 85). Buss would later expand on this research when two exhibitions on Versace were held in Como in 1998 in two different locations. One, simply titled Gianni Versace, was a re-edition of the 1997 exhibition at the Metropolitan Museum of Art in New York, curated by Richard Martin. Another, held at the Fondazione Antonio Ratti, titled Gianni Versace. The Reinvention of Materials, was curated by Chiara Buss, by then appointed as the director of the textile museum of the foundation. The second display was exclusively focused on materials and divided into four sections: Woven Pattern, Printed Fabric, Non-Woven Fabric, Mixed Technique (Buss and Martin, 1998). In 1999 the exhibition toured to the Museum of Modern Art in Miami and in 2002 it was updated and transformed for the V&A, where it was curated by Claire Wilcox with Chiara Buss. As described by Stevenson (2008), the show was enlarged to fit the spaces and featured a section dedicated to Donatella Versace. Versace's close relationship with celebrities was also stressed, and the show opened with dresses worn by British celebrities such as Princess Diana and actress Elizabeth Hurley. Valerie Cumming would later criticize the focus on celebrity both in this exhibition and in the 2004 retrospective on Vivienne Westwood, also curated by Claire Wilcox at the V&A. Cumming objected to the potential consequences of shifting towards contemporary designers and celebrities as she linked them to the increasing depletion of resources for the collection, preservation and research of historical dress (Cumming, 2004). Yet, what brought praise to the Versace show was the technical analysis of Versace's work and the discussion on fabrics and construction. As Valerie Steele (director of the Museum at the Fashion Institute of Technology in New York) observed: 'The exhibition also featured a wealth of historical and technical information that contributed to raising it beyond the banal paradigm of designer-as-artist' (Steele, 2008: 16). Fashion scholar Liz Mason also highlighted the unusual narrative for a fashion exhibition in her review for *Fashion Theory*:

> In the accompanying publication the essay by Chiara Buss, 'The Craft of Gianni Versace', focuses entirely on his interventions in the production processes and manipulation and printing of materials, and the exhibition also drew our attention to the complexity of this process. (Mason, 2005: 87)

As the director of a prestigious textile corporate institution in Como, one of Italy's main textile production districts, and as Versace was one of the clients of the Ratti silk manufactory, Buss had special access to information and artefacts critical to the research on the technical side of Versace's work.

Displays of garments in the late nineteenth and early twentieth century had already presented these artefacts as products of specific techniques and crafts, especially when installed within international exhibitions (Petrov, 2019). However, in the second half of the twentieth century, a shift towards historical and artistic perspectives was detected in the displays held in arts museums. To argue that a focus on technique has reappeared only because of corporate institutions or that it can be found only in corporate institutions would be incorrect. Nevertheless, corporate institutions are uniquely positioned to endorse this approach because of their very corporate nature, as parent companies are the repositories of the technical knowledge unfolded in exhibitions. When discussing exhibitions organized by brands themselves, Petrov stated that these can 'provide access to the craftsmanship and tradition that otherwise only a very privileged few would have' (2019). For instance, in 2014 the Fondazione Antonio Ratti held *Emilio Pucci e Como. 1950–1980* (Emilio Pucci and Como. 1950–1980) which investigated the relationship between the designer and the silk manufacturers of Como, where Pucci had his textiles printed. The exhibition did not just present Emilio Pucci as an individual artist, but highlighted the agency of the manufacturers in the development of Pucci's visions and how their technical skills influenced Pucci's success (Rosina and Chiara, 2014).

Most importantly, high-quality textile production is one of the key differentiating traits of Italian fashion and focusing on technique is a recognition of the centrality of the textile industry in the Italian fashion system (Stanfill, 2014; Steele, 2003; White, 2000). This element was indeed given prominence in the exhibition *The Glamour of Italian Fashion 1945–2014* curated by Sonnet Stanfill and held at the V&A in 2014. This display presented a balance between celebrity and technical information – as the 2002 Versace show did – and

Figure 5.2 The exhibition *Emilio Pucci e Como. 1950–1980* (*Emilio Pucci and Como. 1950–1980*) investigated the relationship between the designer Emilio Pucci and silk manufacturing district of Como. Fondazione Antonio Ratti, Como, 2014. Photograph by Giacomo Introzzi. Courtesy Giacomo Introzzi.

one of its three sections was entirely dedicated to industrial and artisanal manufacturing, exploring the variety of production methods (Stanfill, 2014). Furthermore, as the catalogue attests, the curator worked closely with corporate museums and archives, and scholars from these institutions were asked to contribute to the publication. In particular, Margherita Rosina (then director of the Museo Studio del Tessuto of the Fondazione Antonio Ratti, Como) and Filippo Guarini (director of the Museo del Tessuto, Prato) were commissioned essays on the Italian textile industry and its relationship with the fashion system.

The focus on technique may also respond to a precise communication strategy, as evidenced by the work of the Museo del Tessuto in Prato. When describing the contemporary collection in 1999, the then director Tamara Boccherini highlighted that the selection not only operated on artistic criteria but included 'even fabrics that have seemingly no artistic value and that elsewhere would not be considered worthy of attention'[11] (Boccherini, 1999: 8) in order to illustrate 'the long process of scientific and technological research from those who had to get a competitive product to reach the maximum effect with the minimum cost'[12] (Boccherini, 1999: 8). Their focus on technique can be detected in many exhibitions. For instance, the display dedicated to *Vintage. L'irresistibile fascino del vissuto* (Vintage. The irresistible charm of the past) (Guarini, 2012) investigated the recycling process of wool and the rug trade which had characterized the Prato area since the thirteenth century (Museo del Tessuto, 2013). Another example is provided by the Fondazione Gianfranco Ferré, which became the Centro di Ricerca Gianfranco Ferré in 2021 and is now run by the university Politecnico di Milano. In 2014 the institution worked with the Museo del Tessuto in Prato and organized the exhibition *La camicia bianca secondo me. Gianfranco Ferré* (The White Shirt According to Me. Gianfranco Ferré), which toured to Milan in 2015 (Airaghi, 2014). The display focused on the interpretations of the white shirt which Ferré included in all his collections. The installation placed the attention on the shirts, and photographs were commissioned and displayed alongside sketches and technical drawings to explain the complex constructions of the garments. Through these operations, the museum positions the Prato textile industry as an element of the Italian fashion system and can then leverage the value and competitiveness of Italian fashion to market its products both nationally and internationally.

Using exhibitions as promotional tools to culturally frame fashion and textile products is a strategy which has been employed systematically by Italian companies since the 1950s. In the first decades, there was a marked differentiation between curation and industry, with the latter providing financial support and

Figure 5.3 The display *Vintage. L'irresistibile fascino del vissuto* (*Vintage. The Irresistible Charm of the Past*) investigated the recycling process of wool and the rug trade which had characterized the Prato area since the thirteenth century. Museo del Tessuto, Prato, 2012. Courtesy *Museo del Tessuto, Prato*.

resources to promote scholarship of the field. With the 1980s and the boom of the Italian fashion industry, alongside the growing interest of academics and institutions in fashion, there was an increase in the breadth of cultural projects which the industry could support and benefit from sponsoring. The exchange with scholarship contributed to the industry's awareness of the potential of corporate heritage as an operational resource for companies and of exhibitions as strategic tools for marketing campaigns, such as the relaunch of Florence as the cultural centre of Italian fashion. In this respect, since the 1950s the Florence fashion system had demonstrated prowess in the use of the past to define its position within the broader national and international fashion systems. With the pioneering corporate cultural policies conceived by Carlo Rivetti in the 1990s and later the establishment of the Fondazione Pitti Immagine Discovery, and through the curatorship of respectively Giannino Malossi and Maria Luisa Frisa, there emerged an approach to curation which could be defined as *corporate curation*, that is the employment of curatorial tools to address corporate needs. I argue that these operations cannot be described as the import of 'fashion-world values into a museum's decision-making process' (Muschamp in Steele, 2008: 17), which is the criticism that had been directed at the Armani exhibition,

Figure 5.4 The exhibition *La camicia bianca secondo me. Gianfranco Ferré* (*The White Shirt According to Me. Gianfranco Ferré*) was a collaboration with the Fondazione Gianfranco Ferré and the Museo del Tessuto in Prato, where it was held in 2014. This photograph shows the display when it was installed in the Sala delle Cariatidi of Palazzo Reale in Milan. Photograph by Leonardo Salvini. Milan, 2015. Courtesy *Archivio Fondazione Gianfranco Ferré*.

but can instead be interpreted as the employment of curatorial practices and museum values into fashion-world decision-making process.

The exhibitions of Malossi and Frisa were not devised for the dissemination of research findings – though they were rooted in research – but as a form of criticism: the displays used visual juxtapositions to trigger reflection and discussion on the fashion industry. Exhibitions were effectively used as a visual critical commentary to themes in line with the current trends and interests of the industry and professionals attending the fair. The aesthetic driven, non-narrative approach was also detected at the Metropolitan Museum of New York in the 2000s, where displays could be used to assess 'a new layer of visual sources by which to interpret the staging of fashion in an interior' (McNeil in Petrov, 2019). These displays were commissioned by the industry but the themes were often proposed by curators who were able to detect current trends and preoccupations and elaborate upon them through the use of multiple artefacts. In the publication celebrating sixty years of the CFMI, fashion journalist Angelo Flaccavento wrote that these exhibitions captured 'the very essence of contemporary fashion: the construction of the future out of the reutilization of the past, the disregard for hierarchies and chronologies, the inexorable emphasis on pure visuality' (2015: 135). Because these are commentaries on what is happening in the industry, themes evolved with the industry. For example, after the 2008 financial crisis and the increased importance of heritage marketing, Frisa looked at the history of Italian fashion and curated two historicizing displays: *Bellissima!* (2014) was dedicated to Italian couture from the 1940s to the 1960s; and *Italiana* (2018) to the rise of Italian ready-to-wear from the 1970s to the 1990s. In 2008, Frisa declared that she does not aim to 'achieve historical fidelity to fashion, but rather a critical exercise' (Frisa, 2008: 172). In a conversation with the author in 2021, she also noted that she had not previously engaged with a historicizing exhibition because she needed to be an established curator to be able to embark on such broad-ranging projects which required the extensive support of corporate archives and, therefore, existing relationships with them which she had built in the previous decades.[13] Once again, curatorial narratives are devised in response to specific needs and evolve as these needs evolve. It is, however, essential to state that many of these projects did not only address corporate needs but also civic ones (Xu, 2017), since fashion as a subject and corporate heritage were interpreted from collective perspectives. In the next section, I will ponder the value of scholarship resulted from corporate cultural policies and how corporate institutions can manage corporate and civic needs, providing benefits to both.

5.4 Managing corporate and civic needs

From the 1950s to the 1980s, there was a clear distinction between sponsored projects and industry, the contribution of the industry was limited to patronage and sponsorship, and the preoccupation of scholars was to highlight the rigour of the research into the study of fashion as its value was not yet universally acknowledged. As shown by the approach of CISST, museums and scholars could not be seen as passive agents exploited for commercial gain (Petrov, 2019), but were in fact benefitting from the exchange as the industry provided more than financial resources, but also access to the objects of study, which also allowed for specific curatorial narratives (see previous paragraph). Furthermore, the extensive use of exhibitions made by the industry as communication tools contributed to the popularity of fashion exhibitions, which eventually impacted on the presence of these displays in the programming of traditional institutions.

This is a relationship of mutual benefit which creates 'reciprocal value in exhibitions' (Petrov, 2019: 31–62).

As Petrov has already discussed (2019), fashion exhibitions situate visitors as consumers and this broadens the dimensions with which visitors engage in exhibitions, thus increasing the value and potential of fashion curation as a practice. The problem with the 2000 Armani exhibition was not the presence of fashion in a museum but the overtly commercial and intellectually shallow nature of the exhibition (Petrov, 2019). Commercial interests can be beneficial to curation, as argued in this book, not only because they may be the key to more resources, but because they may trigger experimentation, as was the case of the exhibitions commissioned by Pitti in the 1990s and 2000s: curation became a form of visual criticism that suggested socio-cultural contextualization and critical observations of themes relevant to current trends and issues in the industry. This must be viewed not as a sign of lower 'academic' quality of these projects: the catalogues of these exhibitions evidence extensive research but they were not intended as academic monographs but instead as publications with the appeal of fashion magazines and coffee table books. In the same way, the main focus of exhibitions was not the dissemination of scholarship – which nevertheless informed the work of curators – but the presentation of an engaging experience that would make fashion consumers aware of the cultural dimensions of fashion. In fact, as markets and consumers have evolved and physical stores are drastically changing their role in the industry, corporate curation and institutions can provide models on how to use these physical spaces. Corporate curatorial practices can therefore guide and inform retail configurations.

The effectiveness of corporate cultural policies lies precisely in the ability to fulfil corporate needs whilst also framing their consumers as members of a community, as discussed in Chapter 3. Corporate museums are the best-suited example to highlight the successful outcomes when companies equally address corporate and civic needs. The Museo del Tessuto in Prato is a key example of the exchange between a museum and the industry. In 1975 the Museo was founded following the donation of the collection of the textile industrialist and alumnus Loriano Bertini to the specialist textile college Istituto Tecnico Industriale Statale Tullio Buzzi (the Tullio Buzzi State Technical-Industrial Institute). The collection included 612 textile fragments from the Middle Ages to the eighteenth century and had a 'double function: both to historically orient the young designer and to stimulate the creation of new designs' (Bonito Fanelli, 1975: 2). Initially, the museum was a conglomerate of different collections and the increment in the collections relied mainly on private donors, though it was already intended as a resource for the local industry and was supported by entrepreneurs and industry associations. In 1997, the museum moved to a bigger location in the city hall and broadened its scope from an educational collection of a school to a civic museum: collecting policies were devised to shape the collections through the new perspective. One collection was, in fact, created *ex-novo* and aimed at documenting the contemporary productions of fabrics for fashion. An agreement was stipulated between local manufacturers and the museum for the systematic selection of 100 samples – operated by the museum staff and in response to the collections plan – displayed at each edition of the biannual trade fair Prato Expo. The resulting collection cannot be technically considered corporate as it is independent from manufacturers, who have their own archival policies in place. However, though operated independently by the museum, the selection aims at portraying the current state of the local production district and is instrumental for its cultural communication through exhibitions.

Pearce wrote that 'the making of a collection is one way in which we organize our relationship with the external physical world of which collections are a part ... Collections are a significant element in our attempt to construct the world' (1992: 37). This statement suits the collecting policy for contemporary textiles at Prato, where both the museum's management and the local manufacturers' association agree that the museum should become the cultural interface of the district. This can be detected in the statute, which declares that the main mission of the institution is education but, in article 2, outlines secondary functions:

- collaborate in the preservation of the memory of textile production of the Prato district, through the recovery, safeguard and collect testimonies, advise companies holding historical archives, undertake studies and research;
- actively participate – within its competences – in initiatives for the cultural, tourist, economic and image relaunch of the area and district. (Museo del Tessuto, 2003: 2)[14]

Filippo Guarini, director of the museum, has pointed out how the promotion of the district as the indirect promotion of the community:

> It is important for the museum, within the bounds of its limited resources, to be able to offer the city and the district small, and if possible great, opportunities both for a revival of the image of the district (particularly with regards to the strategic role it plays in providing the global fashion industry a know-how and a product of the highest level) and for its development into a 'new' cultural and tourist attraction. (Guarini, 2013: 136)

Its collections both inform the sense of self of the community (social and industrial) (Belk, 1995) and are informed by the identity that the community wishes to construct: it is a reciprocal relationship of exchange between a community and its industry. The museum interprets corporate heritage as collective heritage and makes it tangible to the community through its operations (Urde, Greyser and Balmer, 2007). Because of such close ties with the industry, the institution can be considered a corporate museum (Amari, [1997] 2001; Bulegato, 2008).

The Museo Salvatore Ferragamo, though originated from the corporate archive of a company, equally engaged with collective selves and its interaction with the community takes place through exhibitions. The museum presents a different exhibition every year, which is developed in relation to the holdings of the corporate archive and the preoccupations of the brands (sustainability) but is unfolded through a broader perspective, aimed at stressing the cultural and social relevance of the brand. Collaborations with national and international museums were established 'with the aim of building multi-disciplinary displays in which fashion and the life of Ferragamo are an important element of a deliberately richer history' (Ricci in Fulco, 2015).[15] The event which signalled this shift was the 2015 exhibition *A Palace and the City*, dedicated to the history of the building where Ferragamo headquarters are located, on the occasion of the 150th anniversary of Florence as the capital of Italy. It was a history of the city told from the perspective of a palace which has played a focal role in the city since the thirteenth century. The catalogue mirrors both the curatorial approach and the scientific rigour of the museum: specialists are commissioned essays according to the themes included in the exhibitions, while Stefania Ricci authors the essays on Ferragamo, as the expert on the shoemaker. This has since become a model for the museum's catalogues. Fashion scholars are often credited as co-curators, such as Enrica Morini and Maria Luisa Frisa for *Across Art and Fashion* in 2016 (Ricci, 2016a).

If initially (1980s and 1990s) corporate institutions were only limitedly addressing civic needs, they are now 'mature enough to house the same kinds of major functions that "official" museums do' (Xu, 2017: 51). One of the ways in which to assess the contribution to scholarship is not only through publications but also to evaluate the connections and interactions with established institutions. For example, the 2016 exhibition *Across Art and Fashion* was a collaboration with four other local institutions: Galleria d'Arte Moderna, Biblioteca Nazionale Centrale, Museo Marino Marini in Florence; and Museo del Tessuto in Prato. Each institution investigated a different

Figure 5.5 This room of the exhibition *Un Palazzo e la Città* (*A Palace and the City*) recreated the art gallery of Luigi Bellini, which was located in Palazzo Spini Feroni in the 1930s, before Salvatore Ferragamo there set up his workshop. Museo Salvatore Ferragamo, Florence, 2015. Courtesy *Museo Salvatore Ferragamo*.

element of the exhibition's theme in accordance with its own collection and nature. The Museo Salvatore Ferragamo was the project leader and the company was the main sponsor. The displays featured an impressive number of international loans of iconic pieces from historical couturiers such as Yves Saint Laurent and Elsa Schiaparelli, as well as leading designers such as Hussein Chalayan and Alexander McQueen. The resources made available by the company allowed for an ambitious project to take place which would have not otherwise been possible. The Florentine museological landscape concentrates a vast number of visitors in a small number of fine arts museums. Projects of this kind stimulate an increase in visitor numbers, especially since Museo Salvatore Ferragamo has twice more visitors (40,000 visitors in 2017) than Museo Marino Marini in Florence (19,000 in 2017) or Museo del Tessuto in Prato (20,000 in 2017). The 2017 and 2018 exhibitions continued this trend by proposing loans from the Museo nazionale delle arti e tradizioni popolari (National Museum of Popular Arts and Customs) in Rome for the exhibition *1927. The Return to Italy* (Sisi and Ricci, 2017) or the Museo Enrico Caruso in Lastra a Signa for the exhibition *Italy in Hollywood* (Ricci, 2018). The Museo Salvatore Ferragamo demonstrated the ability of corporate museums to stimulate museum networks and favour inter-institutional exchange, both of artefacts and scholarship.

The main challenge is given by the need to balance corporate needs with the scholarship and intellectual freedom expected of museums (Petrov, 2019) but I would argue that these limitations, though differently manifested, equally exist in traditional museums, where the presence of sponsors and the interests of lenders can equally impact the extent of critical analysis presented in fashion exhibitions, as evidenced by previously reported criticism to exhibitions at the V&A and the Metropolitan Museum of Art. The effectiveness of fashion curation then lies in how interests and limitations are managed and how the transparency with which corporate needs are declared. In 2015, Ferruccio Ferragamo, President of the brand and the museum, openly discussed the marketing benefits of the institution as well as its relevance as a public service: 'it is the location ideal to compare different artistic disciplines, to research and reflect, to train the new generations'[16] (Ferragamo, 2015: 5).

I argue that this transparency is the key to resolve the problematic commercial nature of fashion exhibitions. Not all corporate events are transparent and not all corporate institutions interpret collections from collective perspectives and address civic needs, yet they can provide successful models on how to equally benefit industry and scholarship. This is not a prerogative of Italian fashion curation but, due to the contextual reasons highlighted in Chapters 2 and 3, and to the strategic use of heritage intrinsic to the Italian fashion industry and its marketing, corporate institutions are particularly developed in Italy and the industry has largely contributed to the development of fashion curation in Italy.

6

Concluding remarks

What's Italian about fashion curation?

This book delineates a relationship between heritage, industry and institutions which is led by diverse needs and results into a broad range of operations. No curatorial traits or approaches can be considered exclusively Italian but are nevertheless intrinsic to the complex system of textile and fashion industries in Italy and to the centrality of this system in Italian society and culture.

Reviewing the history of fashion curation highlighted the agency of the industry and the concept of *corporate cultural policy* is introduced to identify all the activities of a company for cultural communication, ranging from financial support of external projects to in-house development and curation. This book frames fashion curation as an intersection between two poles, industry and scholarship (institutions and academia) and indirectly invites to move away from the preoccupation of defining boundaries between these two poles in favour of identifying strategies to develop curatorial approaches that can be beneficial to both poles. This inevitably leads to questioning the purpose of exhibitions and publications, an essential step to explore the full potential of institutions in current and future environments.

The binary opposition between industry and 'culture' or even 'art', as writers often define the world of exhibition-making and museums, was formed dialogically and academically, rather than emerging from the field. The separation between industry and scholarship was triggered by early fashion scholars who aimed at providing authority to fashion studies. Interpretative bias is present across the institutional landscape and, though differently, traditional and corporate institutions are equally biased. Museums are not neutral and have always been platforms used to produce meaning as well as consensus: it would be misleading to consider them objective interpreters of material culture. The narrations there contained are prompted by surrounding pressures and regulated by political, social and cultural values. There is an ontological difference between traditional and corporate museums: the former aim at addressing civic needs but, as institutions, are inevitably intertwined with corporate needs; the latter aim at fulfilling corporate needs and may also address civic needs. For this reason, the French term *museal* could be employed to identify institutions that engage in museological operations, and the not-for-profit museums described by the definition of the International Council of Museums (ICOM) are only one manifestation of a *museal* institution. This term was first introduced in English by ICOM's *Key Concepts of Museology* (Desvallées and Mairesse, 2010) where the authors advocated for the overcoming of the not-for-profit nature that museums should have, according to ICOM. Not-for-profit and for-profit museums are equally limited in their operations: the limitations on scholarly activity do not undermine the quality of the activity itself, but simply provide boundaries within which the activity must be carried out. In traditional museums, these limitations are posed by institutional patrons and sponsors, as well as by local and national associations that monitor inclusivity and accessibility. Within this group, public institutions may be more subject to political expectations while private ones may be more exposed to economic pressures. In corporate museums, the limitations are circumscribed by corporate needs. The analysis of corporate institutions in Italy has highlighted where their limitations stand but it has also underlined the academic level of research undertaken in (some of) these institutions and the transparency with which they address their limitations.

In the shift from sponsor to cultural producer, the industry also impacted on curatorial narratives: corporate institutions are often repositories of technological knowledge and communicate it through displays and publications, as well as employing it for internal training and educational programs. Though not always present, narratives focused on manufacture have characterized the operations of fashion and textile corporate institutions. In the future, this narrative will likely take on a central role for brands in their move towards a sustainable and ethical continuation of their operations. Materials and making in general are playing a fundamental role in the restructuring of the industry so corporate institutions are repositories of knowledge which must be communicated and harnessed. For example, the Museo Salvatore Ferragamo is already in charge of internal training on corporate heritage, develops educational programmes to promote the importance of crafts in Italian culture and recently dedicated a large exhibition to *Sustainable Thinking* (2019). The Museo del Tessuto in Prato has long served as the cultural interface of the local production districts and has the visibility and tools to provide interpretative clues to the industry on present issues as well as suggesting possibilities for future solutions.

Italy is scattered with small museums with niche interests; for example, there are two museums dedicated to cork, one in Central Italy (Cervarezza) and one in Sardinia (Calangianus), as well as museums on umbrellas, glasses and taps. These institutions run on limited funds and are not part of a system with a strategic plan and resources to support their operations. They can be integrated in the local industry and used to raise awareness of the cultural relevance of their production and to provide technical knowledge and inspiration to the industry. Trade associations are uniquely positioned to develop a network between institutions (private and public) and industry for the promotion of a local district or national industry, serving marketing purposes as well as enhancing the cultural cachet of fashion. This was eminently demonstrated by Pitti Immagine and how their varied corporate cultural policy contributed to the revival of Florence as a capital of fashion in Italy. A similar framework could be employed to investigate curatorial practices in other countries such as Belgium: Antwerp is a fashion hub where the MoMu museum was established in 2002 and is closely connected to both the Royal Academy and the Antwerp fashion district. MoMu is considered a cutting edge institution and its exhibitions have gained critical acclaim, and it could be interpreted as a corporate museum. Similar to the Museo del Tessuto di Prato, MoMu is the cultural interface of Belgian fashion: it has developed an avant-garde curatorial approach precisely because of the avant-garde approach associated with the local fashion design, and whose operations are crucial to the current industry and the preservation of this identity.

What was and remains crucial to curatorial practices is broadening the management of heritage beyond corporate perspectives and shift the purpose of curatorial projects from promotion to sense-making. There are inevitably many examples of exhibitions solely dedicated to the promotion of a brand but it is highlighted throughout this publication that there are also many corporate cultural events which solicit in the viewers a critical response (Loscialpo, 2016). These events will not go against the brand by presenting negative views but they can frame visitors as members of a sociocultural community, not only as customers, and thus address extended levels of the self (Belk, 1995). While this approach is a requirement of traditional museums, it is not of corporate institutions; however, they can become museal institutions when the narratives they construct and disseminate are relevant to social groups and not only to corporate interests. Corporate institutions are effective structures to manage corporate cultural policies, and outputs like exhibitions can be used as platforms through which brands can engage with consumers and society at large. They can be used to raise awareness of the cultural dimension of fashion and brands can address complex issues, such as sustainability and inclusivity, and articulate their positions.

One of the themes which can be addressed by corporate institutions is national identity. This book highlights the role of fashion and curation in the construction of what is 'authentically Italian' and how exhibitions and publications are great tools to contextualize a practice within a defined cultural heritage whose marketing power is still harnessed by communication strategies. In the current environment, when many efforts are made to move away from fashion as a globalized, Euro-centric discourse, it is essential to discuss the extent to which cultural stereotypes are perpetuated by Western fashion brands. Developing projects dedicated to the relationship between fashion and national identity may be an effective strategy to contribute towards the shifting of fashion from a globalized industry towards fashion as a locally constituted, social practice. Further research is warranted for example on France, a country with a long tradition of commodification of its own culture. Luxury brands such as Hermès and Dior commodify Frenchness not only through their products but also through their corporate cultural policies. Since the late 2000s, they have increased their staff dedicated to heritage operations as well as the number of publications – which are used as the lowest-priced entry point to luxury brands and have a huge potential in building intimate relationships with consumers as well as communicating the symbolic value of luxury products. Another examination could focus on Louis Vuitton, which has greatly diversified its corporate cultural policy and now operates an archive with a display facility and a corporate art foundation, as well as large touring exhibitions. This could result in a deeper understanding of the differences between these facilities, their interconnections and the processes governing their operations.

Writing in 2022, fashion is undergoing systemic changes with small brands emerging as successful organizations which can guarantee sustainability across their operations and have a solid ethical ground. This group of brands are smoothly adapting to new paradigms, in which transparency is an essential requirement for consumers who align to brands because of their values. In this context, heritage brands are at a crossroad: either they focus their corporate cultural policies on an elitarian artification which may likely not be relevant in the long-term, or they focus on providing cultural services to social groups beyond their consumers. The latter already have platforms such as social media which they engage in meaningful interactions with brands, though the interactions are limited in duration or depth, while exhibitions and publications can allow for deeper and more complex exchanges because of their nature.

Corporate institutions can be used as places where brands make the space and time for themselves as well as for visitors to reflect on current debates and, at the same time, they are uniquely positioned to question the role of museums and exhibitions in general.

The binary division between scholarship (academia and museums) and industry was more detrimental than beneficial both to the practice of fashion curation and to fashion studies. As shown throughout the book, corporate heritage projects can be beneficial to brands, consumers and society alike – and this intertwining of corporate and civic needs has been at the core of corporate cultural policies from the 1950s. Corporate agency and resources are greater than in academia or traditional institutions, and can be harnessed to contribute to scholarship, by way of increasing the accessibility to critical tools through which to make sense of society and fashion. For what concerns the industry, corporate curation is an essential tool for companies not only to market their past but to reflect critically on their history and identify solutions to the changes currently happening in the industry. From a corporate perspective, cultural operations inevitably have corporate interests at heart, whether the return on investment may be only symbolic as in the case of patronage; companies and trade associations should then not worry about the corporate nature of their own operations. Their choice is deciding whether to make their projects relevant beyond corporate interests and frame visitors as consumers, addressing mainly existing and potential customers. If they frame visitors as social agents, they can also provide a service to people who may not become their customers but who would be enriched by understanding the complexity of fashion and its centrality in their lives, eventually raising awareness of the cultural and social relevance of their industry.

Notes

1 Constructing Italian fashion heritage

1 'Ed allora perché imitare e riprodurre servilmente le acconciature d'oltr'alpe, quando l'Italia può tentare di fare da sé e molto meglio? … Non è questione soltanto di patriottismo, che potrebbe far sorridere trattandosi di moda, ma è questione di storia, perchè nulla di più caratteristico che l'arte del vestire, la quale, altrettanto come il linguaggio, ha sempre segnato il genio di una razza, d'un popolo, d'una stirpe: e nessun paese, come l'Italia, che viene chiamata la terra classica dell'arte' (Genoni, 1906: 3).
2 'per lottare contro la produzione straniera, per affinare le loro concezioni, per affermarsi con un carattere di schietta ed originale italianità, per creare insomma un'arte decorativa veramente nazionale' (Genoni, 1908: 6).
3 Conversation with author, 2021.
4 'Quel che il committente voleva per promuovere (forse per dimostrare ancora una volta) il talento, l'originalità, la creatività del *made in Italy*' (Aulenti, 1992: 7; emphasis in the original).

2 Industry and corporate heritage in Italy

1 'ogni manufatto in grado di testimoniare in modo adeguato e significativo la cultura sia spirituale che materiale dell'uomo: sono beni culturali le fotografie, le opere cinematografiche, audiovisive o sequenze di immagini la cui produzione sia anteriore ai 25 anni; I mezzi di trasporto con più di 75 anni; I beni e gli strumenti della tecnica e della scienza con più di 50 anni' (Montemaggi, 2007: 49).
2 'Cultura d'impresa significa il racconto condiviso di quel fare quotidiano che caratterizza l'impegno delle aziende, la sua proiezione verso l'insieme delle imprese e verso l'intera società. Un racconto che esca dai confini aziendali e sappia rappresentare compiutamente e con forza il valore reale dell'impresa per lo sviluppo economico, sociale e civile del Paese' (Confindustria, 2010: 1).
3 'La conoscenza diffusa e puntuale del mondo dell' impresa, delle sue storie e dei suoi progetti è il miglior strumento per creare consapevolezza del valore dell'impresa per il progresso economico e civile' (Confindustria, 2010: 10).

4 'legittimazione culturale dell'impresa' (Sapelli, 1998: 48).
5 'permetta una relazione interattiva e che nello stesso tempo offra a chi si presta a essere soggetto di questa relazione diversi piani di analisi che sono poi quelli dell'impresa' (Sapelli, 1998: 48).
6 n'Quando … si è posto il problema di tutelare la memoria industriale sono state le aziende in prima persona ad occuparsene' (Amari, [1997] 2001: 13).
7 'piena deducibilità dal reddito d'impresa delle erogazioni liberali a favore sia dei beni che delle attività culturali, a fronte dei requisiti dell'articolo di legge' (Martino, 2010: 47).
8 'un nuovo sistema di agevolazioni fiscali al fine di incentivare le erogazioni liberali per la realizzazione di iniziative di interesse culturale e favorire il mecenatismo' (Università Bocconi, 2003: 11).
9 'cultura di un'impresa è quel complesso, stratificato nel tempo e peculiare, di conoscenze, competenze e professionalità che determinano il successo di un'azienda, la comunicazione è l'immagine di sé che l'impresa intende presentare' (Robotti, 2012: 68).
10 'Linguaggio – quello della cultura – più di ogni altro universale è in grado di dare corpo alla "reputazione" d'impresa' (Martino, 2010: 14).
11 'modelli mutuamente esclusivi e sequenziali sul piano storico, prodotto cioè di un'evoluzione lineare' (Martino, 2010: 41).
12 'imprenditore-mecenate, per il quale la cultura rappresenta un veicolo di promozione sociale e uno status symbol' (Martino, 2010: 66).
13 'un coinvolgimento pragmatico e strumentale, che si traduce nel consapevole orientamento alla comunicazione' (Martino, 2010: 66).
14 'caratterizzata da un basso tasso di coinvolgimento dell'impresa, e dunque, da scarsi margini di autonomia gestionale, ivi incluso il controllo sugli stessi esiti della comunicazione' (Martino, 2010: 42).
15 'l'insofferenza di alcune delle maggiori imprese nel 'mettere il loro marchio su manifestazioni organizzate da altri' triggered the 'loro tendenza a intervenire direttamente nell'organizzazione di eventi culturali, forti della loro cultura d'impresa' (Trezzini in Martino, 2010: 43).
16 'contraddistinte dalla ricerca di una più profonda interazione fra partner privato e iniziativa culturale' (Martino, 2010: 42).
17 'al fine di incentivare le erogazioni liberali per la realizzazione di iniziative di interesse culturale e favorire il mecenatismo' (Assolombarda, 2003: 11).
18 'instaurare con il mondo esterno (e anche interno) un rapporto più complesso e articolato, consapevoli che il valore della loro identità e della loro storia hanno un peso pari a quello dei loro prodotti o servizi' (Bondardo, 1999: 39).
19 'oggi le aziende vogliono più investimenti strategici che eventi spettacolari, che, tradotto in altre parole, significa passare dalla sponsorizzazione alla politica culturale' (Bondardo, 1999: 43).

20 'capaci di creare valore sia per l'azienda che per la collettività' (Bondardo, 1999: 45).
21 '• interventi a favore dalla cultura da parte di imprese aderenti ad Assolombarda;
   • i risultati eventualmente rilevabili o le osservazioni comunque formulabili su tali interventi;
   • motivazioni / modalità per una migliore collaborazione tra imprese e cultura' (Università Bocconi, 2003: 3).
22 'la spesa delle famiglie italiane per cultura e tempo libero è passata dai 48 miliardi annui del 1998 ai 64 miliardi del 2008, con un incremento del 34% lungo il decennio considerato' (Martino, 2010: 54).
23 'consentire margini di autonomia decisamente più ampi sul piano sia economico, che gestionale e della comunicazione' (Martino, 2010: 82).
24 'razionalizzazione – a un tempo economica e comunicativa – dell'investimento aziendale' (Martino, 2010: 83).
25 'incoraggiare e stimolare coloro che ne hanno la volontà ad intraprendere la strada degli studi, sostenendo la serietà e il merito' (Amatori, 2004).
26 'una libera associazione di studiosi che concede spazio ad ogni orientamento culturale, senza remore e limiti, se non quello dell'elementare correttezza nei rapporti fra studiosi' (Amatori, 2004).
27 'il riconoscimento del fatto che un investimento del privato nella valorizzazione della cultura torna sì a vantaggio di chi lo ha fatto' (Benedini, 1998: 1).
28 'Non a caso, la localizzazione del futuro Centro è stata individuata in un contesto museale, e in particolare nel museo che per eccellenza riflette e "rappresenta" la cultura e il patrimonio dell'impresa sul suolo nazionale: il Museo della Scienza e della Tecnica a Milano ... il Museo "Leonardo da Vinci" metterà a disposizione non solo i propri locali, ma anche e soprattutto la propria *expertise* in materia di conservazione, ricerca, interpretazione, didattica ed esposizione' (Camerana, 1998: 65).
29 'valorizzazione e promozione dei musei d'impresa in Italia ed eventualmente in Europa' (Camerana, 1998: 66).
30 'Abbiamo la fortuna di partecipare allo sviluppo di una nuova forma di valorizzazione culturale; una forma che può e deve imparare dalla museologia e dall'archivistica, ma che, al tempo stesso, può offrire un contributo autonomo e originale. Penso che questo sia uno degli aspetti più avvincenti del nostro lavoro: stiamo costruendo delle realtà inedite, potenzialmente libere di strutturarsi secondo intenzioni proprie, grazie alle indicazioni di una preziosa tradizione metodologica' (Appiani, 1999: 116).
31 'L'approccio alla gestione di un archivio di moda debba oggi essere molto articolato e richieda competenze specifiche che non si limitino a ragioni e prospettive prettamente aziendali, né a quelle rigorosamente archivistiche o museali, ma che sappiano trovare un equilibrio tra esigenze storico-documentarie

e conservative, quelle di lettura critica e culturale dei registri "visuali", iconici, stilistici e creativi e quelle di utilizzo strategico dei materiali' (Arezzi Boza, 2012: 148).
32 'per autonoma volontà del mondo imprenditoriale' (Martino, 2013: 109).
33 'acquisisce, riordina e rende fruibili gli archivi economici riconosciuti di notevole interesse storico, in collaborazione con le locali Sovrintendenze' (CCI, 2008).
34 'consolida i rapporti di collaborazione tra il MiBACT e Museimpresa, Associazione italiana archivi e musei d'impresa, con l'intento di integrare la rete dei Musei d'impresa nel Sistema museale nazionale' (Museimpresa, 2017).

3 Corporate heritage and institutions

1 'Le fondazioni d'impresa nate tra il 1996 e il 2005 rappresentano il 64,1% delle fondazioni esistenti al 2005' (Monteverdi, 2009: 27).
2 'Nelle fondazioni è essenziale l'esistenza di un nucleo iniziale di beni destinati dal fondatore o dai fondatori al conseguimento di un determinato scopo' (Bartesaghi, 1999: 62).
3 'disporre di un rilevante patrimonio, bibliografico, archivistico, museale, cinematografico, musicale, audiovisivo pubblicamente fruibile in forma continuativa' … di svolgere e fornire servizi, di accertato e rilevante valore culturale, collegati all'attività di ricerca e al patrimonio documentario' (Demarie, 2004: 3).
4 'un contenitore più ampio e più libero rispetto al Museo, che non può e non deve allontanarsi dalla *mission* aziendale' (Ricci in Fulco, 2015).
5 'Credo che la relazione tra museo e Fondazione si chiarirà nel tempo, trattandosi di un'azienda familiare tutto avviene a piccoli passi' (Ricci in Fulco, 2015).
6 'sebbene le imprese spesso propongano svariate denominazioni come "percorso storico", "galleria", "galleria storica", "museobottega", "centro documentazione", "centro culturale", "fabbrica casa museo", l'istituzione si qualifica in ogni caso come museo' (Gilodi, 2002: 7).
7 'in letteratura non si annovera al momento una definizione condivisa [di museo d'impresa] ed è, pertanto, in corso un dibattito che porta a definire il museo d'impresa per differenza rispetto ad altre due tipologie di interventi simili posti in essere dall'impresa … :la *collezione d'impresa* … e *l'archivio d'impresa*' (Gilodi, 2002: 7; emphasis in the original).
8 'Per *collezione aziendale* s'intende un insieme di oggetti relativi all'attività e alla produzione di una o più aziende appartenenti ad uno stesso settore merceologico' (Amari, [1997] 2001: 72; emphasis in the original).

9 'Un archivio è un insieme di documenti, senza riguardo alla forma o al supporto, automaticamente e organicamente creati e/o accumulati nel corso delle attività e funzioni da un soggetto produttore' (Museimpresa, 2021).

10 'al privato (ovvero l'azienda) è fatto l'obbligo di conservare l'archivio e di sottoporre ad autorizzazione alcuni atti straordinari quali lo spostamento, il trasferimento ad altre persone giuridiche, l'alienazione, l'eliminazione e lo scarto' (Delfiol, 2012: 6).

11 'una virtuosa combinazione tra sensibilità dell'imprenditore, vigilanza delle istituzioni preposte (Soprintendenze) e ricercatori allo scopo di ottenere i risultati più fruttuosi e positivi' (Fanfani, 2012: 24).

12 'una struttura permanente che raccoglie, inventaria e conserva documenti ufficiali e originali di interesse storico prodotti da un'impresa nell'espletamento delle sue attività e funzioni, assicurandone la consultazione per finalità di studio e di ricerca' (Martino, 2013: 180).

13 'hanno dimostrato come un archivio può essere fonte di idee innovative oppure diventare un attore importante nel marketing aziendale e nei rapporti con i clienti per accrescere la conoscenza del brand e la reputazione dell'impresa' (Costa, 2012: 133).

14 'estremamente eterogenei per qualità e quantità' (Fanfani, 2012: 20–1).

15 'non solo scritti su carta, ma pure oggetti, sia materiali che digitali e soprattutto ibridi' (Robotti, 2012: 67).

16 'progetto scientifico sugli archivi (e il plurale è d'obbligo)' (Arezzi Boza, 2012: 151).

17 'La collezione, la quale rimane spesso il punto di partenza per una futura struttura museale, non è assolutamente da confondere con l'archivio, il quale per definizione raccoglie esclusivamente documenti ufficiali' (Amari, 2001: 73).

18 'materiali che possono essere testimonianza della produzione e della vita dell'impresa' (Amari, 2001: 72).

19 'espressione di gusti e tendenze artistiche personali e non rappresenta di certo l'evoluzione della società' (Amari, [1997] 2001: 72).

20 'può essere visitata da studiosi del settore e in alcuni casi venire utilizzata come supporto didattico per corsi di formazione' (Amari, 2001: 73).

21 'funzionale, estetico, storico' (Amari, 2001: 74).

22 'La costituzione e l'arricchimento dell'archivio storico è quasi sempre la base e il presupposto, nonché il nucleo iniziale, del museo d'impresa' (Kaiser, 1998: 4).

23 'è una struttura che nasce per la comunicazione culturale' (Robotti, 2012: 68).

24 'la stretta relazione che ci deve essere tra archivio e museo della stessa impresa: l'uno è la miniera di informazioni dell'altro e l'altro un potente strumento di divulgazione dell'uno … il museo d'impresa è un potente apparato di comunicazione e di fruizione e può benissimo essere utilizzato come "introduzione" all'archivio' (Robotti, 2012: 73).

25 'Capita che la decisione di progettare e allestire un museo abbia origine in seguito al successo riscosso presso l'opinione pubblica di mostre temporanee relative alle collezioni storiche dell'azienda, mostre che vengono inizialmente concepite ed organizzate come momento promozionale di una o più aziende coinvolte' (Amari, 2001: 75).
26 'Ciò su cui vorrei insistere è questo: in molti casi il grado di apertura al pubblico dei musei d'impresa è solo "quantitativamente" diverso da quello dei musei tradizionali. I musei d'impresa sono spesso archivi operativi, quotidianamente utilizzati da chi lavora nelle aziende, allocati nel cuore delle fabbriche e in spazi ristretti: tutto questo non favorisce una fruizione pubblica. È il caso del nostro museo, ed è il motivo per cui è visitabile solo su appuntamento. In Italia vi sono molti piccoli musei, il cui accesso è regolato nel modo appena ricordato, e ciò non suscita particolare stupore, come non dovrebbe meravigliare il fatto che l'accesso a un'azienda sia controllato' (Appiani, 1999: 118).
27 'Innanzitutto possiamo operare una distinzione tra museo *dell'*impresa e *nell'*impresa, e museo *generato* dall'impresa. Alla prima categoria appartiene il museo aziendale classico, realizzato da un'impresa attiva, preferibilmente all'interno di una sua sede (in genere la principale o quella storicamente più rappresentativa). Alla seconda appartengono molti altri musei la cui storia è indissolubilmente legata a una vicenda aziendale e che da questa sono stati generati' (Negri, 2003: 18).
28 'come principale vocazione quella di sviluppare la densità concettuale della moda [as exhibitions do, but the] valorizzazione della pregnanza estetica della marca' (Marchetti, 2017: 87).
29 'originati a diverso titolo da un'azienda e il cui patrimonio sia strettamente connesso all'attività *specifica* dell'impresa' (Negri, 2003: 19).
30 'emanazione di un'attività economica' (Museimpresa in Negri, 2003: 36).

4 A history of fashion curation in Italy

1 'più appariscenti che lussuosi, più solleticanti che estetici, più scenografici che signorili, più impressionanti che armonici' (Genoni, 1906: 3).
2 'collaborare nel proficuo sforzo, per vincere il misoneismo e la consuetudine di copiare servilmente il modello di Parigi; e così anche in questo ramo d'arte, l'Italia potrà in modo originale affermarsi, come è in procinto di farlo vittoriosamente in tutti gli altri campi dell'Arte Decorativa' (Genoni, 1906: 4).
3 'L'abito da ballo, è ispirato dalla Primavera del Botticelli, che si ammira nella Galleria degli Uffizi a Firenze. Cercando di conservare al vestito la freschezza e la vaporosità del modello, l'espositrice ha sostituito alle solite spumeggianti mussole una artistica festonatura di tessuto, come si ammira nel quadro stesso. Ha voluto

poi, colla massima naturalezza, riprodurre in ricamo i fiori di campo nella loro svariata gamma di disegno, nella loro inesauribile tavolozza di tinte, in parte caduti, in parte strappati, in parte sfogliati, in parte soffiati dal vento; e così attenersi simbolicamente al tema della Primavera stessa' (Genoni, 1906: 6).

4 'più fine, più ideale, più mistico, più italiano'(Genoni, 1906: 8).
5 'per nulla adatti alla nostra indole etnica e storica, alle nostre tradizioni d'arte, al nostro tipo di fisico, ed alla rinnovellata vita nazionale' (Genoni, 1908: 9).
6 'adattare questi classici modelli alle esigenze del costume moderno e del nostro tempo, conservando loro però tutta la vaga nobiltà dello stile ed il sapore del ricordo classico' (Genoni, 1908: 10).
7 Available at https://amshistorica.unibo.it/rosagenoni [Last accessed in May 2022].
8 'Genoni ha avuto un ruolo pionieristico utilizzando la storia della moda per leggere la società del suo tempo e più in generale nel tempo e anche per contribuire alla costruzione di una nuova società' (Muzzarelli, 2016: 74).
9 'sul costume, sulla moda, sull'economia e sull'arte che il Centro acquistava da tutto il mondo ... La biblioteca del CIAC diventò un rinomato punto di incontro e di studio per tutti i ricercatori interessati ad approfondire il tema del costume e della moda' (MUVE, 2021).
10 'una sintetica presentazione dei temi che il Centro Internazionale delle Arti e del Costume intende affrontare e svolgere nelle mostre degli anni venturi e vuole nel contempo dare, con una presentazione panoramica di "momenti di arte e di vita", una dimostrazione della importanza del costume nel tempo e della vastità del soggetto' (CIAC, 1951: 3).
11 For an in-depth discussion of exhibition design and the CIAC, see Collicelli Cagol (2013, 2015).
12 'un musée destiné à accueillir et à conserver les documents concernant le passé du costume' (Segati, 1952: 18).
13 'la première organisation possédant des perspectives internationals – à mon avis la seule conception correcte en matière de mode' (Langley Moore, 1952: 214).
14 'conferire all'appena costituito CIAC un ruolo centrale nelle ricerche internazionali sulla storia della moda' (Rizzini, 2016: 17).
15 'una colta autodidatta che amava studiare gli abiti ma anche collezionarli' (Muzzarelli, 2016: 75).
16 'un utile mezzo d'informazione per chi deve orientare tempestivamente il pubblico nel campo della moda, e quindi uno strumento destinato al servizio del mercato per aiutare quelle scelte decisive che trasformano la moda in costume' (Marinotti in Archivio Luce, 1969).
17 'di stabilire una base proficua per le sue esigenze di lavoro ed una fonte di informazioni precise ed aggiornate per quanti s'interessano a questi studi al più

largo settore del Costume inteso nel suo significato umano e sociale' (CIAC, 1970: 5).
18. 'storici italiani delle arti applicate, e in particolare dei tessuti, costumi e merletti [che erano stati spinti da] l'esigenza di costruire un organismo che unisse gli sforzi dei singoli in un tentativo di incidere sulla attuale situazione del patrimonio tessile italiano' (CISST, 1980: 3).
19. 'per i ruoli istituzionali che ricoprivano in musei, centri di ricerca e soprintendenze, strutture già in quel periodo sensibili al problema della conservazione del patrimonio tessile italiano, il meno considerato delle già poco studiate arti decorative' (Rizzini, 2016: 26).
20. 'il primo museo statale italiano dedicato interamente alla conservazione e allo studio della moda, abiti e accessori del costume e del tessuto' (Butazzi in Rizzini, 2016: 28).
21. 'come proposta per un museo della moda a Milano' (dell'Acqua, 1980: 9).
22. 'nella ricerca di standard e pratiche condivisibili, nella comune consapevolezza della necessità di una attiva ed efficace riflessione museale sulla moda' (Monti, 2019: 69).
23. 'Fu l'inizio ufficiale di un lungo e tormentato percorso che avrebbe coinvolto numerose persone e istituzioni pubbliche e private' (Rizzini, 2016: 30).
24. 'un grande sviluppo di studi e ricerche, tramite mostre, convegni, costituzioni di musei, progetti e pubblicazioni ormai entrati nella storia degli studi sulla moda e sul tessile in Italia' (Rizzini, 2016: 30).
25. 'un insieme di segni, ognuno dei quali aveva implicazioni e significati differenti (culturali, artistici, sociali, psicologici, psicanalitici ecc.) che potevano essere analizzati solo facendo ricorso a fonti diverse (la stampa di moda, ma anche la letteratura, i diari, i manuali di danza, i galatei, i testi monografici, e così via). Le immagini facevano parte di questa molteplicità di fonti, ma non come semplice conferma o illustrazione di quello che in altre sedi veniva documentato' (Morini, 2016: 82).
26. For a detailed account on fashion research at CSAC, refer to Fava and Soldi (2018).
27. 'furono coinvolti docenti universitari, ma anche studiosi alle prime armi di ogni parte del paese' (Rizzini, 2016: 31).
28. 'fu probabilmente l'inizio degli studi italiani sulla moda contemporanea' (Rizzini, 2016: 31).
29. 'uno spettacolo delle idee, delle invenzioni, degli oggetti che intendeva essere percepito come un evento profondamente inserito nella contemporaneità' (Monti, 2019: 70).
30. 'protagonista del progetto sono la sensibilità e lo sguardo dell'insider' (Monti, 2019: 75).
31. 'studiare e organizzare la ricchissima raccolta di documenti, fotografie, filmati e calzature del fondatore dell'azienda, Salvatore Ferragamo' (Ricci, 2016b: 47).

32 The catalogue presented texts in Italian and English, however the following extract is my translation, for the original translation misses the subtle references that are evidence of this approach.

'Con questa mostra sulla figura, ma soprattutto sull'opera, di Salvatore Ferragamo, anche il Centro Mostre di Firenze produce un'esposizione dedicata ad un argomento davvero di moda, come le recenti mostre di Milano e di Venezia, consacrate rispettivamente al costume teatrale e all'abito da sera, dimostrano: e niente sembra oggi essere più di moda, come mostra, di una mostra appunto sulla moda. Certo, Firenze ha il vantaggio di essere riuscita ad istituire per prima, tra tutte le città italiane che ne covavano da tempo il desiderio legittimo, il proprio museo della moda, cioè la prestigiosa Galleria del Costume di Palazzo Pitti: e può godere così del conforto di una struttura seria e di una équipe di specialisti preparati ed oculati. E siccome la mostra di Ferragamo è nata in collaborazione con la Galleria del Costume, essa appare, oltre che seducente per gli oggetti esposti, anche filologicamente inappuntabile, come prova del resto il catalogo davvero bellissimo che l'accompagna ... Questo "taglio", che potremo definire perfino "scientifico" (con tutto il rispetto che dobbiamo alle fisiche chimiche e matematiche) è indubbiamente favorito dal fatto che la figura di Ferragamo è ormai conclusa e consegnata per intero alla storia così che la mostra, senza abdicare alla propria contemporaneità, può essere definita una retrospettiva antologica, svincolata dunque dall'ipoteca di un presente troppo a ridosso (anche se appare utilissima quale esempio insigne proprio per il presente e addirittura per il futuro)' (Salvi, 1985: 8).

33 'la produzione e la diffusione di libri, riviste e pubblicazioni inerenti la moda (cura i cataloghi delle manifestazioni Pitti]' (CFMI, 2018).

34 'numerose occasioni di approfondimento culturale e stimoli per analizzare criticamente il suo passato, presente e futuro' (Rivetti, 1992: xi).

35 'Sono temi di grande interesse che suggeriscono spunti di riflessione sui problemi attuali' (Rivetti, 1992: xi).

36 Conversation with author, 2021.

37 Conversation with author, 2021.

38 'Che un'iniziativa del genere sia stata concepita e si tenga in Italia è tuttavia il segno che in questo paese la riflessione sulla moda va di pari passo con le affermazioni internazionali delle sue aziende e dei suoi stilisti famosi' (Rimbotti, 1996: xiv).

39 'Indagare sui rapporti tra la moda e gli altri linguaggi creativi contemporanei' (Rimbotti, 1996: xiv).

40 'nell'ottica di porre maggiore rilievo istituzionale alle attività del Gruppo legate alla contemporaneità' (Pitti Immagine, 2021).

41 Conversation with author, 2021.

42 'L'operazione di Pitti era semplice: fare pubblicità attraverso Barney e Juergen Teller, Pipilotti Rist, Susan Ciancolo, Shirin Neshat, insomma il mondo dell'arte, invece che investire in pagine pubblicitarie' (Frisa in Tozzi, 2015).
43 'di scoprire, valorizzare e rendere fruibile un ampio ventaglio di fonti, finora inesplorate, del patrimonio archivistico, bibliografico, iconografico, audiovisivo relativo alla moda italiana' (SAN, 2021).
44 'L'Associazione deve riflettere i grandi cambiamenti avvenuti nel sistema della moda … l'Associazione si propone quindi di essere efficace strumento non solo di promozione di ricerche e attività culturali' (MISA, 2013).

5 Industry and curation: A critical commentary

1 'portavoce in un ruolo molto affine a quello di Pitti Immagine' (Napoleone, 2015: 9).
2 'I soci, il consiglio direttivo nazionale, le segreterie regionali, il presidente del CISST, pur puntando soprattutto alla conoscenza dei tessili antichi, per ragioni di sopravvivenza di questi, hanno però sempre tenuto contatti di scambio reciproco anche con la produzione contemporanea di tessuti e moda e con i suoi operatori' (Mottola Molfino, 1990: 2).
3 'In futuro, con il sostegno dei nostri mecenati (tra i quali anche aziende produttrici sempre più interessate alla storia dei tessili) vorremmo quindi mettere in cantiere alcune ricerche mirate' (Mottola Molfino, 1991: 2).
4 Conversation with author, 2021.
5 'hanno offerto in questi anni agli operatori del settore (ma anche a un pubblico sempre più largo) numerose occasioni di approfondimento culturale e stimoli per analizzare criticamente il suo passato, presente e futuro' (Rivetti, 1992: xi).
6 Conversation with author, 2021.
7 Conversation with author, 2021.
8 'la moda ha un'enorme influenza sulla nostra cultura e tuttavia non viene ufficalmente riconosciuta come facente parte della *vera* cultura' (Celant, Settembrini and Sischy, 1996: xxxi).
9 'investire in cultura vuol dire dunque continuare a mantenere produttivi per la contemporaneità contenuti, modi e forme di un passato che altrimenti sarebbe destinato a perdere di valore rendendo postumo il presente' (Settembrini, 1996: 8).
10 'sia sempre delicata, rischiosa e tuttavia carica di futuro la mutazione della filosofia d'impresa da soggetto esclusivamente economico a soggetto anche culturale' (Paolucci, 2015: 9).
11 'anche tessuti che all'apparenza non hanno alcun valore artistico e che altrove non sarebbero stati considerati degni di attenzione' (Boccherini, 1999: 8).

12 'un lungo processo di ricerca scientifica e tecnologica da parte di chi doveva ottenere un prodotto concorrenziale per raggiungere il massimo effetto con il minor costo' (Boccherini, 1999: 8).
13 Conversation with author, 2021.
14 'collaborare alla conservazione della memoria produttiva tessile del distretto pratese, attraverso attività di recupero, salvaguardia e raccolta di testimonianze, consulenza alle aziende detentrici di archivi storici, svolgimento di studi e ricerche; /partecipare attivamente – per quanto di propria competenza – alle iniziative di rilancio culturale, turistico, economico e di immagine del territorio e del distretto' (Fondazione Museo del Tessuto, 2003: 2).
15 'con l'obiettivo di costruire mostre multidisciplinari in cui la moda e la vita di Ferragamo siano un tassello importante di una storia volutamente più ricca' (Ricci in Fulco, 2015).
16 'è il territorio dove confrontare discipline artistiche diverse, dove fare ricerca e riflettere, dove educare le nuove generazioni' (Ferragamo, 2015: 5).

References

Aiello, G., Donvito, R., Grazzini, L. and Petrucci, E., 2016. The Relationship between the Territory and Fashion Events: The Case of Florence and Pitti Immagine Fashion Fairs, *Journal of Global Fashion Marketing*, 7(3), pp. 150–65.

Airaghi, R., ed., 2014. *La Camicia Bianca Secondo Me. Gianfranco Ferré*. Milan: Skira.

Altaroma, 2021. *Our Mission*. Available at: https://www.altaroma.it/ [Last accessed August 2021].

Amari, M. [1997] 2001. *I musei delle aziende. La cultura della tecnica tra arte e storia*. Milan: Franco Angeli.

Amatori, F., 2004. *La memoria non mi inganna: l'Assi 1981–2004*. Available at: http://www.assi-web.it/governance/storia-assi/ [Last accessed August 2021].

Anderson, F., 2000. Museums as Fashion Media. In S. Bruzzi and P. Church Gibson, eds, *Fashion Cultures: Theories, Explorations and Analysis*. London: Routledge, pp. 371–89.

Appiani, F., 1999. Museo Alessi. In L. Kaiser, ed., *Musei d'impresa. Identità e prospettive*. Milan: Assolombarda, pp. 116–21.

Archivio Luce, 1969. *Venezia – Centro internazionale arte e costumi* [online video]. Available at: patrimonio.archivioluce.com/luce-web/detail/IL5000072111/2/venezia-centro-internazionale-arte-e-costumi.html [Last accessed August 2021].

Arezzi Boza, A., 2012. Gli archivi delle imprese di Moda: conservare e valorizzare la creatività. In R. Baglioni and F. Del Giudice, eds, *L'impresa dell'archivio. Organizzazione, gestione e conservazione dell'archivio d'impresa*. Florence: Edizioni Polistampa, pp. 145–58.

Aschengreen Piacenti, K., 1992. *La Sala Bianca. Nascita della moda italiana*. Exhibition catalogue, 25 June–25 September. Milan: Electa.

Aschengreen Piacenti, K. and Pinto, S., 1979. *Curiosità di una reggia. Vicende della guardaroba di Palazzo Pitti*. Florence: Centro Di.

Aschengreen Piacenti, K., Ricci, S. and Vergani, G., eds, 1985. *I protagonisti della moda. Salvatore Ferragamo (1898–1960)*. Florence: Centro Di.

Ashworth, G. and Larkham, P. J., eds, 1994. *Building a New Heritage: Tourism, Culture and Identity in the New Europe*. London: Routledge.

Aulenti, G., 1992. Foreword. In K. Aschengreen Piacenti. *La Sala Bianca. Nascita della Moda Italiana*. Milan: Electa, pp. 7–8.

Baglioni, R. and Del Giudice, F., eds, 2012. *L'impresa dell'archivio. Organizzazione, gestione e conservazione dell'archivio d'impresa*. Firenze: Edizioni Polistampa.

Balmer, J. M. T., 2013. Corporate Heritage, Corporate Heritage Marketing, and Total Corporate Heritage Communications. What Are They? What of Them? *Corporate Communications: An International Journal*, 18(3), pp. 290–326.

Bandera, S. and Canella, M., eds, 2017. *La Rinascente. 100 Anni 1917–2017.* Milan: Skira.

Bartesaghi, M. C., 1999. Il Museo d'Impresa: realtà e modelli giuridici. In L. Kaiser, ed., *Musei d'impresa. Identità e prospettive*. Milan: Assolombarda, pp. 59–63.

Belfanti, C. M., 2015a. History as an Intangible Asset for the Italian Fashion Business (1950–1954). *Journal of Historical Research in Marketing*, 7(1), pp. 74–90.

Belfanti, C. M., 2015b. Renaissance and 'Made in Italy': Marketing Italian Fashion through History (1949–1952). *Journal of Modern Italian Studies*, 20(1), pp. 53–66.

Belk, R. W., 1995. *Collecting in a Consumer Society*. London: Routledge.

Benedini, B., 1998. Assolombarda per la cultura. In L. Kaiser, ed., *I musei d'impresa tra comunicazione e politica culturale. La memoria nel futuro*. Milan: Assoservizi, pp. 1–2.

Berta, G., ed., 1989, *Appunti sull'evoluzione del gruppo GFT: un'analisi condotta sui fondi dell'archivio storico*. Turin: Gruppo GFT.

Bertola, P. and Linfante, V., eds, 2015. *Il Nuovo Vocabolario della Moda Italiana*. Florence: Mandragora.

Bertoli, G., Busacca, B., Ostillio, M. C. and Di Vito, S., 2016. Corporate Museums and Brand Authenticity: Explorative Research of the Gucci Museo. *Journal of Global Fashion Marketing*, 7(3), pp. 181–95.

Bianchino, G., 1984. *Sorelle Fontana*. Parma: UNIPR.

Bianchino, G., 1987. *Disegno della moda italiana 1945–1980*. Parma: UNIPR.

Bianchino, G., 1988. *Walter Albini*. Parma: UNIPR.

Bocca, N. and Buss, C., eds, 1989. *Gianni Versace. L'abito per pensare*. Milan: Mondadori.

Boccherini, T., ed., 1999. *Il Museo del Tessuto di Prato*. Milan: Skira.

Bodo, C., ed., 1994. *Rapporto sull'economia della cultura in Italia 1980–1990*. Rome: Presidenza del Consiglio dei ministri.

Bodo, R. and Monteverdi, A., eds, 2009. *Rapporto di Ricerca. Le Corporate Foundations in Italia*. Milan: Fondazione Sodalitas.

Bonami, F., Frisa, M. L. and Tonchi, S., eds, 2000. *Uniforme. Ordine E Disordine 1950–2000*. Milan: Charta.

Bondardo, A. M., 1999. Valore & Cultura: i termini di uno scambio virtuoso. In L. Kaiser, ed., *Musei d'impresa. Identità e prospettive*. Milan: Assolombarda, pp. 38–46.

Bondardo Comunicazione, 2000. *Porta lontano investire in cultura: l'opinione degli italiani sul rapporto impresa-cultura*. Milan: il Sole 24 ore.

Bonetti, F., 2005. Directed by Venice … Souvenir d'Italie. In M. L. Frisa, F. Bonami, and A. Mattirolo, eds, *Lo sguardo italiano: fotografie italiane di moda dal 1951 a oggi*. Milan: Charta, pp. 60–5.

Bonfiglio-Dosio, G. 2003. *Archivi d'impresa: studi e proposte*. Padua: CLUEP.
Bonito Fanelli, R., ed., 1975. *Il museo del tessuto a Prato. La donazione Bertini*. Florence: Centro Di.
Bonti, M., 2014. The Corporate Museums and Their Social Function: Some Evidence from Italy. *European Scientific Journal* (1), pp. 141–50.
Boucher, F., 1965. *Histoire du costume en Occident de l'Antiquité à nos jours*. Paris: Flammarion.
Bulegato, F., 2008. *I musei d'impresa: dalle arti industriali al design*. Roma: Carocci.
Buss, C., 1992. *Silk, Gold and Silver*. Milan: Fabbri Editore.
Buss, C., 1996. *Velvets*. Como: Ratti.
Buss, C., ed., 1997. *Silk and Colour*. Como: Ratti.
Buss, C., ed., 2001. *Silk: The 1900's in Como*. Cinisello Balsamo: Silvana Editoriale.
Buss, C. and Martin, R., 1998. *The Reinvention of Materials*. Milan: Leonardo Arte.
Butazzi, G., 1976. *Costumi dei secoli XVII e XIX*. Milan: Cordani.
Butazzi, G., ed., 1980. *1922–1943: Vent'anni di moda italiana. Proposta per un museo della moda a Milano*. Florence: Centro Di.
Butazzi, G., 1981. *Moda: storia, arte, società*. Milan: Gruppo Editoriale Fabbri.
Butazzi, G., 1987. Introduction. In G. Bianchino, G. Butazzi, A. Mottola Molfino and A C. Quintavalle, eds, *The Origins of High Fashion and Knitwear*. Milan: Electa, pp. 7–10.
Butazzi, G., 2008. Fashion and Costume Research and Study: The Situation in Italy. Paper presented to the *Costume Colloquium I: A tribute to Janet Arnold*, Florence, 6–9 November. Audio recording previously available at: http://www.costume-textiles.com/past-costume-colloquiums/costume-colloquium-a-tribute-to-janet-arnold/programme/ [Last accessed May 2016].
Butazzi, G. and Mottola Molfino, A., eds, 1986. *La moda italiana. Dall'antimoda allo stilismo*. Milan: Electa.
Butazzi, G., Mottola Molfino, A. and Quintavalle, A. C., eds, 1985. *La moda italiana. Le origini dell'alta moda e la maglieria*. Milan: Electa.
Butazzi, G., Mottola Molfino, A. and Soli, P., 1983. *Gianni Versace: dieci anni di creatività*. Verona: Studio la Città.
Camerana, C., 1998. La proposta di Assolombarda per i musei d'impresa. In L. Kaiser, ed., *I musei d'impresa tra comunicazione e politica culturale. La memoria nel futuro*. Milan: Assoservizi, pp. 64–8.
Caratozzolo, V. C., 2014. Reorienting Fashion: Italy's Wayfinding after World War II. In S. Stanfill, ed., *The Glamour of Italian Fashion Since 1945*. London: V&A Publishing, pp. 48–57.
Caratozzolo, V. C., Clark, J. and Frisa, M. L., 2008. *Simonetta: la prima donna della moda italiana*. Venice: Marsilio.
Carroll, A. B., 1999. Corporate Social Responsibility: Evolution of a Definitional Construct. *Business & Society*, 38(3), pp. 268–95.

Carù, A., Leone, G. and Ostillio, M. C., 2016. L'autenticità come driver strategico per il brand value. Il caso Salvatore Ferragamo. *Economia & management: la rivista della Scuola di Direzione Aziendale dell'Università L. Bocconi* (1), pp. 67–79.

Carucci, P., 2006. Alcune osservazioni sul Codice dei beni culturali. *Archivi*, 1(1), pp. 23–40.

Cavicchi, A., 2017. The Quest for a Brief Eternity. In O. Saillard, ed., *The Ephemeral Museum of Fashion*. Venice: Marsilio, p. 14.

Celant, G., and Koda, H., 2000. *Giorgio Armani*. New York: Abrams.

Celant, G., Settembrini, L. and Sischy, I., eds, 1996. *Biennale di Firenze. Il Tempo e la Moda*. Milan: Skira.

Centro per la cultura d'impresa, 2014. *Archivio economico territoriale*. Available at: http://www.culturadimpresa.org/archivio-economico-territoriale/ [Last accessed October 2017].

CFMI, 2021. *Chi Siamo*. Available at: http://www.cfmi.it/ [Last accessed April 2021].

CIAC, 1951. *Mostra del costume nel tempo … Dall'età ellenica al romanticismo*, 25 August–14 October. Venice: Palazzo Grassi.

CIAC, ed., 1952. *Actes du 1er Congrès international d'histoire du costume*, 30 August–7 September. Venice: Palazzo Grassi.

CIAC, ed., 1954. *Teatro Mito e Individuo. I Convegno-Laboratorio*, 15–17 January. Venice: Palazzo Grassi.

CIAC, ed., 1957. *Termine e Concetto di Costume. II Convegno-Laboratorio*, 27–9 September. Venice: Palazzo Grassi.

CIAC, 1970. *Guida internazionale ai musei e alle collezioni pubbliche di costumi e di tessuti*. Venice: Centro Internazionale delle Arti e del Costume.

Chiara, F., 2013. Antonio Ratti and His Textile Collection. In M. Rosina, ed., *Collecting Textiles. Patrons Collections Museums*. Turin: Allemandi & C., pp. 11–32.

Chiarelli, C., 2009. *Dal guardaroba al museo: dinamismo e metamorfosi della Galleria del Costume*. Livorno: Sillabe.

CISST, ed., 1980. *Notizie CISST*, 1(1).

CISST, ed., 1981. *Atti della conferenza 'Per un museo della moda'*, 27 March.

CISST, ed., 1983. *Aspetti e problemi degli studi sui tessili antichi: II Convegno C.I.S.S.T., Firenze 1981*. Florence: CISST.

CISST, ed., 1988. *Le tappezzerie nelle dimore storiche: studi e metodi di conservazione*. Turin: Umberto Allemandi.

CISST, ed., 1990. *Arte Tessile*, 1. Florence: Edifir.

CISST, C., ed., 1991a. *Arte Tessile*, 2. Florence: Edifir.

CISST, ed., 1991b. *Per una Storia della Moda Pronta. Problemi e Ricerche*. Florence: Edifir.

CISST, C., ed., 1992. *Arte Tessile*, 3. Florence: Edifir.

CISST, C., ed., 1993. *Arte Tessile*, 4. Florence: Edifir.

CISST, C., ed., 1994. *Arte Tessile*, 5. Florence: Edifir.

Clark, J. and de la Haye, A., 2014. *Exhibiting Fashion: Before and After 1971*. New Haven, CT: Yale University Press.

Clark, J. and Frisa, M. L., 2012. *Diana Vreeland after Diana Vreeland*. Venice: Marsilio.

Codice dei Beni Culturali e del Paesaggio, D. Lgs. 42/2004, Rome: MiBACT.

Coleman, L. V., 1943. *Company Museums*. Washington: The Association.

Colaiacomo, P. and Caratozzolo, V. C., 2010. The Impact of Traditional Indian Clothing on Italian Fashion Design from Germana Marucelli to Gianni Versace, *Fashion Theory*, 14(2), pp. 183–213.

Collicelli Cagol, S., 2013. *Towards a Genealogy of the Thematic Contemporary Art Exhibition: Italian Exhibition Culture from the Mostra della Rivoluzione Fascista (1932) to the Palazzo Grassi's Ciclo della Vitalità (1959–1961)*. PhD thesis, Royal College of Art: London.

Collicelli Cagol, S., 2015. Exhibition History and the Institution as a Medium. *Stedelijk Studies*, 2. Available at: https://stedelijkstudies.com/journal/exhibition-history-and-the-institution-as-a-medium/ [Last accessed April 2018].

Confindustria, 2010. *Manifesto della Cultura d'Impresa*. Available at: http://www.assolombarda.it/servizi/cultura-d-impresa/documenti/manifesto-della-cultura-dimpresa/view [Last accessed October 2017].

Corbellini, E. and Saviolo, S., 2004. *La scommessa del Made in Italy e il futuro della moda italiana*. Milan: Etas.

Costa, B., 2012. Comunicare e interagire con gli utilizzatori dell'Archivio: una sfida per l'archivistica d'impresa. In R. Baglioni and F. Del Giudice, eds, *L'impresa dell'archivio. Organizzazione, gestione e conservazione dell'archivio d'impresa*. Florence: Edizioni Polistampa, pp. 131–44.

Crane, D., 2012. Boundaries: Using Cultural Theory to Unravel the Complex Relationship between Fashion and Art. In A. Geczy and V. Karaminas, eds, *Fashion and Art*. London: Bloomsbury, pp. 99–110.

CSAC, 1990. *Moda media storia: incontri di lavoro*, 3–4 November. Parma: CSAC.

CSAC, 2021. *Chi Siamo*. Available at: https://www.csacparma.it/chi-siamo/ [Last accessed August 2021].

Cumming, V., 2004. *Understanding Fashion History*. London: Batsford.

Dahlsrud, A., 2008. How Corporate Social Responsibility Is Defined: An Analysis of 37 Definitions. *Corporate Social Responsibility and Environmental Management*, 15(1), pp. 1–13.

Danilov, V. J., 1991. *Corporate Museums, Galleries, and Visitor Centers: A Directory*. New York: Greenwood Press.

Danilov, V. J., 1992. *A Planning Guide for Corporate Museums, Galleries, and Visitor Centers*. New York: Greenwood Press.

de la Haye, A., 2010. Introduction: Dress and Fashion in the Context of the Museum. In J. B. Eicher, ed., *Berg Encyclopedia of World Dress and Fashion*. Oxford: Berg, pp. 285–7.

de la Haye, A., 2014. Exhibiting Fashion Before 1971. In J. Clark and A. de la Haye, eds, *Exhibiting Fashion: Before and After 1971*. New Haven, CT: Yale University Press, pp. 9–56.

Dell'Acqua, G. G., 1980. Introduzione. In G., Butazzi, ed., *Vent'anni di moda italiana. Proposta per un museo della moda a Milano*. Florence: Centro Di, p. 9.

Delfiol, R., 2012. Un quarantennio di tutela sugli archivi d'impresa: problemi e strategie. In R. Baglioni and F. Del Giudice, eds, *L'impresa dell'archivio. Organizzazione, gestione e conservazione dell'archivio d'impresa*. Florence: Edizioni Polistampa, pp. 1–18.

Desiderio, E., 2015. The Florence Center for Italian Fashion. In M. L. Frisa, ed., *Firenze Fashion Atlas*. Venice: Marsilio, pp. 13–14.

Desvallées, A. and Mairesse, F., 2010. *Dictionary of Museology*. Paris: ICOM.

Donadoni Roveri, A. M., ed., 1993. *Qibti*. Como: Ratti.

Druesedow, J., 2010. Dress and Fashion Exhibits. In J. B. Eicher, ed., *Berg Encyclopedia of World Dress and Fashion*. Oxford: Berg, pp. 304–10.

Ehle, P. and Hauser, O., 2013. History Management. In J. Messedat, ed., *Corporate Museums*. Ludwigsburg: Avedition, pp. 36–43.

Eicher, J. B., 2010. *Berg Encyclopedia of World Dress and Fashion*. Oxford: Berg.

Europeana, 2013. *Europeana Fashion*. Available at: https://www.europeana.eu/portal/en/collections/fashion [Last accessed August 2021].

Fanfani, T., 2012. Archivio storico d'impresa: un complesso percorso di affermazione. In R. Baglioni and F. Del Giudice, eds, *L'impresa dell'archivio. Organizzazione, gestione e conservazione dell'archivio d'impresa*. Firenze: Edizioni Polistampa, pp. 19–48.

Fava, E. and Soldi, M., 2018. Moda media storia. La ricerca di moda allo Csac. In M. Borgherini, A. Mengoni, A. Sacchi and A. Vaccari, eds, *Laboratorio Italia. Canoni e contraddizioni del Made in Italy*. Milan: Mimesis, pp. 174–89.

Fee, S., 2014. Before There Was Pinterest: Textile Study Rooms in North American 'Art' Museums. *Textile Society of America 2014 Biennial Symposium Proceedings: New Directions: Examining the Past, Creating the Future. 10–14 September*. Los Angeles, pp. 1–14.

Ferragamo, F., 2015. Premessa. In S. Ricci, ed., *Museo Salvatore Ferragamo. I nostri primi trent'anni*. Florence: Edifir, p. 5.

Fidolini, M., 1987. *Lucio Venna. Dal Secondo Futurismo al manifesto pubblicitario*. Casalecchio di Reno: Grafis Edizioni.

Finzi, E., 2000. Data. In Bondardo Comunicazione, ed., *Porta Lontano investire in cultura. Building Bridges. Italians' Attitudes to Business and the Arts*. Milan: Il Sole 24 ORE, pp. 91–106.

Flaccavento, A., 2015. Construction Time Again. In M. L. Frisa, ed., *Firenze Fashion Atlas*. Venice: Marsilio, pp. 134–5.

Fondazione Museo del Tessuto, 2003. *Statuto Fondazione Museo del Tessuto di Prato*. Available at: https://www.museodeltessuto.it/fondazione/amminist

razione-trasparente-2/01-disposizioni-generali/atti-generali/ [Last accessed August 2021].

Foroni, L. and Magagnino, M., 2010. *Monografie Istituzionali d'Impresa*. Verona: QuiEdit.

Foster, W. M., Coraiola, D. M., Suddaby, R., Kroezen, J. and Chandler, D., 2017. The Strategic Use of Historical Narratives: A Theoretical Framework. *Business History*, 59(8), pp. 1176–200.

FRI, 2021. *The Foundation*. Available at: https://www.fashionresearchitaly.org/en/foundation/ [Last accessed April 2021].

Frisa, M. L., 2008. The Curator's Risk. *Fashion Theory*, 12(2), pp. 171–80.

Frisa, M. L., 2011. *Italian Fashion Now*. Venice: Marsilio.

Frisa, M. L., ed., 2015. *Firenze Fashion Atlas*. Venice: Marsilio.

Frisa, M. L., Bonami, F. and Mattirolo, A., eds, 2005. *Lo sguardo italiano: fotografie italiane di moda dal 1951 a oggi*. Milan: Charta.

Frisa, M. L., Mattirolo, A. and Tonchi, S., eds, 2014. *Bellissima. L'Italia dell'alta moda, 1945–1968*. Milan: Electa.

Frisa, M. L., Monti, G. and Tonchi, S., eds, 2018. *Italiana. L'Italia vista dalla moda, 1971–2001*. Venice: Marsilio.

Fukai, A., 2010. Dress and Fashion Museums. In J. B. Eicher, ed., *Encyclopedia of World Dress and Fashion*. Oxford: Berg, pp. 288–93.

Fulco, E., 2015. A piccoli passi: il rapporto tra Museo Ferragamo e Fondazione Ferragamo. *Il Giornale delle Fondazioni* [online], 14 April. Available at: http://www.ilgiornaledellefondazioni.com/content/piccoli-passi-il-rapporto-tra-museo-ferragamo-e-fondazione-ferragamo [Last accessed August 2021].

Gabbuti, G., 2000. No Business Is an Island. In Bondardo Comunicazione, ed., *Porta Lontano investire in cultura. Building Bridges. Italians' Attitudes to Business and the Arts*. Milan: Il Sole 24 ORE, pp. 115–16.

García, L. N., 2018. Fashion: Cultural Heritage and the Made in. *ZoneModa Journal*, 8(1), pp. 63–75.

Genoni, R., 1906. *Al visitatore*. Milan: Officina tipo-litografica Augusto Campanella.

Genoni, R., 1908. *Per una moda italiana: relazione al 1. congresso nazionale delle donne italiane in Roma (sezione letteratura ed arte) della signora Rosa Genoni delegata della Società Umanitaria di Milano*. n.p.

Genoni, R., 1909. *Per una moda italiana: modelli saggi schizzi di abbigliamento femminile: 1906–1909*. Milan: Alfieri & Lacroix.

Genoni, R., 1918. *Storia del costume femminile: brevi cenni illustrativi della serie di diapositive*. Roma: Istituto Minerva.

Genoni, R., 1925. *La storia della moda attraverso i secoli: (dalla preistoria ai tempi odierni)*. Bergamo: Istituto Italiano d'Arti Grafiche.

Ghersetti, F. and Gamba, G., 2017. The Benetton Archive: Problems and Solutions Integrating Databases and Archives. In F. Pino, ed., *Creating the Best Business Archive. Achieving a Good Return on Investment*. Milan: Hoepli, pp. 117–25.

Gilodi, C., 2002. *Il museo d'impresa: forma esclusiva per il corporate marketing.* Castellanza: Liuc Papers.

Giumelli, E., 2016. The Meaning of the Made in Italy Changes in a Changing World. *Italian Sociological Review*, 6(2), pp. 241–63.

Google, 2017. *We Wear Culture.* Available at: https://artsandculture.google.com/project/fashion [Last accessed April 2022].

Goria, C. and Merlotti, A., eds, 2011. *Moda in Italia. 150 anni di eleganza.* Milan: Condé Nast.

Gorman, L., 1989. Corporate Culture. *Management Decision*, 27(1), pp. 14–19.

Griffiths, J., 1999. In Good Company? Do Company Museums Serve the Company, Its Marketing Department, Its Employees or the Public? *Museum News*, 10, p. 35–8.

Guarini, F., 2013. Which Role for a Textile Museum in a Contemporary Textile Manufacturing District? The Example of Prato. In M. Rosina, ed., *Collecting Textiles. Patrons Collections Museums.* Turin: Allemandi & C., pp. 123–38.

Hesmondhalgh, D. and Pratt, A. C., 2005. Cultural Industries and Cultural Policy. *International Journal of Cultural Policy,* 11(1), pp. 1–13.

Hollenbeck, C. R., Peters, C. and Zinkhan, G. M., 2008. Retail Spectacles and Brand Meaning: Insights from a Brand Museum Case Study. *Journal of Retailing*, 84(3), pp. 334–53.

Horsley, J., 2014. An Incomplete Inventory of Fashion Exhibitions Since 1971. In J. Clark and A. de la Haye, eds, *Exhibiting Fashion Before and After 1971.* New Haven, CT: Yale University Press, pp. 169–245.

Iannone, F., 2016. Quando il museo comunica l'impresa: identità organizzativa e sensemaking nel museo Salvatore Ferragamo. *IL CAPITALE CULTURALE. Studies on the Value of Cultural Heritage* (13), pp. 525–53.

ICA, 2022. *What Are Archives?* Available at: https://www.ica.org/en/what-archive [Last accessed May 2022].

ICOM, 2007. *Museum Definition.* Available at: https://icom.museum/en/activities/standards-guidelines/museum-definition/ [Last accessed August 2021].

Impresa Cultura, 2001. *Guggenheim Impresa & Cultura Prize, Fifth Edition.* Available at: http://www.impresacultura.it/premioguggenheim/english/pg_Vediz.html [Last accessed August 2021].

Jackson Jowers, S., 2013. *Theatrical Costume, Make-Up and Wigs: A Bibliography and Iconography.* London: Routledge.

Kaiser, L., ed., 1998. *I musei d'impresa tra comunicazione e politica culturale. La memoria nel futuro.* Milan: Assoservizi.

Kaiser, L., ed., 1999. *Musei d'impresa. Identità e prospettive.* Milan: Assolombarda.

Kaiser, L., ed., 2000. *Musei d'impresa in Europa. Modelli e prospettive.* Milan: Assolombarda.

Kapferer, J. N., 2014. The Artification of Luxury: From Artisans to Artists. *Business Horizons*, 57(3), pp. 371–80.

Kottasz, R., Bennett, R., Savani, S. and Ali-Choudhury, R., 2008. The Role of Corporate Art in the Management of Corporate Identity. *Corporate Communications: An International Journal*, 13(3), pp. 235–54.

Kozinets, R. V., Sherry, J. F., DeBerry-Spence, B., Duhachek, A., Nuttavuthisit, K. and Storm, D., 2002. Themed Flagship Brand Stores in the New Millennium: Theory, Practice, Prospects. *Journal of Retailing*, 78(1), pp. 17–29.

Kurkdjian, S., 2020. Paris as the Capital of Fashion, 1858–1939: An Inquiry. *Fashion Theory*, 24(3), pp. 371–91.

Langley-Moore, D., 1952. *Constitution d'un musée du Costume*. In CIAC, ed., *Actes du 1er Congrès international d'histoire du costume*, 30 August–7 September. Venice: Palazzo Grassi, pp. 214–23.

Laurenzi, L., 1985. Con le pellicce dei sogni Roma celebra il gran lusso. *La Repubblica*, 6 October. Available at: https://ricerca.repubblica.it/repubblica/archivio/repubblica/1985/10/06/con-le-pellicce-dei-sogni-roma-celebra.html [Last accessed August 2021].

Laver, J., 1952. *Séanche D'ouverture*. In CIAC, ed., *Actes du 1er Congrès international d'histoire du costume*, 30 August–7 September. Venice: Palazzo Grassi, p. 19.

Laver, J. and de la Haye, A., 1995. *Costume and Fashion: A Concise History*. London: Thames and Hudson.

Lazzeretti, L. and Oliva, S., 2020. Exploring the Marriage between Fashion and 'Made in Italy' and the Key Role of G. B. Giorgini. *European Planning Studies*, pp. 1–20.

Legge n.534, 1996. Nuove norme per l'erogazione di contribute statali alle istituzioni culturali. *Gazzetta Ufficiale*, 248, 22 October.

Lehman, K. F. and Byrom, J. W., 2007. Corporate Museums in Japan: Institutionalizing a Culture of Industry and Technology. *9th International Conference on Arts & Cultural Management* [online] Valencia, 8–11 July 2007. Available at: http://eprints.utas.edu.au/8528/2/AIMAC_paper_Lehman_and_Byrom.pdf [Last accessed August 2021].

Levi-Pisetzky, R., 1964–8. *Storia del Costume in Italia*. Milan: Treccani.

Levi-Pisetzky, R., 1973. *Moda e costume*. Turin: Einaudi.

Levi-Pisetzky, R., 1978. *Il costume e la moda nella società italiana*. Turin: Einaudi.

Levi-Pisetzky, R. and Butazzi, G., 1995. *Il costume e la moda nella società italiana*. Turin: Einaudi.

Lévi-Strauss, M., 1995. *Cachemire*. Ratti: Como.

Liggeri, D., 2015. *La comunicazione di musei e archivi d'impresa*. Bergamo: Lubrina-LEB.

Livingstone, P., 2011. Is It a Museum Experience? Corporate Exhibitions for Cultural Tourists. *Exhibitionist*, 1, pp. 16–21.

Loscialpo, F., 2016. From the Physical to the Digital and Back: Fashion Exhibitions in the Digital Age. *International Journal of Fashion Studies*, 3(2), pp. 225–48.

Maddaluno, P., 2015. Inscrivere la moda nel design: Alessandro Mendini e Domus Moda 1981–85. *A/I/S/Design. Storie e ricerche*, 5. Available at: http://

www.aisdesign.org/aisd/inscrivere-la-moda-nel-design-alessandro-mendini-e-domus-moda-1981-85 [Last accessed August 2021].

Malossi, G. ed., 1992. *The Sala Bianca. The Birth of Italian Fashion*. Milan: Electa

Malossi, G., ed., 1993. *La regola estrosa: cent'anni di eleganza maschile italiana*. Milan: Electa.

Malossi, G., ed., 1998. *The Style Engine: Spectacle, Identity, Design, and Business: How the Fashion Industry Uses Style to Create Wealth*. Florence: Monacelli Press.

Malossi, G., ed., 1999. *Volare: The Icon of Italy in Global Pop Culture*. New York: Monacelli Press.

Malossi, G., ed., 2000. *Material Man: Masculinity, Sexuality, Style*. New York: H. N. Abrams.

Mannucci, E., 2015. 5 ragazze possono bastare a rivoluzionare la moda. *La Repubblica*, 14 May. Available at: https://www.corriere.it/14_maggio_15/roma-5-ragazze-posson-bastare-rivoluzionare-moda-76583c18-dc4d-11e3-8893-5231acf0035c.shtml [Last accessed August 2021].

Marchetti, L., 2017. Il curating della moda nella cultura del consumo: lo spazio della marca. In L. Marchetti and S. Segre Reinach, *Exhibit! La moda esposta: lo spazio della mostra e lo spazio della marca*. Milan: Bruno Mondadori, pp. 84–104.

Marenzi, C., 2017. A Necessary Noncurrentness. In O. Saillard, ed., *The Ephemeral Museum of Fashion*. Venice: Marsilio, p. 17.

Martino, V., 2010. *La comunicazione culturale d'impresa*. Milano: Guerini.

Martino, V., 2013. *Dalle storie alla storia d'impresa*. Acireale-Roma: Bonanno.

Masè, S. and Cedrola, E., 2017, Louis Vuitton's Art-Based Strategy to Communicate Exclusivity and Prestige. In B. Jin and E. Cedrola, eds, *Fashion Branding and Communication. Core Strategies of European Luxury Brands*. New York: Pelgrave Pivot, pp. 155–84.

Mason, L., 2005. Exhibition Review: The Art and Craft of Gianni Versace. *Fashion Theory*, 9(1), pp. 85–8.

Massi, M. and Turrini, A., eds, 2020. *The Artification of Luxury Fashion Brands: Synergies, Contaminations, and Hybridizations*. Cham: Palgrave Pivot.

Mazzotta, S., 2018. Le fondazioni culturali delle corporate del lusso. Collezioni d'arte aziendali, mecenatismo e sponsorizzazione. *ZoneModa Journal*, 8(1), pp. 43–61.

McNeil, P., 2008. 'We're Not in the Fashion Business': Fashion in the Museum and the Academy. *Fashion Theory*, 12(1), pp. 65–81.

Melandri, G., 2000. Business, Culture and Institutions. In Bondardo Comunicazione, ed., *Porta Lontano investire in cultura. Building Bridges. Italians' Attitudes to Business and the Arts*. Milano: Il Sole 24 ORE, pp. 117–20.

Mendini, A., 1981. Musei della moda? Considerazioni teoriche a proposito di un museo della moda per Milano. *Domus Moda*, supplement *Domus*, 621, p. 1.

Merlo, E. and Perugini, M., 2020. The Determinants of the Emergence of Turin as the First Capital of Italian Fashion Industry (1900–1960). *Fashion Theory*, 24(3), pp. 325–48.

Messedat, J., ed., 2013. *Corporate Museums: Concepts, Ideas, Realisation*. Ludwigsburg: Avedition.

MiBACT, 2011. *Portale Archivi d'Impresa*. Available at: http://www.imprese.san.beniculturali.it/web/imprese/home;jsessionid=9CA884E35AF910CB57D34E240EB73822.sanimprese_JBOSS [Last accessed August 2021].

MISA, 2013. *Associazione Italiana degli Studi di Moda*. Website expired. Formerly Available at: www.misa.it [Last accessed September 2016].

Miller, T., 2010. Cultural Policy. In M. Ryan, ed., *The Encyclopedia of Literary and Cultural Theory*. Available at: https://onlinelibrary.wiley.com/doi/10.1002/9781444337839.wbelctv3c014 [Last accessed August 2021].

Mondadori, L., ed., 1998. *Fashion/Cinema. Biennale di Firenze 1998*. Milan: Electa.

Montella, M., and Dragoni, P., eds, 2010. *Musei e valorizzazione dei Beni culturali. Atti della Commissione per la definizione dei livelli minimi di qualità delle attività di valorizzazione*. Bologna: CLUEB.

Montemaggi, M. and Severino, F., 2007. *Heritage marketing. La storia dell'impresa italiana come vantaggio competitivo*. Milan: FrancoAngeli.

Monteverdi, A., 2009. Le fondazioni d'impresa nella relazione Istat sulle fondazioni: una panoramica. In R. Bodo, and A. Monteverdi, eds, *Rapporto di Ricerca. Le Corporate Foundations in Italia*. Milan: Fondazione Sodalitas, pp. 27–33.

Monti, G., 2019. Moda, curatela, museo: un dibattito lungo un decennio, un decennio lungo quarant'anni. *ZoneModa Journal*, 9(1), pp. 61–89.

Morel, C., 2005. Will Businesses Ever Become Legitimate Partners in the Financing of the Arts in France? *International Journal of Cultural Policy*, 11(2), pp. 199–213.

Morelli, O., 1987. The International Success and Domestic Debut of Postwar Italian Fashion. In G. Bianchino, G. Butazzi, A. Mottola Molfino, A. C. Quintavalle, eds, *The Origins of High Fashion and Knitwear*. Milan: Electa, pp. 11–57.

Morini, E., 2016. La moda raccontata attraverso le immagini. Una lezione di metodo. In E. Morini, M. Rizzini and M. Rosina, eds, *Moda Arte Storia Società. Omaggio a Grazietta Butazzi*. Como: Nodo Libri, pp. 77–84.

Morini, E., 2020. *Interazioni fra moda e arte. Boldini, Poiret, Genoni*. Milan: Mimesis Edizioni.

Morini, E. and Rosina, M., 2005. *La moda come passione e come professione. La donazione Bernasconi*. Cinisello Balsamo: Silvana Editoriale.

Morini, E., Rizzini, M. and Rosina, M., eds, 2016. *Moda Arte Storia Società. Omaggio a Grazietta Butazzi*. Como: Nodo Libri.

Mottola, Molfino, A., 1990. I fili di un discorso. *Arte Tessile*, 1, pp. 2–3.

Mottola, Molfino, A., 1991. Dal filo alla trama. *Arte Tessile*, 2, pp. 2–3.

Museimpresa, 2017. *Accordo di collaborazione tra Museimpresa e MiBACT*. Available at: https://www.museimpresa.com/firma-dellaccordo-di-collaborazione-tra-museimpresa-e-mibact/ [Last accessed August 2021].

Museimpresa, 2021. *Museimpresa*. Available at: https://www.museimpresa.com/museimpresa/ [Last accessed August 2021].

Museo del Tessuto, 2007. *Thirty Years of Donations*. Prato: Museo del Tessuto Edizioni.

Museo del Tessuto, ed., 2013. *Vintage, l'irresistibile fascino del vissuto*. Cinisello Balsamo: Silvana Editoriale.

MUVE, 2021. *Biblioteca del Centro Studi di Storia del Tessuto e del Costume di Palazzo Mocenigo*. Available at: http://mocenigo.visitmuve.it/it/il-museo/servizi-agli-studi osi/biblioteca/ [Last accessed April 2021].

Muzzarelli, M. G., 2016. Ancora su moda, arte, storia e società. In E. Morini, M. Rizzini and M. Rosina, eds, *Moda Arte Storia Società. Omaggio a Grazietta Butazzi*. Como: Nodo Libri, pp. 71–6.

Napoleone, R., 1999. Foreword. In G. Malossi, ed., *Volare: The Icon of Italy in Global Pop Culture*. Florence: Monacelli Press, p. 23.

Napoleone, R., 2015. Foreword. In P. Bertola and V. Linfante, eds, *Il Nuovo Vocabolario della Moda Italiana*, Florence: Mandragora, p. 9.

Negri M., 2003. *Manuale di museologia per i musei aziendali*. Soveria Mannelli: Rubbettino Editore.

Nissley, N. and Casey, A., 2002. The Politics of the Exhibition: Viewing Corporate Museums through the Paradigmatic Lens of Organizational Memory. *British Journal of Management*, 13, pp. S36–S45.

Ogbonna, E. and Harris, L. C., 1998. Organizational Culture: It's Not What You Think. *Journal of General Management*, 23(3), pp. 35–48.

OMA, 2018. *New York Prada Epicenter*. Available at: http://oma.eu/projects/prada-epicenter-new-york [Last accessed July 2018].

OMI, 2018. *Osservatorio Monografie D'Impresa*. Available at: http://www.monografie impresa.it/ [Last accessed July 2018].

Ortoleva, P., 1999. Buying Italian: Fashion, Identities, Stereotypes. In G. Malossi, ed., *Volare: The Icon of Italy in Global Pop Culture*. Florence: Monacelli Press, pp. 46–54.

Palais Galliera, ed., 1986. *Gianni Versace: Dialogues de Mode: Des Photographes Autour D'une Création*. Milan: Electa.

Paletta, G., 2009. Fondazioni d'Impresa: lo stato dell'arte. In T. Fanfani, ed., *Cultura d'impresa, creatività, arte*. Quaderni della Fondazione Piaggio, 13(1,2), pp. 43–56.

Palmer, A., 2008. Untouchable: Creating Desire and Knowledge in Museum Costume and Textile Exhibitions. *Fashion Theory*, 12(1), pp. 31–63.

Paolucci, A., 2015. Introduzione. In S. Ricci, ed., *Museo Salvatore Ferragamo. I nostri primi trent'anni*. Florence: Edifir, pp. 7–11.

Paulicelli, E., 2004. *Fashion Under Fascism. Beyond the Black Shirt*. London: Berg.

Paulicelli, E., 2014. Fashion: The Cultural Economy of *Made in Italy*. *Fashion Practice*, 6(2), pp. 155–74.

Paulicelli, E., 2015a. *La moda è un cosa seria. Milano Expo 1906 e La Grande Guerra*. Milan: Deleyva Editore.

Paulicelli, E., 2015b. Italian Fashion: Yesterday, Today and Tomorrow. *Journal of Modern Italian Studies*, 20(1), pp. 1–9.

Paulicelli, E., 2016. *Writing Fashion in Early Modern Italy: From Sprezzatura to Satire*. London: Routledge.

Pearce, S., 1992. *Museums, Objects and Collections: A Cultural Study*. Leicester: Leicester University Press.

Peter-Muller, I., 1994. *Cravates: Women's Accessories in the 19th Century*. Como: Ratti.

Petrov, J., 2019. *Fashion, History, Museums: Inventing the Display of Dress*. London: Bloomsbury Visual Arts.

Phillips, M. and Woodham, A., 2009. Museums, Schools and Geographies of Cultural Value. *Cultural Trends*, 18 (2), pp. 149–83.

Piatkowska, K., 2014. The Corporate Museum: A New Type of Museum Created as a Component of Marketing Company. *The International Journal of The Inclusive Museum*, 6(2), pp. 29–37.

Pinchera, V. and Rinallo, D., 2017. The Emergence of Italy as a Fashion Country: Nation Branding and Collective Meaning Creation at Florence's Fashion Shows (1951–1965). *Business History*, 62(1), pp. 151–78.

Pino, F., ed., 2017. *Creating the Best Business Archive. Achieving a Good Return on Investment*. Milan: Hoepli.

Pitti Immagine, 2021. *Fondazione Pitti Discovery*. Available at: http://www.pittimmagine.com/en/corporate/fondazione-pitti-discovery.html [Last accessed April 2021].

PleaseDisturbNow, 2013. *Allestimenti temporanei. Pitti Immagine e la Stazione Leopolda.* https://creativefashiondesignart.wordpress.com/2013/10/24/allestimenti-contemporanei-pitti-immagine-e-stazione-leopolda/ [Last accessed August 2021].

pptArt, n.d. *About pptArt*. Available at: https://www.pptart.net/about-pptart [Last accessed August 2021].

Prele, C., 2008. *La Fondazione. Evoluzione Giuridica di un Istituto alla Ribalta*. Turin: Fondazione Giovanni Agnelli.

Protezione delle cose di interesse artistico e storico. D. Lgs. 1089/1939. Rome: Ministero dei Beni Culturali.

Quintavalle, A. C., 1987. Fashion: The Three Cultures. In G. Bianchino, G. Butazzi, A. Mottola Molfino and A. C. Quintavalle, eds, *The Origins of High Fashion and Knitwear*. Milan: Electa, pp. 11–57.

Rentschler, R., 2002. *The Entrepreneurial Arts Leader: Cultural Policy, Change and Reinvention*. Brisbane: University of Queensland Press.

Ricci, S., ed., 1995. *Palazzo Spini Feroni e il suo museo*. Milan: Mondadori.

Ricci, S., ed., 2008. *Salvatore Ferragamo. Evolving Legend 1928–2008*. Milan: Skira.

Ricci, S., ed., 2015a. *Museo Salvatore Ferragamo. I nostri primi trent'anni*. Florence: Edifir.

Ricci, S., ed., 2016a. *Tra Arte e Moda*. Florence: Mandragora.

Ricci, S., 2016b. Grazietta Butazzi e Salvatore Ferragamo. In E. Morini, M. Rizzini and M. Rosina, eds, *Moda Arte Storia Società. Omaggio a Grazietta Butazzi*. Como: Nodo Libri, pp. 47–50.

Ricci, S., ed., 2018. *L'Italia a Hollywood*. Milan: Skira.

Ricci, S. and Spinelli, R., eds, 2015. *A Palace and the City*. Milan: Skira.

Ricci, Stefano, 2015. Introduzione. In M. L. Frisa, ed., 2015. *Firenze Fashion Atlas*. Venice: Marsilio, pp. 9–10.

Riegels Melchior, M. and Svensson, B., 2014. *Fashion and Museums. Theory and Practice*. London: Bloomsbury Academic.

Rimbotti, V., 1996. Prefazione. In G. Celant, L. Settembrini and I. Sischy, eds, *Biennale di Firenze. Il Tempo e la Moda*. Milan: Skira, p. xvi.

Rivetti, M., 1991. Prefazione. In CISST, ed. *Per una Storia della Moda Pronta. Problemi e Ricerche*. Firenze: EDIFIR, p. xi.

Rizzini, M., 2016. Grazietta Butazzi. Le origini di un metodo. In E. Morini, M. Rizzini and M. Rosina, eds, *Moda Arte Storia Società. Omaggio a Grazietta Butazzi*. Como: Nodo Libri, pp. 13–32.

Robotti, D., 2012. L'archivio del prodotto come 'cuore' dell'archivio d'impresa. In R. Baglioni e and F. Del Giudice, eds, *L'impresa dell'archivio. Organizzazione, gestione e conservazione dell'archivio d'impresa*. Florence: Edizioni Polistampa, pp. 67–76.

Rocamora, A., 2006. *Fashioning the City: Paris, Fashion and the Media*. London: I. B. Tauris.

Romani, G., 2015. Fashioning the Italian Nation: Risorgimento and its *costume all'italiana*. *Journal of Modern Italian Studies*, 20(1), pp. 10–23.

Rosina, M., ed., 2013. *Collecting Textiles. Patrons Collections Museums*. Turin: Allemandi & C.

Rosina, M. and Chiara, F., eds, 2014. *Emilio Pucci e Como 1950–1980*. Como: NodoLibri.

Rurale, A. and Prestini, S., 2020. Trussardi Art and Fashion: A Long-Distance Relationship? In M. Massi and A. Turrini, eds, *The Artification of Luxury Fashion Brands: Synergies, Contaminations, and Hybridizations*. Cham: Palgrave Pivot, pp. 63–87.

Ryan, N., 2007. Prada and the Art of Patronage. *Fashion Theory*, 11(1), pp. 7–24.

Saillard, O., ed., 2017. *The Ephemeral Museum of Fashion*. Venice: Marsilio.

Saint Laurent, Y. and Vreeland, D., eds, 1983. *Yves Saint Laurent*. London: Thames and Hudson.

Salvi, S., 1985. Il calzolaio prodigioso. In K. Aschengreen Piacenti, S. Ricci and G. Vergani, eds, *I protagonisti della moda. Salvatore Ferragamo(1898–1960)*. Florence: Centro Di, p. 8.

SAN, 2010. *Pitti, non solo immagine*. Available at: http://www.moda.san.beniculturali.it/wordpress/?percorsi=1988-nasce-pitti-immagine [Last accessed April 2021].

Sapelli, G., 1998. Il ruolo della formazione nella tutela e nella valorizzazione del patrimonio d'impresa. In L. Kaiser, ed., *I musei d'impresa tra comunicazione e politica culturale. La memoria nel futuro*. Milan: Assoservizi, pp. 48–50.

Scarpellini, E., 2019. *Italian Fashion since 1945: a Cultural History*. Cham: Palgrave Macmillan.

Schnapp, J. T., 1997. The Fabric of Modern Times. *Critical Inquiry*, 24(1), pp. 191–245.

Schuster, J. M., 2003. *Mapping State Cultural Policy: The State of Washington*. Chicago, IL: University of Chicago Press.

Segati, G., 1952. *Séanche D'ouverture*. In CIAC, ed., *Actes du 1er Congrès international d'histoire du costume*, 30 August–7 September. Venice: Palazzo Grassi, p. 18.

Segre Reinach, S., 2010. If You Speak Fashion You Speak Italian: Notes on Present Day Italian Fashion Identity. *Critical Studies in Fashion & Beauty*, 1(2), pp. 203–15.

Segre Reinach, S., 2011. National Identities and International Recognition. *Fashion Theory*, 15(2), pp. 267–72.

Segre Reinach, S., 2014. The Italian Fashion Revolution in Milan. In S. Stanfill, ed., *The Glamour of Italian Fashion Since 1945*. London: V&A Publishing, pp. 58–73.

Segre Reinach, S., 2017. Fashion Museums and Fashion Exhibitions in Italy: New Perspectives in Italian Fashion Studies. In A. Vänskä and H. Clark, eds, *Fashion Curating: Critical Practice in the Museum and Beyond*. London: Bloomsbury Academic, pp. 171–8.

Settembrini, L., 1996. La Biennale di Firenze. Un progetto culturale sulla contemporaneità. In G. Celant, L. Settembrini and I. Sischy, eds, *Biennale di Firenze. Il Tempo e la Moda*. Milan: Skira, pp. 5–12.

Shapiro, R. and Heinich, N., 2012. When Is Artification? *Contemporary Aesthetics (Journal Archive)*, 0 (4): article 9.

Silverman, D., 1986. *Selling Culture: Bloomingdale's, Diana Vreeland, and the New Aristocracy of Taste in Reagan's America*. New York: Pantheon Books.

Sisi, C. and Ricci, S., eds, 2017. *1927. Il ritorno in Italia. Salvatore Ferragamo e la cultura visiva del Novecento*. Milan: Skira.

Soldi, M., 2018. Una fonte per la storia della moda italiana: l'Archivio Rosa Genoni. *ZoneModa Journal*, 8(1), pp. 17–26.

Soli, P., ed., 1984. *Il genio antipatico. Creatività e tecnologia della moda Italiana 1951–1983*. Milan: Mondadori.

Stanfill, S., ed., 2014. *The Glamour of Italian Fashion Since 1945*. London: V&A.

Steele, V., ed., 2003. *Fashion, Italian Style*. New Haven, CT: Yale University Press.

Steele, V., 2008. Museum Quality: The Rise of the Fashion Exhibition. *Fashion Theory*, 12(1), pp. 7–30.

Steele, V., 2017. *Paris Fashion: A Cultural History*. London: Bloomsbury.

Steele, V., ed., 2019. *Paris: Capital of Fashion*. London: Bloomsbury Visual Arts.

Sterlacci, F. and Arbuckle, J., 2017. *Historical Dictionary of the Fashion Industry*. Lanham: Rowman & Littlefield.

Stevenson, N. J., 2008. The Fashion Retrospective. *Fashion Theory*, 12(2), pp. 219–35.

Stigliani, I. and Ravasi, D., 2007. Organizational Artifacts and the Expression of Identity in Corporate Museums at Alfa Romeo, Kartell and Piaggio. In L.Lerpold, ed., *Organizational Identity in Practice*. London: Routledge, pp. 197–215.

Swann, J., 1977. Proposed Scheme for Cataloguing Shoes. *Costume*, 11(1), pp. 34–7.

Taylor, L., 2002. *The Study of Dress History*. Manchester: Manchester University Press.

Taylor, L., 2004. *Establishing Dress History*. Manchester: Manchester University Press.

Taylor, M., 2005. Culture Transition: Fashion's Cultural Dialogue between Commerce and Art. *Fashion Theory*, 9(4), pp. 445–59.

Thompson, E., 2010. Museum Collections of Dress and Fashion. In J. B. Eicher, ed., *Berg Encyclopedia of World Dress and Fashion*. Oxford: Berg, pp. 295–303.

Touring Club Italiano, 2008. *Dossier Musei 2008*. Available at: http://www.ontit.it/opencms/export/sites/default/ont/it/documenti/archivio/files/ONT_2008-05-01_00487.pdf [Last accessed October 2017].

Tozzi, L., 2015. Interview with Maria Luisa Frisa. *Zero Magazine*, 8 December. Available at: https://zero.eu/persone/intervista-a-maria-luisa-frisa/?lang=en [Last accessed April 2018].

Treccani, 1953–62. *Storia di Milano*. Milan: Treccani.

Trezzini, L., 1994. Il quadro di riferimento dello spettacolo dal vivo. In C. Bodo, ed., *Rapporto sull'economia della cultura in Italia 1980–1990*. Rome: Presidenza del Consiglio dei ministri, pp. 367–83.

Trubert-Tollu, C., Tétart-Vittu, F., Martin-Hattemberg, J. M. and Olivieri F., 2017. *The House of Worth, 1858–1954: The Birth of Haute Couture*. London: Thames & Hudson.

UNESCO, 2021. *Cultural policy*. Available at: http://www.unesco.org/new/en/moscow/culture/cultural-policy/ [Last accessed August 2021].

Università Bocconi, 2003. *Impresa e cultura a Milano. Ricerca Assolombarda. Il ruolo delle imprese per sostenere imprenditorialità, qualità e fruizione nella cultura e nello spettacolo a Milano*. Milan: Università Bocconi.

Urde, M., Greyser, S. A. and Balmer, J. M., 2007. Corporate Brands with a Heritage. *Journal of Brand Management*, 15(1), pp. 4–19.

Vänskä, A. and Clark, H. eds, 2017. *Fashion Curating: Critical Practice in the Museum and Beyond*. London: Bloomsbury Academic.

Viti, P. 1998. L'impresa come soggetto culturale: l'esperienza di Palazzo Grassi. In L. Kaiser, ed., *I musei d'impresa tra comunicazione e politica culturale. La memoria nel futuro*. Milan: Assoservizi, pp. 38–41.

Warnecke, J.-C., 2013. Museum … is forever – Transferring the 'Museum' Format to the Corporate Sphere. In J. Messedat, ed., *Corporate Museums*. Ludwigsburg: Avedition, pp. 26–35.

White, N., 2000. *Reconstructing Italian Fashion: America and the Development of the Italian Fashion Industry*. Oxford: Berg.

Wilcox, C., Mendes, V. and Buss, C., 2002. *The Art and Craft of Gianni Versace*. London: V&A.

Wilson, E., 1985. *Adorned in Dreams: Fashion and Modernity*. London: Virago Press.

Wu, C. T., 2003. *Privatising Culture: Corporate Art Intervention Since the 1980s*. London: Verso.

Xu, X., 2017. *Corporate Museums. From Industry Identity to Exhibition Communication.* Florence: Altralinea Edizioni.
Yarwood, D., 1978. *Illustrated Encyclopedia of World Costume.* New York: Dover.
Zambiasi, M. 1996. *1996 Biennal Art and Fashion Firenze* [online video]. Available at: https://youtu.be/nxkyRE93s6o [Last accessed August 2021].

Index

Note: Page numbers in *italic* indicate figures.

Alberici, Clelia 89, 94, 95
Albini, Walter 97
Alessi 66
Altaroma, Rome 122
Amari, Monica 56, 60–1
Amatori, Franco 45
Anderson, Fiona 52–3
Ansaldo 44
Appel, Karel 87
Appiani, Francesca 46–7, 63
archives *see* corporate archives
Archivi della Moda del Novecento (portal) 124
Arezzi Boza, Alessandra 47, 59, 121, 126
Armani, Giorgio 23, 65, 76, 89–90, 110–11, 113, 151
Arnold, Janet 93, 103, 121
Arte Tessile (CISST) 103, 134, 135
artification 21–4, 54, 160
artificial fibres 79–80, 82, 85–6
Aschengreen Piacenti, Kirsten 19, 25, 92, 99, 100
Associazione di storia e di studi d'impresa (ASSI) 44–5, 47
Associazione Italiana degli Studi di Moda (MISA), Venice 127–8
Assolombarda 31, 38, 39, 42, 45–7, 62–3
Aulenti, Gae 25–6, *105*
authenticity 12, 13, 15, 16, 18, 21, 160
Avedon, Richard 116

Balmer, John 5
Bartesaghi, Maria Cleme 54
Beaton, Cecil 1, 68
Beecroft, Vanessa 67
Belfanti, Carlo Marco 11, 13, 21, 26
Belk, Russell W. 60–1, 65, 67, 70, 72
Benedini, Benito 45
Benetton Archive 56–7

Berg Encyclopedia of World Dress and Fashion 6, 7–8, 53, 75
Bernasconi, Silvana 90
Bertelli, Carlo 94
Bertini, Loriano 151
Bertola, Paola 122, 132
Bianchino, Gloria 97
Biennale di Firenze, Florence 23, 76, 106–10, *109*, 111, 133, 138–9
Binaghi Olivari, Maria Teresa 89, 92
Blahnik, Manolo 23
Blum, Stella 95
Bocca, Nicoletta 116
Boccherini, Tamara 147
Bocconi University, Milan 32, 42, 45
Bonami, Francesco 113, 115, 138, 140
Bondardo Comunicazione 39, 40, 42
Bondardo, Michela 39–40
Bonisoli, Alberto 128
Bonti, Maria Cristina 31, 64
Bossaglia, Rossana 97
Botticelli, Sandro, *La Primavera* 12–13, 77–8
Boucher, François 84
brand equity 37, 60, 69
brand heritage, definition 5
brand museums 68
brand retail spaces 66–9
Brin, Irene 15
Brooklyn Museum, New York 16
Bulegato, Fiorella 56
Bulgari 122
business archives *see* corporate archives
Business School, Libera Università Internazionale degli Studi Sociali (LUISS), Rome 35
Buss, Chiara 92, 102, 111–12, 116–17, 144–5
Butazzi, Grazietta
  cataloguing work 89, 101

conference on 8, 75–6, 97, 135
exhibitions curated 94, 98
on Galleria del Costume at Palazzo Pitti 92
legacy 97–8, 135
organiser of conferences 19, 95, 103, 121, 134
publications 84, 85, 87–8, 96, 97
Byrde, Penelope 95

Calefato, Patrizia 127
Calvino, Italo, *American Lessons* 129
Camerana, Carlo 45–6
Camera Nazionale della Moda Italiana, Milan 122, *123*, 127, 129, 132
Campbell, Thomas 141
Capucci, Roberto (Fondazione) 124
Caratozzolo, Vittoria Caterina 13, 14, 120
Casey, A. (and Nissley, N.) 64
Castello Sforzesco, Milan 89, 101, 116, *118*, 144
Celant, Germano 22, 43, 106, 108, 111, 138–9
Centre for Corporate Museums (project) 46
Centre International d'Etude des Textiles Anciens (CIETA), Lyon 91, 135
Centro di Firenze per la Moda Italiana, Florence 76, 103, 104–5, 112, 139, 140
Centro di Ricerca Gianfranco Ferré (formerly Fondazione Gianfranco Ferré), Milan 124, 147, *149*
Centro Internazionale delle Arti e del Costume (CIAC), Venice 76, 80–8, 90, 133–4
Centro Italiano per lo Studio della Storia del Tessuto (CISST), Rome 18–19, 91–4, 102–3, 111, 121, 134–5
Centro per la Cultura d'impresa, Milan 48
Centro Studi di Storia del Tessuto e del Costume, Venice 88
Centro Studio e Archivio della Comunicazione (CSAC), Parma 96–7
Chiara, Francina 141
CIAC (Centro Internazionale delle Arti e del Costume), Venice 76, 80–8, 90, 133–4

CIETA (Centre International d'Etude des Textiles Anciens), Lyon 91, 135
CISST (Centro Italiano per lo Studio della Storia del Tessuto), Rome 18–19, 91–4, 102–3, 111, 121, 134–5
Civiche Raccolte d'Arte Applicata, Milan 89, 90, 94
Clark, Judith 108, 120, 129
Coca Cola, World of, Atlanta 66, 67
Code of Cultural Heritage and Landscape (consolidated Act, Italy) 29, 33
Colaiacomo, Paola 127
Coleman, Lawrence Veil 51
Collicelli Cagol, Stefano 80, 82, 87
Colonna di Cesarò, Simonetta 120
commodification of culture 110, 160
community, engaging with 72–3, 110, 151–3, 161
Como *see* Fondazione Antonio Ratti, Como
company museums *see* corporate museums
Confederazione Nazionale dell'Artigianato e della Piccola e Media Industria (CNA) 132
conferences
Ansaldo, on cultural heritage, history research and industry (1982) 44
Assolombarda, on corporate museums (1998–2000) 31, 39–40, 45–7, 62–3
CIAC, on history of costume (1952) 82–5
CISST, on ready-to-wear (1990) 19, 102–3, 134, 135
Costume Colloquium (2008), Florence 8, 121
CSAC (1984) 97
Fondazione Antonio Ratti, *Collecting Textile* (2012) 141
Fondazione Antonio Ratti, on Grazietta Butazzi (2014) 8, 75–6, 97, 135
ICA, on corporate archives (2015) 70
MISA, *Insegnare la moda. Modelli e politiche culturali tra formazione e industria* 127
Prima conferenza internazionale per un Museo della Moda (1981), Milan 76, 95

Index

Confindustria 30, 34, 45, 47, 48
constructivist approach to history 19–21
consumption of fashion
   and sense of community 72–3, 110, 151–3, 161
   and stereotypes 14, 15–16, 20
continuity 13, 21, 26, 119–20, 139, 143
corporate archives
   compared to corporate collections 56–7, 60–1
   compared to corporate museums 61, 62–3
   conference on 70
   definitions of 4, 57–9, 71
   digitization projects 124–7
   legal framework 33, 58
   management and study of 44, 47, 111–12, 128, 134
corporate art 35, 36, 60, 67
Corporate Art Awards 35, 41
corporate collections 56–7, 60–1, 72
corporate communication *see* corporate cultural policies
corporate cultural policies
   and corporate archives 61
   and corporate foundations 54, 55
   and corporate museums 63
   definitions of 2, 5, 33–4
   in France 160
   investment (cultural production) 41–4, 136–43
   partnership 38–41
   patronage 22, 32, 35–6, 37, 38, 67, 132–3, 135
   sponsorship 36–8, 42–3, 70, 71, 87, 131–6
   strategic use of the past (*see* Renaissance)
   use of contemporary art 115–16, 138
corporate culture, definition 30, 34
Corporate Culture Week 47
corporate, definition and use of adjective 4, 71
corporate foundations 38, 53–5 *see also* individual foundations (Fondazione, Fondation)
corporate heritage
   collecting 55–7 (*see also* corporate archives; corporate collections)
   cultural and social relevance 159–61
   dual aims of preservation 30–2, 34
   exhibiting 64–8
   interpretative framework 71–3
   investment in 31–3 (*see also* corporate cultural policies)
   Italian perspective on 30–1
   promotion of 47–8
   researching and studying 44–9, 69–71
   training/education in 46–7, 91–2, 104, 127–8, 158
   see also fashion heritage
corporate heritage studies 44–9, 69–71 *see also* fashion studies in Italy
corporate institutions
   categorization attempts 51–2, 55–7, 60, 62, 63, 71, 72
   cultural and social relevance 22, 61, 159–61
   development in Italy 5–6, 53
   in fashion studies 52–3
   future directions 159–61
   inter-institutional exchange 153–5
   legal framework 32–3, 54
   profit motive 33, 72
   tool of social responsibility 30–1
   training/education for professionals in 46–7, 91–2, 104, 127–8, 158
corporate museums
   awards for 40–1
   and civic needs 72–3, 110, 151–3, 161
   compared to corporate archives 61, 62–3
   compared to flagship stores 67–8
   compared to traditional museums 63, 64–6, 72, 157–8
   conferences on 31, 39–40, 45–7, 63
   definitions of 4, 51–2, 56, 64, 70
   in specialist literature 6
   visitors numbers 32, 65–6, 154
   see also individual museums (Museo, Musée)
Costa, Barbara 58–9
costume all'italiana 11–12
Costume and Fashion: A Concise History (Laver) 85
country-of-origin effects 17, 18, 27
Crane, Diane 21

196　　　　　　　　　　　　　　　*Index*

CSAC (Centro Studio e Archivio della Comunicazione), Parma 96–7
Cultural Heritage and Landscape Code (consolidated Act, Italy) 29, 33
cultural heritage, Italian State legislation and management 29, 31, 32–3, 37–8, 48, 53–4, 124, 128
cultural policy *see* corporate cultural policies
cultural studies 137
Cumming, Valerie 1, 6, 7, 8, 144

Danilov, Victor J. 44, 51–2, 55, 60
de Antonis, Pasquale 23
De Benedetti, Carlo 37
de la Haye, Amy 53, 75, 85, 108
Delfiol, R. 58
Delpierre, Madeleine 95
Devoti, Donata 91–2
digital archives 124–7
Dior, Christian 65
Direzione Generale per gli Archivi 48
displacement 23
Dolce&Gabbana 16
Domus 95–6
drawings collections 96–7
Druesedow, Jean 6–7, 53, 103
Dudovich, Marcello 35
Durand, Maximilien 141

Edifir 103, 104, 135
education in corporate heritage 46–7, 91–2, 104, 127–8, 158
Einaudi 85
Establishing Dress History (Taylor) 6, 7, 53
Europeana Fashion (portal) 126
European Foundation Centre (EFC) 54
Exhibiting Fashion: Before and After 1971 (Horsley) 117–18

Fanfani, Tommaso 58, 59
fascist regime, fashion and textiles during 79–80, 94
fashion
　artification 21–4, 25
　challenges 160–1
　definition 7–8

fashion curation
　collaboration with industry 90, 98, 103, 127–9, 134–5, 148, 161
　corporate curation approach 148–9, 151
　definitions of 1, 20
　focus on continuity 117–24, 143
　focus on engagement with contemporary arts 104–10, 113–16, 138
　focus on history of costume 80–90
　focus on manufacture/technology 99, 144–7, 158
　focus on methodology and academic rigour 90–101, 102, 111–12, 139
　in international discourse 6–7
　merchandising techniques 68
　periodization in Italian literature 75–7
　training/education for professionals 46–7, 91–2, 104, 127–8, 158
　use of textiles in 81, 87, 133–4
　as visual criticism 105–6, 115, 149–50, 151
Fashion Engineering Unit (FEU) 106, *107*, 110, 137
fashion exhibitions (in general)
　commodifying culture 110
　criticism of 23, 71, 99, 111, 117, 144, 151
　cultural sponsorship of 131–6
　during fascist regime 79–80
　in flagship stores 66–9
　narrative shift 140
　as promotional tools 77–80, 116–17, 137, 147–8
　responding to civic needs 72–3, 110, 150–5, 161
　touring 26, 65, 82, 86, 116, 118, 122, 138, 144, 147
　transparency of intents 132, 155
　triggering discourse on fashion museums 89–90, 92, 94–5
fashion exhibitions
　1922–1943 Vent'anni di Moda in Italia. Proposta per un museo della moda a Milano (1980–1), Milan 94–5, 129
　L'abito per Pensare (1989), Milan 116, *118*, 144

Index

Across Art and Fashion (2016), Florence 153–4
Antonio Marras: Nulla dies sine linea (2016), Milan 123, *125*
Bellissima. L'Italia e l'alta moda 1945–1968 (2014), Rome 122, 150
Biennale di Firenze (1996–1998), Florence 23, 76, 106–10, *109*, 111, 133, 138–9
La camicia bianca secondo me. Gianfranco Ferré (2014), Prato 147, *149*
Christian Dior, Couturier Du Rêve (2017), Paris; (2019), London 65
Conseguenze impreviste. Arte, moda, design: ipotesi di nuove creatività in Italia (1982–83), Prato 98
Costumi dei secoli XVIII e XIX (1976), Milan 89
Curiosità di una reggia. Vicende della guardaroba di Palazzo Pitti (1979), Florence 92, *93*
Emilio Pucci e Como 1950–1980 (2014), Como 145, *146*
Il genio antipatico. Creatività e tecnologia della moda Italiana 1951–1983 (1984), Rome and Genoa 98
Genoni's at International Exhibition (1906), Milan 12–13, 77–8, *78*
Gianni Versace, dialogues de mode: des photographes autour d'une creation (1986), Paris 116
Gianni Versace: dieci anni di creatività (1983), Verona 98
Gianni Versace. La reinvenzione della materia (1998), Como 116, *119*, 144–5
Giorgio Armani (2000), New York 23, 65, 76, 89–90, 110–11, 151
The Glamour of Italian Fashion, 1945–2014 (2014), London 121, 145–7
Italiana. L'Italia vista dalla moda 1971–2001 (2018), Milan 122, *123*, 150
Italy at work. Her Renaissance in Design Today (1950), New York 16
La leggenda del filo d'oro, le vie della seta (1952), Venice 82, *83*
MEMOS. A proposito della moda di questo millennio (2020), Milan 129
Moda in Italia. 150 anni di eleganza (2011), Turin 121
Mostra del Costume nel Tempo. Momenti di arte e di vita dall'età ellenica al romanticismo (1951), Venice 81–2
Mostra di libri d'arte sul costume (1951), Venice 81
Il motore della moda (1998), Florence 106, *107*
Il museo effimero della moda (2017), Florence 141, *142*
Il Nuovo Vocabolario della Moda Italiana (2015), Milan 122, *124*, 132
Un Palazzo e la Città (2015), Florence 153, *154*
Un percorso di lavoro. Fendi – Karl Lagerfeld (1985), Rome 23, 98–9
Prima rassegna internazionale dell'abbigliamento (1956), Milan 85–6
I protagonisti della moda. Salvatore Ferragamo (1898–1960) (1985), Florence 19, 44, 65, 99–101, *100*, 139
La Regola Estrosa: Cento anni di eleganza maschile italiana (1993), Florence 105
La Sala Bianca: The birth of Italian fashion (1992), Florence 20, 25–6, 76, 104, *105*, 136
Salvatore Ferragamo. Evolving Legend 1928–2008 (2008), Shanghai 118–20, *120*
Seta. Il Novecento a Como (2001), Como 76, 111–12
Simonetta. La Prima Donna della Moda Italiana (2008), Florence 120
Subhuman Inhuman Superhuman (2017), Milan 123
Supermarket of Style (1993), Florence 105, 137
I Tessili dell'Avvenire (1954), Venice 85
Uniforme. Ordine e Disordine (2001), Florence 76, 113–14, *114*
Uomo oggetto. Mitologie, spettacolo e mode della maschilità (2000), Florence 106
Valentino a Roma: 45 Years of Style (2007), Rome 117

Vintage. L'irresistibile fascino del vissuto (2012), Prato 147, *148*
Vitalità nell'arte (1959), Venice 86–7
Volare: The Icon of Italy in Global Pop Culture (1999), Florence 20, 106
Yves Saint Laurent (1983), New York 65, 99, 100, 111
fashion heritage
   continuity with contemporary fashion 16, 21, 26, 119–20, 139, 143
   digitalisation 124–7
   research and study 18–19, 85, 97–8, 102–3, 134
   social and cultural relevance 72–3, 110, 151–3, 161
   and stereotypes 14, 15–16, 20
   support by Italian State 124, 128
fashion industry
   contribution to research 90, 98, 103, 127–9, 134–5, 148, 161
   as cultural producer 41–4, 136–43
   as cultural sponsor 131–6
fashion museums
   discourse in Italy 89–90, 92, 94–5
   Museo della Moda e del Costume (formerly Galleria del Costume of Palazzo Pitti), Florence 6–7, 25, 92, 99, 120, 140–1, *142*
   Palais Galliera, Paris 23, 90, 116
   see also Victoria & Albert Museum (V&A)
fashion photography 15–16, 23, 116
fashion studies in Italy
   collection and cataloguing 81, 89–90, 101
   disseminating specialist knowledge 87
   early development 79
   historical approaches to 19–21
   importance of contemporaneity in 107, 114–15, 138–9
   importance of scholarship-industry interaction for 90, 98, 103, 127–9, 134–5, 148, 161
   importance of scientific rigour in 100–2
   in international discourse 6–7
Fashion Theory 68, 114, 139, 145
Federmoda 128
Fee, Sarah 2
Fendi 23, 98–9

Ferragamo, Ferruccio 155
Ferragamo, Salvatore 35, 47, 73, 153
   exhibitions about 19, 44, 65, 99–101, 118–20, *120*, 139
   see also Fondazione Salvatore Ferragamo; Museo Salvatore Ferragamo
Ferré, Gianfranco 92, 108, *109*, 124, 147, *149*
FIAT 37, 88
Fiesoli, Laura 121
Fiorucci DXing 110, 137
Flaccavento, Angelo 149–50
flagship stores 66–9
Florence
   Biennale di Firenze 23, 76, 106–10, *109*, 111, 133, 138–9
   as birthplace of Italian fashion 24–6, 104
   Centro di Firenze per la Moda Italiana 76, 103, 104–5, 112, 139, 140
   competing as cultural centre of Italian fashion 14, 80
   developing as cultural centre of Italian fashion 16–17, 20, 104–6, 136
   Fondazione Archivio Emilio Pucci 59, 124, 126
   Fondazione per il Rinascimento Digitale 126
   Fondazione Pitti Immagine Discovery 76, 112–16, 120, 136, 138, 139–40, 148
   Fondazione Salvatore Ferragamo 55, 59 (*see also* Museo Salvatore Ferragamo)
   Gallerie degli Uffizi 65, 111, 140
   Gucci Archivio 126–7
   Museo della Moda e del Costume (formerly Galleria del Costume of Palazzo Pitti) 6–7, 25, 92, 99, 120, 140–1, *142*
   Museo Marino Marini 153, 154
   Palazzo Pitti, Sala Bianca 16, 25–6, 76, 92, *93*, 104, *105*, 136
   Palazzo Spini Feroni 153, *154*
   Palazzo Strozzi 19, 25, 89, 99–101, 104, *105*, 139
   Stazione Leopolda 104–6, *107*, 113, *114*, 137
Fondation Louis Vuitton, Paris 67, 160

Fondazione Antonio Ratti, Como
  conferences 8, 75–6, 97, 135, 141
  exhibitions 76, 111–12, 116, *119*, 144–5, *146*
  Museo Studio del Tessuto 102
Fondazione Archivio Emilio Pucci, Florence 59, 124, 126
Fondazione dei Musei Civici di Venezia, Venice 88
Fondazione Fashion Research Italy (FRI) 128
Fondazione Gianfranco Ferré (now Centro di Ricerca Gianfranco Ferré), Milan 124, 147, *149*
Fondazione Micol Fontana, Rome 124
Fondazione Nicola Trussardi, Milan 55
Fondazione per il Rinascimento Digitale, Florence 126
Fondazione Pitti Immagine Discovery, Florence 76, 112–16, 120, 136, 138, 139–40, 148
Fondazione Prada, Milan 22, 43
Fondazione Roberto Capucci 124
Fondazione Salvatore Ferragamo, Florence 55, 59 *see also* Museo Salvatore Ferragamo
Fontana Sisters 97, 124
Ford Museum, Dearborn, Michigan 70
French fashion 12, 77, 79, 160
Frisa, Maria Luisa
  curatorial approach 113–15, 136, 139, 140, 148, 149, 150
  exhibitions curated 113, 120, 122, 129, 150, 153
  founder of the Associazione Italiana degli Studi di Moda (MISA) 127
Fukai, Akiko 6, 7–8, 75

Gabbuti, Gioacchino 42
Galleria del Costume of Palazzo Pitti (now Museo della Moda e del Costume), Florence 6–7, 25, 92, 99, 120, 140–1, *142*
Galleria Nazionale d'Arte Moderna, Rome 23, 98–9
Gallerie degli Uffizi, Florence 65, 111, 140
Gamba, Greta 57
Gattinoni 124
Genoni, Rosa 12–13, 16, 75, 77–9

GFT (Gruppo Finanziario Tessile) 17, 18–19, 97–8, 102–3, 134
Ghersetti, Francesca 56–7
Giacomoni, Silvia 115
Gilodi, Cecilia 56
Giorgini, Giovanni Battista 16–17, 24, 25, 26, 85, 143
Golzio Aimone, Elsa 102, 134
Google Arts & Culture 126
Grand Palais, Paris 66
Grès, Alix (Madame) 23
Greyser, Stephen 5
Gruppo Finanziario Tessile (GFT) 17, 18–19, 97–8, 102–3, 134
Guarini, Filippo 147, 152
Gucci Archivio, Florence 126–7
Guggenheim Award – Industry & Culture (later Industry and Culture Award) 40–1, 43, 110
Guggenheim Foundation 39
Guggenheim Museum, New York 23, 65, 66–7, 76, 90, 110–11
Guggenheim, Peggy (Collection), Venice 39

heritage *see* corporate heritage; cultural heritage; fashion heritage
heritage brands 5, 20, 126, 160
heritage marketing *see* Pitti Immagine; Renaissance
heritagization 27
Histoire du Costume (Boucher) 84
historical archives 58, 61, 62
historical linkages 68, 69
historical narratives 11–18, 79, 138–9 *see also* Renaissance
Hollenbeck, Candice R. 68
Horsley, Jeffrey 117–18

ICA (International Council on Archives) 4, 33, 41, 57
ICOM (International Council of Museums) 4, 33, 46, 64, 68, 69, 72, 158
'imitation museums' 53, 68
industrial heritage *see* corporate heritage
Industry and Culture Award (formerly Guggenheim Award – Industry & Culture) 40–1, 43, 110

InStyle 111
International Council of Museums (ICOM) 4, 33, 46, 64, 68, 69, 72, 158
International Council on Archives (ICA) 4, 33, 41, 57
International Exhibition (1906), Milan 12–13
International Jury Grand Prix 12–13
Intrapresae Collezione Guggenheim 39, 40, 41
investment (cultural production) 41–4, 136–43
Istituto Centrale per il Catalogo 91
Italian fashion
 as expression of Italianness 12–18, 79, 105, 106, 120
 heritagization 27
 originating myth 16, 24–7, 104–6
Italian Fashion Now (Frisa) 115
Italianness through fashion 12–18, 79, 105, 106, 120
Italy
 cultural heritage, State legislation and management 29, 31, 32–3, 37–8, 48, 53–4
 fashion heritage, State support to 124, 128
 national branding 14–15, 17, 21, 27
 national identity 11–12, 20, 24
 statistics on corporate institutions 5–6, 53
 stereotypical representations 14, 15–16, 20
 traditional costume 11–12

Kaiser, Linda 45, 62, 63
Kanai, Jun 95
Kapferer, Jean-Noel 21–2
Key Concepts of Museology (ICOM) 158
Kinmonth, Patrick 117
Koda, Harold 111
Koolhas, Rem 66
Kozinets, Robert V. 66, 68
Krizia 97

Lagerfeld, Karl 23, 98–9
Lampis, Antonio 48
Laver, James 75, 84, 85
Lelong, Lucien 84

Levi Pisetzky, Rosita 75, 84–5, 89, 94, 95
Libera Università Internazionale degli Studi Sociali (LUISS), Rome 35
Linfante, Vittorio 122, 132
Livingstone, P. 67
London
 Museums Association 41
 Victoria & Albert Museum (V&A), London 1, 65, 68, 90, 116, 117, 121, 144–5
Louis Vuitton flagship store, Paris 67
LUISS (Libera Università Internazionale degli Studi Sociali), Rome 35
Lupi, Italo 105
luxury products, artification of 21–2

Made in Italy 17–18, 21, 24, 26, 106
Magagnino, Mario 69
Malossi, Giannino 20, 25, 104–6, 110, 136–7, 138, 148, 149
Manifesto della Cultura d'Impresa (Confindustria) 30, 34
Marchetti, Luca 69
Marenzi, Claudio 141
Marinotti, Franco 80, 81, 82, 85, 87, 102
Marinotti, Paolo 82, 86–7, 133
Marras, Antonio 123, *125*
Martino, Valentina
 on corporate institutions 47, 58, 62
 on industry and culture interactions 34, 36, 38, 39, 41, 43
Martin, Richard 103, 116, 144
Marucelli, Germana 13
Mason, Liz 145
Masotti, Alberto 128
Matteucci Lavarini, Cecilia 92
Mattirolo, Anna 122
MAXXI Museum, Rome 122
'mecenatismo' 36
Melandri, Giovanna 38–9
Mendes, Valerie 95
Mendini, Alessandro 95–6
merchandising display techniques 68
Metropolitan Museum of Art (The Met), New York 65, 70, 99, 102, 111, 116, 144, 149
Milan
 Bocconi University 32, 42, 45

Camera Nazionale della Moda
  Italiana 122, *123*, 127, 129, 132
Castello Sforzesco 89, 101, 116,
  118, 144
Centro di Ricerca Gianfranco Ferré
  (formerly Fondazione Gianfranco
  Ferré) 124, 147, *149*
Centro per la Cultura d'impresa 48
Civiche Raccolte d'Arte
  Applicata 89, 90, 94
competing as centre of Italian
  fashion 14, 80
developing as Italian centre of
  ready-to-wear 88–9
fashion week 122
Fondazione Nicola Trussardi 55
Fondazione Prada 22, 43
International Exhibition (1906) 12–13
Museo Nazionale della Scienza e della
  Tecnica 'Leonardo da Vinci' 46
Museo Poldi Pezzoli 76, 89, 91,
  94–8, 129
Palazzo Reale 116, 122, *123*, *149*
Rotonda della Besana 89
Triennale 118–19, 122–3, *124*, *125*, 132
Minio, Enrico 121
Ministry of Cultural Heritage and
  Activities (and Tourism) 31, 33, 35,
  38, 48, 128
Ministry of Education, University and
  Research 48
MISA (Associazione Italiana degli Studi di
  Moda), Venice 127–8
Missoni 97
Moda: arte, storia, società (Butazzi) 96
Moda Italiana, La (Butazzi, Mottola
  Molfino, Quintavalle) 96, 97
MoMu museum, Antwerp 159
Mondadori, Leonardo 108–10, 133
Monoelli, Roberto 94
Monroe, Marilyn 126
Monti, Gabriele 8, 98, 144
Moore, Doris Langley 84
Morini, Enrica 12, 19, 127, 135, 153
Moschino 97
Mottola Molfino, Alessandra 89, 91, 92,
  94, 96, 98, 134–5
museal, use of term 158
Musée Bourdelle, Paris 23

Musée de la Mode (Palais Galliera),
  Paris 23, 90, 116
Musée des Arts Décoratifs, Paris 26, 65
Musée Yves Saint Laurent, Paris 65–6
Museimpresa 35, 47–8, 57, 64, 68, 71
Museo Civico, Modena 91
Museo della Moda e del Costume
  (formerly Galleria del Costume of
  Palazzo Pitti), Florence 6–7, 25, 92,
  99, 120, 140–1, *142*
Museo dello Scarpone e della Calzatura
  Sportiva, Montebelluna 40
Museo del Tessuto, Prato 41, 141, 147,
  148, *149*, 151–4, 158
Museo Marino Marini, Florence 153, 154
Museo Nazionale della Scienza e della
  Tecnica 'Leonardo da Vinci,'
  Milan 46
Museo Poldi Pezzoli, Milan 76, 89, 91,
  94–8, 129
Museo Salvatore Ferragamo, Florence
  award winner 40
  community engagement 153
  as company/brand cultural
    interface 41, 43
  digitization projects 124, 126
  educational programmes 158
  exhibitions 67, 73, *154*
  inter-institutional exchange 153–5
  opening of 44, 100
  publications 141–3
  visitors number 65
Museo Studio del Tessuto (Fondazione
  Ratti), Como 102
Museum of Contemporary Art,
  Shanghai 118, *120*
museums (traditional)
  compared to corporate museums 63,
    64–6, 71, 72, 155, 157–8
  compared to flagship stores 67–8
  definition 3, 4
  function of 2, 69
  neutrality of 157
  see also individuals museums
    (Museo, Musée)
Museums Association, London 41
Muzzarelli, Maria Giuseppina 8, 75, 79

Napoleone, Raffaello 20, 132

narratives
  focused on manufacture/
    technology 99, 144–7, 158
  historical 11–18, 79, 138–9 (*see also*
    Renaissance)
  socially relevant 72–3, 110,
    150–5, 161
national identity 11–12, 20, 24, 160
nation branding 14–15, 17, 21, 27
Negri, Massimo 63–4
New York
  Brooklyn Museum 16
  Guggenheim Museum 23, 65, 66–7, 76,
    90, 110–11
  Metropolitan Museum of Art 65, 70,
    99, 102, 111, 116, 144, 149
  Prada flagship store 66–7
Niccoli, Bruna 127
Nissley, N. (and Casey, A.) 64
not-for-profit 33, 158

Office for Metropolitan Architecture
  (OMA) 66
Olivetti 36–7
online archives 124–7
Osservatorio Monografie d'Impresa 69
Owens, Rick 123

Palais Galliera (Musée de la Mode),
  Paris 23, 90, 116
Palazzo Grassi, Venice 37, 80–1, *83*, 88
Palazzo Mocenigo, Venice 88, 90
Palazzo Pitti, Florence
  Museo della Moda e del Costume
    (formerly Galleria del Costume of
    Palazzo Pitti) 6–7, 25, 92, 99, 120,
    140–1, *142*
  Sala Bianca 16, 25–6, 76, 92, *93*, 104,
    105, 136
Palazzo Reale, Milan 116, 122,
  123, 149
Palazzo Spini Feroni, Florence 153, *154*
Palazzo Strozzi, Florence 19, 25, 89,
  99–101, 104, *105*, 139
Palmer, Alexandra 2, 53, 68, 103
Panicelli, Ida 98
Paolucci, Antonio 143
Paris
  Fondation Louis Vuitton 67, 160

Grand Palais, Paris 66
Louis Vuitton flagship store 67
Musée Bourdelle, Paris 23
Musée des Arts Décoratifs 26, 65
Musée Yves Saint Laurent 65–6
Palais Galliera (Musée de la Mode) 23,
  90, 116
partnership 38–41
patronage 22, 32, 35–6, 37, 38, 67,
  132–3, 135
Paulicelli, Eugenia 24, 115
Pearce, S. 152
Peggy Guggenheim Collection,
  Venice 39
Pertagato, Francesco 92
Pescucci, Gabriella 121
Petrov, Julia 2, 22, 145, 151
Pinault, François 37
Pinto, Sandra 92
Pitti Immagine
  award winner 110
  corporate cultural policy 20, 76, 132,
    135, 136–43
  relationship with CISST 103, 135
  relaunch of Florence as fashion
    capital 24, 25, 104–5, 136
  see also Fashion Engineering Unit
    (FEU); Fondazione Pitti Immagine
    Discovery
Pitti Uomo 103, 104, 106, 113, 120, 124
Polhemus, Ted 105, 137
Polimoda 104
Portale degli Archivi d'Impresa 48
Portoghese, Lucia 91
pptArt 35
Prada flagship store, New York 66–7
Prada (Fondazione), Milan 22
Prada, Miuccia 22
Premio Guggenheim – Impresa & Cultura
  (later *Premio Impresa e Cultura*)
  40–1, 43, 110
'product archive' 59, 60
publications *see* corporate heritage studies;
  fashion studies in Italy
Pucci, Emilio 13–14, 145, *146*
Pucci, Emilio (Fondazione Archivio),
  Florence 59, 124, 126

Quintavalle, Arturo Carlo 24–5, 96

Radkai, Karen 15
Ratti, Antonio 102, 141 *see also* Fondazione Antonio Ratti
ready-to-wear 19, 29, 88, 102–3, 122, 134, 150
realistic approach to history 19–20
Renaissance
  definition 11
  as Italianness 12–18, 120
  as marketing strategy 16–18, 20, 26–7, 55, 132–3
  as nation branding 14–15, 17, 21, 27
  originating myth of Italian fashion 16, 24–7, 104–6
  promotion through digital tools 126
  representations in fashion design 12–14, 77–8
Renaissance effect 15, 21, 26
retail spaces 66–9
Ribeiro, Aileen 103
Ricci, Stefania 55, 67, 99, 100, 121, 143, 153
Ricci, Stefano 140
Rimbotti, Vittorio 104, 107
Rinascente, La 35, 94
Risorgimento 11–12
Rivetti, Carlo 136, 148
Rivetti, Marco 17, 19, 25, 103, 104, 135
Rizzini, Marialuisa 8, 84, 91, 92, 95
Robotti, Diego 34, 59, 62
Roditi, Fiammetta 102
Romani, Gabriella 12
Rome
  Altaroma 122
  Centro Italiano per lo Studio della Storia del Tessuto (CISST) 18–19, 91–4, 102–3, 111, 121, 134–5
  competing as centre of Italian fashion 14, 80
  Fondazione Micol Fontana 124
  Galleria Nazionale d'Arte Moderna 23, 98–9
  as Italian capital of high fashion 122
  Libera Università Internazionale degli Studi Sociali (LUISS) 35
  MAXXI Museum 122
  textile exhibitions during fascist regime 79–80
Ronconi, Luca 25, *105*

Rosina, Margherita 135, 147
Rotonda della Besana, Milan 89

Saillard, Olivier 141
Saint Laurent, Yves 65–6, 99, 100, 111
Sala Bianca (Palazzo Pitti), Florence 16, 25–6, 76, 92, *93*, 104, *105*, 136
Salvi, Sergio 100–1
Sandberg, Willem 86
Sapelli, Giulio 31
Scarpa, Carlo 87, 133
Schnapp, J. T. 80
scholarship *see* corporate heritage studies; fashion studies in Italy
Segati, Giuseppe 82
Segre Reinach, Simona 8, 20, 127
Settembrini, Luigi 104, 105, 106, 107, 139
Settimana della Cultura d'Impresa 47
Shapiro, Roberta 21
silk 76, 82, *83*, 111–12
Sischy, Ingrid 106
Sistema Archivi Nazionale (SAN) 124
SNIA Viscosa 80–2, 85–7, 133–4
social media 160
Sole 24 Ore, Il, Porta lontano investire in cultura. L'opinione degli italiani sul rapporto impresa-cultura 32, 38, 42
Soli, Pia 98
Solomon R. Guggenheim Museum, New York 23, 65, 66–7, 76, 90, 110–11
Sorelle Fontana 97, 124
souvenir effect 14
Sozzani, Franca 121
sponsorship 36–8, 42–3, 70, 71, 87, 131–6
Stanfill, Sonnet 18, 121, 141, 145, 147
Stazione Leopolda, Florence 104–6, *107*, 113, *114*, 137
Steele, Valerie 144–5
Stevenson, N. J. 144
stores (flagship) 66–9
Storia del Costume in Italia (Levi Pisetzky) 85
studies *see* corporate heritage studies; fashion studies in Italy
Studio La Città, Verona 98
Study of dress history, The (Taylor) 7
sustainability 158, 160
Swann, June 101

Taylor, Lou 6, 7, 53
Taylor, Melissa 131–2
TCI (Touring Club Italiano) 63
textiles industry and production 12, 77, 79–82, *83*, 85–7, 111–12, 133–4, 145
Thompson, Eleanor 53
Tirelli, Umberto 7, 92, 121
Tonchi, Stefano 113, 115, 122, 140
Touring Club Italiano (TCI) 63
touring exhibitions 26, 65, 82, 86, 116, 118, 122, 138, 144, 147
transparency 132, 155, 160
Treccani 85
Tremelloni, Attilio 102
Triennale, Milan 118–19, 122–3, *124, 125*, 132
Trussardi, Nicola (Fondazione), Milan 55
Turin 14, 77, 80

Uffizi Gallery, Florence 65, 111, 140
Understanding Fashion History (Cumming) 6, 7
UNESCO 33
Union Française des Arts du Costume (UFAC) 84
Urde, Mats 5

Valentino 23, 117
V&A (Victoria & Albert Museum), London 1, 65, 68, 90, 116, 117, 121, 144–5
Veltroni, Walter 45
velvet 12
Venaria royal palace, Turin 121
Veneziani, Jole 23

Venice
  Associazione Italiana degli Studi di Moda (MISA) 127–8
  Centro Internazionale delle Arti e del Costume (CIAC) 76, 80–8, 90, 133–4
  Centro Studi di Storia del Tessuto e del Costume 88
  Fondazione dei Musei Civici di Venezia 88
  Palazzo Grassi 37, 80–1, *83*, 88
  Palazzo Mocenigo 88, 90
  Peggy Guggenheim Collection 39
Venna, Lucio 35
Vergani, Guido 99–100
Versace, Donatella 144
Versace, Gianni 116–17, *118*, *119*, 144–5
Victoria & Albert Museum (V&A), London 1, 65, 68, 90, 116, 117, 121, 144–5
visitors of corporate museums
  as members of cultural communities 72–3, 110, 151–3, 161
  number of 32, 65–6, 154
Viti, Paolo 37
Vreeland, Diana 1, 65, 99–101
Vuitton, Louis 67, 160

Warnecke, Jan-Christian 72
Westuff 113
We Wear Culture (portal) 126
Wilcox, Claire 144
Wilson, Elizabeth 96
Wilson, Robert 111
World of Coca Cola, Atlanta 66, 67
Worth, Charles Frederick 12

Xu, X. 61, 68, 72, 73